Working Memory

LIFE WRITING SERIES

In the Life Writing Series, Wilfrid Laurier University Press publishes life writing and new life-writing criticism and theory in order to promote autobiographical accounts, diaries, letters, memoirs and testimonials written and/or told by women and men whose political, literary, or philosophical purposes are central to their lives. The Series features accounts written in English, or translated into English from French or the languages of the First Nations, or any of the languages of immigration to Canada.

The audience for the series includes scholars, youth, and avid general readers both in Canada and abroad. The Series hopes to continue its work as a leading publisher of life writing of all kinds, as an imprint that aims for scholarly excellence and representing lived experience as tools for both historical and autobiographical research.

We publish original life writing which represent the widest range of experiences of lives lived with integrity. Life Writing also publishes original theoretical investigations about life writing, as long as they are not limited to one author or text.

Series Editor
Marlene Kadar
Humanities, York University

Manuscripts to be sent to
Lisa Quinn, Acquisitions Editor
Wilfrid Laurier University Press
75 University Avenue West
Waterloo, Ontario N2L 3C5, Canada

Working Memory

Women and Work in WWII

Marlene Kadar and Jeanne Perreault
editors

WILFRID LAURIER
UNIVERSITY PRESS

Wilfrid Laurier University Press acknowledges the financial support of the Government of Canada through the Canada Book Fund for its publishing activities. This work was supported by the Research Support Fund.

LAURIER
Inspiring Lives.

ONTARIO ARTS COUNCIL
CONSEIL DES ARTS DE L'ONTARIO
an Ontario government agency
un organisme du gouvernement de l'Ontario

Library and Archives Canada Cataloguing in Publication

Working memory : women and work in World War II / Marlene Kadar and Jeanne Perreault, editors.

(Life writing series)
Includes bibliographical references and index.
Issued in print and electronic formats.
ISBN 978-1-77112-035-7 (paperback).—ISBN978-1-77112-037-1 (epub).—
ISBN 978-1-77112-036-4 (pdf)

1. World War, 1939–1945—War work—Women. I. Kadar, Marlene, [date], author, editor II. Perreault, Jeanne, 1945–, editor III. Series: Life writing series

D810.W7W67 2015   940.53082   C2015-902046-8
                                             C2015-902047-6

Front-cover image: Canadian Women's Army Corps (CWAC) members operating the telephone switchboard at Canadian Military Headquarters, London, 1945. Photograph courtesy of Galt Museum & Archives (#19891053017). Cover design by Blakeley Words+ Pictures. Text design by Angela Booth Malleau.

This book is printed on FSC® certified paper and is certified Ecologo. It contains post-consumer fibre, is processed chlorine free, and is manufactured using biogas energy.

Printed in Canada

Every reasonable effort has been made to acquire permission for copyright material used in this text, and to acknowledge all such indebtedness accurately. Any errors and omissions called to the publisher's attention will be corrected in future printings.

FSC
www.fsc.org

MIX
Paper from
responsible sources
FSC® C004071

*We dedicate this volume to every woman who has struggled
to live with integrity through a war. And to the scholars and artists
who make it possible for us to imagine those lives.*

CONTENTS

INTRODUCTION
THE LIVES AND THE ARCHIVES

Jeanne Perreault and Marlene Kadar

We have been moved by the reactions of our researchers and their subjects to World War II almost seventy years after the fact. Popular media, scholarship, and personal histories continue to be steeped in World War II imagery, history, memory, and materiality. Many of us grew up in families in which the stories of that war formed a persistent foreground or background giving shape to the multiple decisions of everyday life. Our mothers or grandmothers or great-grandmothers saved string or paper bags. Our uncles or grandfathers or great-grandfathers talked incessantly or refused to talk at all about their experiences at war—or worse, at home. The intense focus on the material of everyday life—the sugar or coffee, the stockings—helped divert attention from the emotional deprivation (or relief) of the absent brothers or fathers for women at home.

For the women trapped in zones of war or voluntarily at the front, emotional suppression was another story altogether. Those women could not afford to express much of the panic or grief they were feeling and often spoke in metaphors in the languages that helped them migrate. They reconfigured their realities according to what was available to them and what they had within them to bring to the fore. These are the stories of the women who calculated the main chance and took up with the Nazi soldier, or who eagerly dropped the apron at the door and picked up a paintbrush, or who brazenly bargained for their lives with the most feared of tyrants. Many of our women's stories are about finding ways around or through the tightening grasp of Nazism and planning escapes or migrations. For most, the war was fought in Europe rather than the Pacific, and the essays here reflect that reality. Sometimes stories chronicle compromise or collapse, and now and then, great courage. This is not the courage of bravado and hype and big guns, but rather the courage of the kinds of sacrifices that make sense of the life given, even when that life seems to offer only madness. We are still hungry to hear those stories, and this collection demonstrates our contributors' ability to see the absences as opportunities.

Our title speaks to the work women did in the war: the labour of survival, resistance, or collaboration, or the labour of recording, representing, and/or memorializing these experiences. The relation of our contributors to their subjects is also labour: the researchers trace the sweep of events determining specific occurrences in the subjects' lives, or retrace those and recreate the movement. The essays attempt to deepen our understanding of the experiences and their meanings from the imprints left behind. These efforts are a part of the making of history, and when the process is as personal, and even intimate, as many of our contributors' research has been, it is also the working of memory. The implication here is that memory is indeed intimate, and that the layering of narrative fragments that recovery requires or involves brings us within touching distance of ourselves.

The essays in this collection discuss little-examined aspects of women's work during the war. One of our contributors, Patrick Taylor, observed in his response to our Call for Papers, "When I think of women's war I think of women starving in concentration camps, producing ammunition in brutal conditions in factories all over Europe, vainly working fields devastated by marauding armies, performing sexually for unknown men, and so forth. And yet your volume seems to call for something different, little known." Taylor's words pinpoint the specific wish we have to bring scholarly attention to that part of the historical narrative about the role of women in World War II that may have been overwritten in masculinist code, or simply ignored in favour of other, brasher tales.

The scholars represented here examine a variety of media to get at the forgotten or dismissed parts of the well-known story, and to probe political, intellectual, creative, or personal limit cases.[1] Memory and disguise, evasion and exposure, and courage and corruption appear in the lives of the women examined. The process of discovering, researching, imagining, and recreating aspects of those women's lives has been the work of our contributors. All investigators into the past are painfully aware of the fragmentary nature of our discoveries, as Marlene Kadar's evocative musings in "'Things gone astray'—the Work of the Archive" suggest. But that incompleteness of knowledge is only partially painful to us. The gaps in knowledge and information allow us two intense, though familiar, pleasures: the searching and the recreating—the making of a narrative about and with those fragments. This collection, like others before it, seeks to recognize this. And overarching the whole project is that powerful feminist impulse: the will to ensure that women's lives in their particularities are not submerged in the blur of the past. Richard Terdiman observes, "Inevitably the effort to make sense [of the past] aims at *changing* things" (1993, 345). Like others before us, we wish to change things in the present by working memory.

Our primary aim, then, is to continue the project of recognizing, remembering, and then remembering again the multiple, contested, and contradictory roles women played in World War II. Many of the essays look at life writing—memoir, diary, and other auto/biographical texts and materials—while others focus on representation in art, film, or propaganda. The collection examines a cross-section of women subjects who were compromised, or at least challenged, by necessity and desire in the period of World War II both here and abroad. The project focuses on the specificities or specific surprises a story offers rather than on how fully it represents some national or geopolitical agenda.

Our authors complicate the conventional descriptors of "home front" and "battlefront," using an interdisciplinary methodology whenever possible, and are attentive to the unexpected story folded over within a war story. In the last decade, at least twenty books on some particular moment in women's war experiences have appeared, focusing, for instance, on women in the American Civil War, World War I Berlin, Mennonite refugees of World War II, and US nurses imprisoned in the South Pacific. For us, this plethora of material indicates the ongoing interest in the subject. In contrast to the great number of narratives gathered by veterans' affairs offices (for example), we have no interest in narratives that prop up national reminiscences. Rather, we have sought each author's unique perspective to stir something else—we have looked for some kind of instrument to crack open the familiar cadence of war stories. In every instance, contributors have seen subjects not just as workers or victims caught in the great machinery of war, but as agents of creative responses to necessity, however limited their alternatives. The researchers and writers are also workers. Here, we find them following trails, making memories come to the surface, which is the work of making history.

We have structured the collection to reflect the range of perspectives the chapters explore. We gather essays in rough groupings: essays that examine those who represented war, and essays that examine those who lived the war. Many of the subjects inhabited necessary or expedient compromises, evasions, or deceptions to make their way through war years and family complexities. The war disrupted the normal course of life and our subjects made creative bargains to ensure their survival. We realize that those categories overlap and blur—the writer of a memoir of war has both lived and represented war, for example, and a photojournalist has lived the war while recording it. Some papers are the result of rigorous archival investigation. Others bring close attention to the life writings or graphic representations of the subjects. Several essays focus on the Holocaust, others focus on familial or domestic connections, and still others concentrate on the politics of making memory. Some papers touch all these links. They share a recognition of what has been hidden, folded, layered, and even camouflaged.

Eva Karpinski reads Zofia Nałkowska's wartime and postwar diaries and writes a complex theoretical analysis of the self-conscious observer attempting to forge a place from which to see. Nałkowska, a Polish Gentile, responds to the horrors of the Holocaust, the Warsaw ghetto, and postwar accounts of her life in this analysis of the ethical and moral imperative to witness a nightmare against which one is helpless. In her scrupulously detailed discussion of this too-little-known writer, Karpinski considers the distinctions between textually mediated witnessing and embodied witnessing as crucial aspects of the "constant claims of the past on the present."

Lesley Ferris and Mary Tarantino allow us to see their own processes at work as they create a memorial to the lives of women working as British spies in Nazi-held territory. This essay foregrounds the politics of memorializing while it details the complexities of camouflage, disguise, and secrecy. Ferris and Tarantino guide readers through the details of their intellectual and artistic labours as they show the multi-layered training and practice of tradecraft and the appalling outcomes of the women's capture by the enemy. The power of feeling experienced by the researchers (and audiences) as they recreate this history brings another kind of doubleness—the layering of past and present—to our attention.

In a different kind of doubling or pairing, Charmian Brinson and Julia Winckler take us through the lives of two German sisters on opposite sides of the conflict in Europe during World War II. Mounting an exhibition of photographs and documents, Brinson and Winckler seek to discover the process of recreation and reconciliation the sisters undertook in the postwar period. They consider the inconsistencies of memory as it is manifested in documents and personal connections in their narrative reconstruction of these lives. The authors' intimate connection to their subjects and painstaking efforts to tell a partially available story wholly offer insights into the work of recomposing the past.

Patrick Taylor also brings us his family's history—despite his elder relative's cautionary words: "It might not be a good thing to dig too deeply into the past." Taylor parallels his own story with that of white Barbadian women breaking out of their given roles and, in this case, taking an active part in the war effort by nursing British wounded. The post-colonial history of the island and its fraught relationship to Britain, and the place of World War II in that dynamic history, forms the backstory of this essay. Taylor requires us to acknowledge that our poking around in history may serve us in ways our seniors may not prefer.

Hermine Braunsteiner is one person who would very much have preferred obscurity and erasure. Marlene Kadar investigates the most unsavoury of our subjects, a National Socialist overseer who made her way from the Nazi prison camps to the safety of postwar Canada and the United States, even after having been convicted of war crimes in Europe. Kadar's careful tracking of this fractured history is a model of scholarly research and a fierce grappling with the values, beliefs, and ideologies that inhabit, and perhaps inhibit, our memories, particularly those we and they might like most to forget. The essay becomes a meditation on our reaching after elusive truths.

In contrast to the brutal narrative of Hermine Braunsteiner, Natalie Robinson's subject shows exemplary imagination and courage, even in the face of a frustrating postwar aftermath as she is refused the right to reclaim her paintings. Robinson provides a multi-tiered examination of Dina Gottliebova-Babbitt's use of her art to save herself and her mother under Josef Mengele's authority in Auschwitz. Robinson examines conflicting rights of ownership as the proprietors of historical memory battle for possession of the artwork. Crucial questions of property rights that inflect all participants in history making and telling resurface here.

As principal curator of documentary photography in the Prints and Photographs Division of the Library of Congress, Beverly Brannan is acutely aware of the responsibilities of those who hold public memory in trust. Brannan's focus on American women photographers and photojournalists makes a great contribution to the preservation of women's work in World War II. Women journalists, artists, and photographers on the Allied side were said to have an alibi to go everywhere and do everything. Her essay presents the artists and shows us her own ongoing labour to recover and preserve, and even recreate, the work of women artists of the past. This essay offers a tantalizing invitation to scholars—the not-perfectly-raw material of the archive is ready for the next generation of workers.

Tanya Schaap, an active member of that generation, reads official Canadian war artist Molly Bobak's art and her wartime diary—a parodic account of the absurdities of military life for women—as a challenge to the public image of women in the military. Bobak's work as an artist focused on Canadian servicewomen actively engaging in their jobs. Linking the diary and the paintings, Schaap analyzes the contradictions servicewomen faced during the war years and gives us insight into the everydayness of women's lives. Her analysis of how gender was understood and articulated by servicewomen is an introduction to an unusual Canadian artist. Molly Bobak died at the age of ninety-one, just as this collection was being prepared for publication.

James Stone also brings attention to gender representation in images, examining the film portrayal of Dutchwomen as resistance fighters. Stone marks the powerful role women played in the Resistance and notes that the propaganda functions of such films seem less significant than their challenge to conventional views of women. Like other contributors here, Stone introduces us to little-known aspects of women's experiences in the war, layers the history with an understanding of how it is shaped by representation, and demonstrates that the most obvious story (in this case, making propaganda) may not be the most important one.

We conclude the volume with Catherine Speck's essay on Australian war artist Stella Bowen. Speck examines Bowen's haunting paintings, contextualizing the artist's work in historical and aesthetic terms and focusing on the difficulties women war artists face. Speck invites us to see the psychological power of these paintings, and addresses the effects on both artist and viewer. Seeing these quiet paintings of young men and women, some of them dead before the work was complete, through the eyes of a commonwealth artist helps us frame our understanding of memory's work. By placing her subject's work in context with such precision, Speck suggests we might see in Bowen "a statement about how war itself is irrational."

It is with pride and humility that we present the work of these scholars. Many of them create crossover generic projects (exhibitions, theatre performances, archival websites); several reposition life-writing materials; others use diverse, often individually articulated analytic strategies like seeing camouflage as miasma or opportunity; and all, reaching into the unworked places of art, history, and memory, might be seen as pioneers at the crossroads of the present, going in at least two directions—the past and the future. It has been said that history happens to people while they are living their lives. Our contributors are bringing those lives into a context the subjects did not have. In doing this work, they invite us to imagine ourselves differently into the future.

NOTE

1   Leigh Gilmore's important study brought our attention to the concept of limit cases in life writing. See Gilmore's *The Limits of Autobiography: Trauma and Testimony* (Ithaca, NY: Cornell University Press, 2001).

WORK CITED

Terdiman, Richard. 1993. *Present Past: Modernity and the Memory Crisis.* Ithaca, NY: Cornell University Press.

"THINGS GONE ASTRAY"
The Work of the Archive

Marlene Kadar

When we think of archives, we usually think about large buildings with regulations and professional staff that sort, protect, and distribute collections of unpublished documents and accounts for researchers to read, think about, and interpret. Certainly, anyone who has read Jacques Derrida's *Archive Fever: A Freudian Impression* assumes that the archive is global and illuminating on many levels, but that in its essence it speaks to us about life writing in its most poignant position: as death writing, as my colleague Ian Balfour used to jest ten years ago. (Death writing appears more commonplace as an autobiographical genre now.) Derrida uses Freudian concepts to argue that the archive is the seat of writings that yearn towards that moment of death and dying that we all approach and think about, whether with resolve or panic, or some other emotion or faith altogether.

Part of the archive writ large is the family's "private" archive, a collection that is no less subject to these drives and may in fact be more revealing of the subject, and of those aspects of humanity that we do not always want to reveal when we are alive, or when our beloved friends and relatives are alive (such as how afraid we are to approach the end of life, to know who we really are, and to die alone or forgotten, and how afraid we are that we do not know from whence we come). Richard Teleky, a Canadian-Hungarian poet and scholar, spoke to me about a collection of letters his mother and grandmother had saved for a few generations—letters exchanged between his grandfather (back in Hungary) and the grandfather's daughters (now in Cleveland) who had left for "Amerika" in search of another sister, newly married and reportedly dejected as a consequence of being away from home and family. The young women were emissaries of the father; they were to bring the lost soul back to the homeland, which in this case was Hungary.

Ironically, the daughters never returned to the homeland themselves, and it seems almost in exchange for the bad deal dealt their father that they saved the correspondence that was the evidence of their non-return, the evidence of the death of their parents and the death of their homeland such as it was. With a melancholic beauty, Teleky discussed a kind of muted address to these letters, which would include showing them to the world by publishing them. With his own pen, however, Teleky would give the letters peace, a resting place, or, as he called it, "a context." As Teleky writes in the plaintiff poem "Plainsong," death approaches as each day of life passes. The last three stanzas of his six-stanza poem go like this:

Make a space in your heart for the hour
of departure, cling to breath, stay the minute
as you must—night will pass. Break of day;
morning's over. See how longing can last.

Old men fall on the sidewalk, women shit in their beds,
the dog still snores contented, how much time is ahead?
No refrain can console me, rather bitter, bitter blight,
we are lost in the morning, afraid of the light.

Find a space in your heart for the thought
that life's over, learn to carry the night
like a gift overdue. Reap and sow, the sun
warns us, at end's end your death's you.
(Teleky 2011, 79)

If we follow the poetic justice of these verses, we might more easily anticipate that private archives, uncatalogued archival collections passed from one generation to another, family letters, and the like can provide a therapeutic crutch on which to balance (romantic) family lore and its inevitable difficult memories—both of which are sources of the stories we need in order to interpret our lives. We have to admit that the relationships between documents are often mysterious, enigmatic, unexplained, or unexplainable, and yet assumed to be "of the blood" (although this assumption, too, can be overturned with probing archival research that unveils family secrets, clandestine sexual adventures, or religious and political secrets that question a received truth). Why descendants feel the need, often the deep longing, to read and interpret the lack that Freud speaks so often about is a question without an answer, and yet a question always worth asking. Terry Eagleton closes one of his pensive invectives against the death drive by saying, "It is only because we carry death in our bones that we are able to keep on living" (2007, 160).

I wish to take these bones into a metaphor of context, a place of belonging, where life's longings interpenetrate with death's desire. Can we see the letters kept in Teleky's care, for example, as the skeleton for the story that exists out there but can never in its totality be told? There is always something missing, always a lack in remembering family stories. Yet there is more of a desperation to know when blood is at stake, or when the continuity of life is threatened and we desire to know its roots. For Teleky, the subject's (self-imposed?) exile is a rich source of knowledge about these themes, which he explores narratively in his profoundly compassionate 1998 novel *The Paris Years of Rosie Kamin*.

It almost sounds mystical or irregular, but in fact it is normal, vernacular, that words are used in one present, discovered in another, and interpreted in yet another, so that the private lives of ordinary persons are intelligible to their descendants. Indeed, so desperate is the desire that hundreds of websites have opened declaring that one family archive is here, another there. Other websites offer tools for the preservation of family archives, the conservation of the paper on which words are written and thus saved in an archive, either public or private. But try as we might, we can never archive everything. Paul Ricoeur reminds us of this in *Memory, History, Forgetting*, translating what he calls Pierre Nora's "exclamation"—"Archive as much as you like: something will always be left out" (2004, 169).

Contemporary life-writing theorists and memoirists desire to address this lack, this missing part of the greater story, and in doing so, try to also pay homage to neglected peoples and their communities. Like Teleky, life-writing theorists long to find "all the lost things and names, whatever they may be: things gone astray, mislaid, squandered, wasted" (Steedman 2005, 16). For better or worse, the part that is "left out" changes, but it never goes away.

WORKS CITED

Derrida, Jacques. [1995] 1998. *Archive Fever: A Freudian Impression*. Translated by Eric Prenowitz. Chicago: University of Chicago Press.

Eagleton, Terry. 2007. *The Meaning of Life*. Oxford: Oxford University Press.

Ricoeur, Paul. 2004. *Memory, History, Forgetting*. Translated by Kathleen Blamey and David Pellauer. Chicago and London: University of Chicago Press.

Steedman, Carolyn. 2005. "Archival Methods." In *Research Methods for English Studies*, edited by Gabriele Griffin, 16–29. Edinburgh: Edinburgh University Press.

Teleky, Richard. 1998. *The Paris Years of Rosie Kamin*. South Royalton, VT: Steerforth Press.

———. 2011. *The Hermit in Acadia: Poems*. Holstein, ON: Exile.

"PEOPLE DEALT THIS FATE TO PEOPLE"

The War and the Holocaust in Zofia Nałkowska's Life Writing

Eva C. Karpinski

In early 1945, Zofia Nałkowska, a celebrated Polish modernist writer, author of socially and politically conscious fiction and essays, and doyenne of pre-war literary and cultural salons, was invited by the newly formed Communist government to participate in the unprecedented task of assisting the Central Commission for the Investigation of German Crimes in Poland. What resulted from her exposure to eyewitness accounts, survivors' testimonies, and visits to multiple sites of extermination was a slim volume of documentary narratives called *Medallions*. She distilled some of her experiences into this incredibly economical, restrained, and powerful text that deserves to be placed next to Primo Levi's *Survival in Auschwitz* or Tadeusz Borowski's *This Way for the Gas, Ladies and Gentlemen*. In addition to publishing *Medallions*, Nałkowska was a prolific diarist whose wartime notebooks contain a record of everyday life in German-occupied Warsaw and a rare contemporaneous response by a Polish Gentile writer to the Holocaust, in particular to the liquidation of the Warsaw ghetto.[1] Because *Medallions* became available in English only in 2000, with Diana Kuprel's translation,[2] and Nałkowska's diaries have not yet been translated, her work has not been fully recognized in the Anglo-American canon of world Holocaust literature. Unfortunately, the only article in English that I have been able to locate that discusses Nałkowska's work, Magdalena Opalski's critique of wartime diaries, significantly distorts facts and uses Nałkowska's writing to reinforce the widespread stereotype of Poles' anti-Semitism and indifference to the plight of their Jewish neighbours under the Nazi occupation.[3]

I want to complicate this picture by reading the vast body of Nałkowska's war-related life writing and tracing a trajectory that corresponds to the movement from incomplete witnessing to becoming what Arthur W. Frank calls a "communicative body" (1995, 143)—a receiver and transmitter of difficult knowledge. This trajectory runs from sparse, cryptic remarks in her wartime diaries to the adoption of a conscious testimonial stance in *Medallions* and in the commission's activities. The challenge of my approach lies in viewing Nałkowska's practice of witnessing as spread across three different sites, each constructing a different knowledge about the Holocaust: her wartime diaries (1939–1945) and her post-liberation diaries (1945–1954); the short narratives collected in *Medallions* (1946); and her participation in the work of the commission (1945–1947). These specific forms of life writing and documenting must be read as intertexts that resonate with one another as they span different modalities of the testimonial act, from an intimate diary entry to an aestheticized literary reportage, and, finally, to an act of listening to eyewitness testimonies.

Attending to her role as witness prompts several questions: How has Nałkowska been able to forge a standpoint from which to define her attitude to the surrounding reality, her own person, and the human condition—a standpoint, we must remember, that she captures in the formula, "People dealt this fate to people"?[4] What kind of collective "postmemory" has been produced by the traces of the Holocaust preserved in her private and public texts?[5] How has this difficult knowledge that she unveiled been repressed and/or ideologized through collective denial and amnesia in Polish representations of the Holocaust? How can we translate her personal pain of bearing witness into the national trauma of surviving in the land that has been a forensic locus of the most horrific mass murder in recent history? Occupied Poland, after 1941, was turned into "an 'archipelago' of death-factories and camps, the scene of executions, pacifications, and exterminations which surpassed anything so far documented in the history of [humanity]" (Davies 1981, 454). How does one inhabit this place defiled by violence, chosen by the Nazis to become synonymous with the gas chamber and the crematorium? Describing Nałkowska's autobiographical project, her editor Hanna Kirchner uses the metaphor of "a tightly folded text" that needed to be pried open (quoted in Marszałek 2003, 11). What I am looking for in the folds of Nałkowska's measured language is some insight into a life *in extremis*, some answers to the haunting question: How was it even possible to live and work next to the Holocaust?

The six volumes of Nałkowska's diaries, contained in sixty-seven notebooks, cover almost sixty years of writing, from age twelve to seventy. They are available thanks to the monumental effort of Hanna Kirchner, who edited them after the author's death in 1954, investing decades of research into their preparation. *Wartime Diaries* (1970) was the first volume to be published, and the final sixth volume focusing on the postwar years appeared in 2000. Kirchner took this vast, handwritten, heterogeneous, and chaotic life-writing material, often scribbled on loose sheets and stitched together in a "sartorial manner,"[6] and turned it into a book equipped with a truly encyclopedic historical and biographical apparatus of notes and annotations decoding most of the references hidden in the text. Commenting on the editorial process of turning the "intimate journal" into a more accessible text, Magdalena Marszałek notes the resulting tension between the homogenizing effect of these smoothing interventions and the heterogeneity and fragmentariness inherent in diary record (2003, 13). Another tension is generated by a relative absence of a wider political perspective, an almost claustrophobic confinement to the here and now of Warsaw and its vicinity, along with an inward exploration of the world of books, conversations with people, or glimpses of the past, with a very limited analysis of the events in the outside world. The requirement of contextualization heeded by Nałkowska's editor, and especially the challenge posed by the frequent use of indexical pronouns, arises partly from the quick, momentary notation of the journal, and partly from the writer's wish to encrypt the information and some personal data (Rodak 2011, 245). The specific features of the intimate genre are amplified in the wartime journal by the conspiratorial conditions of its production.

The importance of Nałkowska's war and Holocaust witnessing must be understood in the context of Nazi censorship, prohibition on writing, and destruction of evidence that made any attempt to document atrocities illegal. Any writer expressing forbidden content lived under the threat of arrest, deportation to a camp, or execution. Writing was hazardous and curtailed because of the fear of searches and informants, in addition to regular hardships of daily life such as hunger, curfew, inflation, diseases, and the constant possibility of death. Arbitrary seizures of hostages taken from the streets in reprisal for underground actions were commonplace. In Warsaw, the Nazis adopted communal punishment on a mass scale. The hostages were publicly executed to instill terror and discourage resistance. Decrees were posted all over the city, and the names of the condemned could be heard from loudspeakers that German authorities had installed in public spaces. Private gatherings of more than three people were illegal, so Polish cultural life and education had to be done in secret. Told about a Gestapo search in the neighbours' apartment, Nałkowska, in a moment of panic, burned one notebook of her diary as well as the texts deposited at her place, written by participants of one of the clandestine literary meetings that she hosted (Kirchner 2000, 107). In the entry from 15 January 1943, she says only, "I've lost the whole notebook in the stupidest way." A year later, from the relative safety of her friend's country house in Adamowizna, she adds, "It's regrettable because there was a lot about Mother and everything about those people behind the wall, about their cause, indeed the most horrific one in this horrific world" (4 February 1944). This burned notebook casts a shadow on the extant diary, a haunting trace of what had been destroyed, a remnant constantly negotiating absence and presence, memory and loss. The cryptic nature of the reference to "those people behind the wall"—a recurrent phrase in the diary—reflects a hushed tone of fear, related to a total prohibition of any contact between Poles and Jews. German law in occupied Poland made helping or sheltering Jews punishable by death that was meted out to the rescuer and his or her entire family.

What the diary does not dare to reveal but the reader can reconstruct thanks to Kirchner's generous editorial assistance is that while eking out a living from a small tobacco shop, Nałkowska was engaged in the underground cultural life. She helped organize aid for her protegé, Bruno Schulz, who was locked in the Drohobycz ghetto. She participated in the committee assisting Polish Jewish writers on "the Aryan side," and offered them temporary shelter (Kirchner 2000, 108). Moreover, for Nałkowska, the Holocaust had a personal dimension through the suicide of her Jewish brother-in-law, Maksymilian Bick, whose tragic death in faraway France she had been hiding from her sister, as she mentions in her entries from 15–24 August 1941, and 3 August 1942. Before the war, Nałkowska, a member of the left-leaning intelligentsia, sympathized with Jews. She was supportive of Jewish cultural presence in Polish life and promoted her Polish Jewish colleagues such as Bruno Schulz and Adolf Rudnicki. She publicly condemned any form of anti-Semitism, especially in the Polish Academy of Literature, where in 1938 she fought for inclusion of Julian Tuwim, boasting in her pre-war diary that she remained "faithful" to him in her crusade against reactionary nationalist writers (Nałkowska, ed. Kirchner, 1970, 409n).[7] Besides her strong opposition to anti-Semitism, nationalism, and xenophobia, there is ample evidence of her empathy and compassion for the suffering of others.

When the wall around the Warsaw ghetto was completed in November 1940, it marked not only a significant stage in the development of the Nazi politics of extermination with regard to the Polish Jewish population, but also a completely new chapter in the modern history of Polish–Jewish coexistence. Half a million people were squeezed into a tiny area of the city, living in the most crushing conditions. The ghetto was set up as part of the enforcement of racialized spatial segregation between Jews and "Aryans." But this spatial segregation, apart from making the Nazi genocidal violence possible and invisible, also constructed the power of the Polish gaze to racialize—to scan bodies and speech for traces of meaning in the process of differentiation between self and other. The segregated racialized space constructed the identity of the self as well as the other in deadly proximity that imposed and required a temporal, spatial, and emotional separation (Shallcross 2011, 9), which ultimately led to the exclusion of the racialized other from the imagined community of the nation. From then on, any Jewish person hiding on the "Aryan" side would live in the terror of the Polish gaze encoded with the power of life and death. On the other hand, Jews were forbidden to look at the "Aryan" streetcar that passed through the enclosed space of the ghetto. Jacek Leociak describes the view of the ghetto from "the Aryan streetcar": "It was really a different world, in which the walls, barbed wire, and guarded gates acquire the character of the final borders between life and death. It was a closed space, disconnected and isolated from the space continuum so that it could be degraded and excluded from normal life, so that it could be veiled" (2001, 78). The wall facilitated the dehumanization of the Jewish community through their literal and symbolic exclusion from the public space, establishing the "otherness" of "those behind the wall." Consequently, the elliptical phrases and silences in Nałkowska's diary, albeit due to self-censorship, can hardly be exempted from this "wall effect." She records her impressions from the first months of the ghetto: "The streetcar is passing through the exotic Jewish district, with horrible streets crowded despite the cold, with boarded up shops, burnt houses. Now it's really only Jews and all Jews who live there, the guards stand at the entrance and exit, the streetcar doesn't stop any time. It is extremely strange—as an image and as a thought about it" (8 January 1941). The moments of such spatial transgression into the segregated space of the other reminded the "Aryan" passengers who they were not. The sense of exoticism and strangeness experienced by non-Jews is a sign of their distance and isolation from the life of the ghetto, which allowed them to cultivate their indifference to the misery of the Jews. For Nałkowska, however, such expressive rhetoric was a way to communicate the enormity of the sight, its "monstrous strangeness, incomprehensible either to thought or to this excruciating sadness" (15 April 1943).[8] She provides examples of the tragic contrast between the meaning of spatial segregation for those within the walls and those without. When her friend Leo Belmont died in the ghetto, his wife could follow the coffin "only to the ghetto wall" (2 November 1941). But for those on the outside, "The distance across the street or the thickness of the wall, or another district, separates us temporarily from reality, spares us its horror" (15 January 1944).

Deportations to the Treblinka death camp, one hundred kilometres northeast of Warsaw, started in the summer of 1942. During the first mass liquidation of the ghetto, Nałkowska spent a lot of time at the cemetery mourning her mother's death. This Catholic cemetery, whose walls were adjacent to the ghetto, became her observation point from which she may have recorded information about "those people behind the wall," the information that had been lost together with her burnt diary. She obsessively returns to the lost notebook as "the dark patch of silence [that] cut short my contact with a certain reality. Facts are difficult and must be excluded" (26 January 1943). What are left are mostly cryptic comments registering her increasing horror at the escalating violence: "I leave [the place] with sorrow and intense terror. I suppress tears on the street and give a lot of money to every old beggar" (19 August 1942). After the recent July transports, she describes the ghetto as "the dead city, the city of horrors and suffering....

All windows and balconies ... empty today" (31 August 1942). When the ghetto rises up in resistance in April 1943, and continues fighting until 16 May 1943, she announces the uprising in an enigmatic way: "One can hear and one can see.... Above the cemetery wall ... black clouds, ascending clouds of smoke. Sometimes one can see the flames—like a red, flickering banner in the wind" (25 April 1943). Three days later she adds, "The fate of these people far away, these people near. The dead, the dead. Grim parades of the resigned, the leaps into the flames, leaps into the abyss.... The boy in the window, children carried in the arms" (28 April 1943). And in another entry, she writes, "The depth of sadness, pure horror, pure evil. The smoking ovens, crackling logs. This doesn't change, this continues" (7 May 1943). While the uprising is being brutally squashed and the Germans are razing the ghetto, she describes the scene: "The drowned ones [Jews] are passing by, drawing one into the abyss. The suffering of others becomes sharper, more piercing than one's own, the suffering that transforms people into specters and ghosts. And deadly fear.... It's devastating to see their love, burning at the stake, tenderness against the odds and courage that nobody knows of, that is invisible" (14 May 1943). She felt it necessary to annotate her entries, and in several footnotes written after the war she added explanatory words: Jews, the burning of the ghetto, daily mass murder, firebombs, smoke, and gunshots (Nałkowska, ed. Kirchner, 1970, 280–83).

Nałkowska seemed to be acutely aware of her silences, as well as "the silence of the entire reality" (14 October 1943) that implicated her and other bystanders in what was going on around them. Early on, in October 1940, she talks about feelings of panic and dread at "one's own powerlessness in the face of reality falling apart into multiple horrible events. Astonishment that this is how it is, that it is true. And again, one's own role in it, one's unbelievable place, bad fate." The self emerging from these entries is pained by a sense of futility and plagued with negative affects such as shame and guilt, as she ponders people's "common acquiescence" to suffering "on this side and on the other, on both sides of today's dividing line" (21 March 1942). Hanna Kirchner says that the Holocaust is deeply entrenched in Nałkowska's wartime diaries, not as concrete facts that were impossible for her to articulate, but rather as "the internalized pain, the moral wound" (2000, 121). This wound is gaping in several passages, including this one: "How can I be forced to be a part of this, to acquiesce by a mere fact of living in it! It's also a disgrace, not just torture. It's a horrible shame, not just compassion. All the efforts, to endure, not to go mad, somehow to preserve oneself amidst this dread—it feels like guilt" (29 April 1943). She writes from a horrific space of war from which she cannot exempt herself, from which there is no desertion (Galant 2010, 93). Although she does not want to be drawn into the abyss opened up by the ongoing genocide, she knows that she cannot take a break from this history and reality and—cautiously at first—she undertakes the role of witness. Her descriptions of the burning of the Warsaw ghetto reveal a deepening crisis and a heightened consciousness of the need to bear witness and to preserve the traces of what is being wiped out.

In her wartime diaries, Nałkowska models a certain testimonial stance adopted gradually as a result of witnessing catastrophe engulfing one's own group and others and leading to increasing identification and empathy across difference. The diaries begin and end with extensive reporting on war: the heroic defence of Warsaw against Germany in September 1939, followed by her return to the city after an attempted escape to the south, and the Warsaw Uprising from August to September 1944, the city's final agony witnessed from Adamowizna. These two events frame more than five years of daily existence and struggle for survival, the physical and mental strain of running her tobacco shop under the German occupation and participating in clandestine activities, during the escalating terror against the civilian population. There is a trajectory in her writing about the occupation and the Holocaust that follows a notable change in attitude: as the repression against the Polish population grows, she identifies her fate with the fate of the Jews.[9] While references to the murder of the Jews are muted at first, the comparisons to "those behind the wall" become more frequent with her growing awareness of the anticipated scale of the atrocities and her own sense of impending doom. On 27 January 1943, she writes, "I wondered about others [after the war she added "Jews"]—always felt so tormented by their fate, ready to substitute myself into the tangle of their immense suffering.... Today, when this fate is mine, I act in the same way. There are days when I live as if there was tomorrow and a day after tomorrow." In the months following the final liquidation of the ghetto, with executions of Polish hostages on the rise in retaliation for underground anti-German resistance, when walking on the street is like "brushing against death," she becomes one of the condemned: "It's already the same as it was with them [a footnote explains "Jews"]—what at the time filled us with dread and compassion, and even astonishment. We are acting in the way we couldn't understand in them. We live despite it, we live next to it, and in it" (20 October 1943). She reports the emotions of a man digging in the ruins of the ghetto:

> Wherever he looks, nothing but death and ruins, rubble and debris. He brought home a pair of scissors and a sugar bowl, possibly silver, found there, as well as some firewood. That's all left from the life that swarmed there, from the people who used to walk, talk, work. Who got up in the morning, washed, and got dressed, then undressed in the evening and went to bed. Just like us today. 'It's a cemetery,' he says. And he can't calm down. (14 December 1943)

In contrast to her reticence during the Ghetto Uprising in the spring of 1943, she is eloquent in her accounts of the Warsaw Uprising and does not shy away from descriptions of horrible scenes such as a ten-year-old girl brutally gang-raped by the Ukrainian soldiers. She is severe in her evaluation of the uprising: "Like these people behind the wall, no longer alive, so are we deluding ourselves that each of us will be spared, will survive" (15 August 1944). After the defeat, while Warsaw is being razed, she still draws comparisons: "Now, like before from the cemetery of those others, they are removing marble and headstones.... One can think that I live to be a witness to the death of others" (6 November 1944).

In her early reflection on war, in which she tries to distance herself from the present, she wants to believe that "Nothing changes—only the war equipment, only the weapons are improved" (4 July 1940). However, what happens during World War II, a total war, is a transition from the detached civilian "I" to "we" in the collective approach to the limit of existence. Living literally "on the edge of being," surrounded by the ubiquity of death, she lists litanies of names of dead people: "The number of the dead is countless—not only strangers, but also acquaintances. Sometimes I count in a daze—more than thirty, more than fifty. Sometimes they die from natural causes—and it seems indecent" (9 October 1943). In a constant turn to mourning, obsessed also with her own aging, her imagination is consumed by thanatological themes and images of her mother's dying, the deaths of people in the ghetto, the deaths of innumerable hostages, and the deaths of people in the Warsaw Uprising. As an archive of memory, the diary absorbs these daily losses while also preserving life, keeping it "from being lost or destroyed," and memorializing a portrait of life in time (15 January 1943). Accordingly, her metaphor for the diary is "a bag of memory" filled with the living and the dead (Rodak 2011, 254). The archive of memory becomes archival memory—layering material traces and bodies. In contrast to a composed memoir, her diary writing is not a creation from memory, but rather a depositing (of people, bodies) in the archival space of memory—documentation rather than literary production.

Under the extreme conditions of its making, Nałkowska's wartime diary never loses what has been a persistent feature of her writing: her fascination with people. While her diary can be seen as an existential project of recording a biography while conscious of the dangers she risked in the writing, she constructs what Paweł Rodak calls "the communicative 'I'"—always oriented toward a person rather than text or narrative (2011, 313).[10] She frequently gives expression to her "sense of wonder about others."[11] People are the focus of her consciousness: "People's fate is my reality.... I can't stop thinking about all that is now, and people in it, always people" (21 March 1942). Declaring that it is "through people" that she takes part in the world (19 March 1943), she records intense moments of "love for another human being, the joy and inexpressible happiness of finding oneself through others" (10 November 1943). For Nałkowska, "others" are indispensable to the self. In her vision of a human being as "social and interactive," the interpersonal is at the core of identity, bringing together the ethics and aesthetics of writing, which is humanitarian in form and mindful of the social and existential contexts (Galant 2010, 73). The imbrication of self and others explains the centrality of dialogue and conversation in her life, and also foregrounds the importance of reading as a connection to the dead and the living (9 October 1943).[12] Throughout her life, Nałkowska enjoyed a reputation as a brilliant conversationalist and collected interesting interlocutors from all social ranks and classes, including beggars and prisoners. After the liberation, she actively solicited interviews with the survivors, even stopping them on the streets. This fascination extends to the archived lives of others, found among her late father's papers and bundles of letters that she was sorting out during the war, dwelling among the dead with the hope of "renewing a dead life" in a biographical book about her father.[13] Yet the presence of "others" in this wartime text, more often than a source of pleasure, is a source of pain (16 July 1944). The pain of history that she experiences "because of people" has two major causes: on the one hand, people who are dying, friends and family, including Jews, whom the diary saves from disappearance; on the other hand, people who perpetrate and condone war atrocities, who provoke her to say that "People dealt this fate to people."

Nałkowska returns to this statement, using it as a motto for *Medallions*, written and published immediately after the war.[14] While the eight reportages contained in this slim volume were inspired by her chance encounters with the survivors and her work for the commission, they owe their stylistic and philosophical crispness to the writing techniques of foreshortening and condensation that she had already established in her wartime diaries. Several stories take up and amplify the themes and moral dilemmas encrypted in the diary. The opening piece, "Dr. Spanner," based on Nałkowska's participation in the investigation of the production of soap from human bodies, foregrounds the recurrent motif of the gaze and the curtain or veil separating bystanders and witnesses (the ones not "seeing" but knowing without seeing) from victims and perpetrators (the ones who looked behind the curtain). "The Cemetery Lady" is a flashback to 1943, to the liquidation of the Warsaw ghetto, whose wall—again, the curtain or veil—muffles the enormity of what is happening behind it and warps perception of the people living "right by the wall," prompting the narrator's comment: "Still, reality is endurable because it is selective. It draws near in fragmented events and tattered reports, in echoing shots, in the distant smoke drifts, in the fires which, history cryptically says, 'turn into ashes.' This reality, at once distant and played out against the wall, is not real—that is, until the mind struggles to gather it up, arrest, and understand it" (Nałkowska, trans. by Kuprel, 2000, 18). The issue of incomprehension recurs in "By the Railway Track" in the testimony of a witness to the death of a wounded Jewish woman, an escapee from the transport train, surrounded by Polish villagers unable to offer her help, until one man, who had previously brought her vodka and cigarettes, volunteers to shoot her. Here "a ring of fear" (25) surrounding the woman forms another wall/curtain separating her from the others. In the final example, "Dwojra Zielona," a Jewish woman survivor articulates a simple truth about the ethics of testimony when she explains her strong will to live: "Why? I'll tell you why: to tell everything just like I'm telling you now. To let the world know what they did" (32).

In this collection, Nałkowska offers startling moments of moral confusion experienced through encounters with abject horror, as well as chilling insights into the Nazi biopolitics of terror and the calculated management of human bodies in the rationalized practice of exploitation and extermination. Bożena Shallcross observes that Nałkowska "revised not only the bio-ontological position of the human subject; she also modified the world, which framed these subjects in terms of radical corpo-reality"—that is, the world of corpses (2011, 62).[15] In her attempts to unveil the horror of the abject—that which, in Julia Kristeva's classic sense, is "ejected beyond the scope of the possible, the tolerable, the thinkable" (1982, 1)—Nałkowska's texts break the boundary between the inside and the outside of the horror and draw us into its impurity, without overly passing any judgment.

The title of *Medallions* refers to those portraits of the dead one finds on tombs while walking through cemeteries. Reading these stories, we encounter the limit of memorializing that necessitates new forms of language and a rejection of conventional "literariness" for the sake of writing as a process of depositing the living and the dead in the archive of memory. Suspended on the border between writing and silence, Nałkowska was indeed preoccupied with the relationship between theme and form, using the aesthetics of silence and understatement, speaking through the unsaid. According to Diana Kuprel, "the raw material that confronted Nałkowska during the hearings [of the commission] required that she adopt a different perspective" (in Nałkowska, trans. by Kuprel, 2000, xiv). She turned an aesthetic problem into a powerful ethical and political statement by opting for a pared-down documentary style that communicates (through) the shrinkage of language and self. Speaking through the silences, hesitations, grimaces, gestures, gaps, and intonations, Nałkowska preserves the opacity of the body in saying the unspeakable and creates the effect of the testimonial presence. The horror of the ongoing genocide is refracted into small fragments, showing incompleteness of perception as a defence mechanism against unbearable knowing. "Shattered statues and medallions" (20) that lay along the cemetery avenue also represent fracturing and fragmentation, broken portraits, and textual *mise en abyme*. There is also the aporia of silence between "us" and "them," represented for Nałkowska by the mutilated human remains from which Spanner extracted fat in his lab, corresponding to the figure of *Muselmann* that

Giorgio Agamben uses to represent the ethical limit of witnessing. Working from Primo Levi's description of the *Muselmann* as the complete witness, the one who "touch[ed] the bottom" but did not "return to tell about it" (Levi 1988, 83–84), Agamben (1999) makes this figure a focal point of his own reflection on the (im)possibility of witnessing. What Nałkowska does can be seen as staging a hermeneutics of reading, a semiotic post-mortem in the practice of documentary life writing as reading fragments, here truncated bodies and paraphernalia of the unspeakable crime.

If the burnt diary represents what remains "on the edge of a silence," reminding us of the incompleteness of any testimony, *Medallions* testifies to the unspeakability of "what remains in excess" of what can be told (Frank 1995, 138). Its silences, understatements, and self-control are meant to protect the person from the overwhelming chaos of what was observed. Nałkowska's writing— including her diary entries and her character portraits in *Medallions*—communicates through "bits and pieces" that make up testimony described as acts that "cannot be constructed as knowledge nor assimilated into full cognition" (Felman and Laub 1992, 5). When experience does not fit "into existing frames of reference," an "'overwhelmed' consciousness" can deal only with bits and pieces (Frank 1995, 139). What kind of ethics is needed to bear witness to the atrocities unveiled in front of the commission and to communicate this abject knowledge to others? How can one attest to the inhuman in the human?

In *Giving an Account of Oneself*, Judith Butler suggests that "when we come up against the limits of any epistemological horizon," such that the other person does not "qualify within the scheme of the human within which I operate," then it may be necessary to "risk ourselves precisely there, at the moments of our unknowingness, when what conditions us and what lies before us diverge from one another, when our willingness to become undone constitutes our chance of becoming human, a becoming whose necessity knows no end" (2005, 80). It seems that Nałkowska's ethics of witnessing does precisely that: embraces the inhuman in the human, taking the risk of becoming the subject of testimony as "the one who bears witness to a desubjectification" (Agamben 1999, 121). In *Medallions*, she produces a testimony on the model of Agamben's *Muselmann* as "remnant"—as that which resides in the very relation between the human and the inhuman and in fact forces us to recognize the ethical imperative to preserve this relation (Chare 2011, 131). In dealing with traumatic experiences that challenge our definitions of the human, *Medallions* performs an act of "bearing witness which refuses to hold the belief that limit experiences are beyond communication" (Chare 2011, 10). Her aphorism "People dealt this fate to people" refuses the moral comfort of separating the human and the inhuman, which would be a mere reversal of the Nazi biopower's dualism of human and subhuman.[16] Nałkowska's sentiments here echo those in her diary, where she speaks from a position of atheism, humanism, and moral (ethical) monism, but one that is free from glib relativism. For her, a full range of the inhuman as part of the human extends from biology to morality, from being "meat" (10 November 1943), to living toward death, to having a capacity for evil and violence. This ethics allows her to overcome her repugnance and inquire into the acts of the perpetrators and bystanders, a task much harder because it requires a suspension of self, different from bearing witness to the survivors. It is the courage to see things as they are, not as they should be.

Arthur Frank speaks of the "concentric quality" of testimony, where those who receive stories of witnesses become witnesses, and, by passing on the stories, can in turn make witnesses of others (1995, 142). Nałkowska assumes her place in this "circle of testimony" (143) by seeking out the survivors, receiving their testimony, and responding to the call to join the commission. The last entry in *Wartime Diaries*, dated 10 February 1945, states that Jerzy Borejsza, a Polish Soviet propagandist and leading animator of culture in postwar Communist Poland, proposed that she become the president of the regional Commission for the Investigation of War Crimes in Auschwitz. The commission was based in Łódź (because Warsaw was completely destroyed after the uprising of 1944), and its assignments brought Nałkowska to the sites of death camps in Auschwitz-Birkenau, Stutthof, Majdanek, and Chełmno. Wacław Barcikowski, her colleague from the commission, reminisces in his memoir essay about their site visits and the hours spent listening to the depositions: "Her courage often surrendered to caution, caution to courage. She always took the side of the victim" (1965, 6). He describes her dedication to the task and recalls her shock in reaction to the horrors discovered during the inspection of Chełmno, when the visitors realized that they were walking on the ashes and scattered bones of the gassed people. Nałkowska first covered her eyes, saying, "Monstrous, monstrous. This couldn't have been done by people," and then requested that some of the ashes from this gigantic ossuary be gathered into a small can to provide "authentic evidence" for other members of the commission (Barcikowski 1965, 23). Her gesture (at once respectful and dubious, making one wonder what happened to the human remains that she collected—whether they have been given a proper burial) magnifies one aspect of her duties: preventing the destruction of evidence and memory before it becomes unrecognizable, undone into ashes.[17]

Nałkowska's direct involvement in the work of "the Commission of horror and astonishment," as she refers to it in her diary on 10 October 1945 (Nałkowska, ed. Kirchner, 2000), makes us aware of the contrast between two modes of witnessing: textually mediated witnessing and embodied witnessing. Witnessing is always relational in that it requires the presence of another body. Her participation in the commission goes beyond witnessing that is mediated by print as experienced by readers of *Medallions*. She literalizes the call to witnessing by giving her embodied presence to listening to the stories of the embodied others. Discussing Dori Laub's view of testimony, Nicholas Chare underscores the importance of this restorative work of witnessing that is "as much a process of restoration of self as a record of the event" (2011, 139–40). Through her work for the commission, Nałkowska fulfilled the enabling role of outsider witness that was vital to rehumanizing the survivors as insider witnesses. Her willingness to risk herself and become involved on behalf of others evokes her ethical ruminations in her early 1916 essay on the Polish romantic tragedy *Kordian* by Juliusz Słowacki, where she makes an important distinction between "the ability for inaction" and "the inability for action" (Janowska 2007, 69). Both were experienced during the war, as a certain disposition of the subject, whether cast in the role of perpetrator, bystander, or victim, which sometimes tragically overlapped. Echoes of this moral reasoning resonate in *Wartime Diaries* in her reflection on the Hungarian and Slovakian soldiers visiting Adamowizna during the Warsaw Uprising: they are kind and harmless, she says, "but they might not be. They haven't received the order yet" (18 September 1944). The question of free will and agency preoccupied her in many entries. She discussed the possibility of refusing to murder (the choice of inaction as an active stance)—of which very few were capable—as well as the problem of passive acquiescence for those who chose inaction out of indifference or were forced to accept inaction as they were unable to act. After the war, this dilemma translated into her conscious choice of witnessing as the impossibility of inaction.

Two grassroots activists who were instrumental in recruiting Nałkowska for the commission were her childhood friend Helena Boguszewska and Boguszewska's partner, Jerzy Kornacki, who envisioned the role of Polish writers in collecting testimonies and gathering evidence. Hanna Kirchner reproduces extensive fragments from Kornacki's unpublished manuscript *Kamieniołomy* (Quarries) in her notes for the sixth volume of Nałkowska's diaries (Nałkowska, ed. Kirchner, 2000). They throw an interesting light on the circumstances that led to the initial launching of the Central Commission for the Investigation of German Crimes,[18] as well as on the politics of remembering and documenting Nazi genocide immediately after the liberation. In a note on the entry from 10 February 1945, Kirchner recounts Kornacki's attempts, together with Boguszewska, to protect the site of the Majdanek camp as early as August 1944. At the same time, the Soviets formed their own commission, which was granted priority access to all materials. The Poles were allowed to start their own investigation of the camps built by the German occupiers on Polish soil only after the Soviets had concluded their inquiry. Not only had the Russian Army removed a lot of archival evidence from Auschwitz, but there were also rumours of looting (reported by one of the former inmates, Arthur Mayer, for whom Nałkowska had romantic feelings). Shallcross writes that the material object world of the

Holocaust was largely destroyed by the withdrawing Nazi troops and the Russian and Polish plundering of sites of former concentration camps that Polish authorities failed to prevent (2011, 129). In her unpublished memoir, Boguszewska recalls the difficulties they encountered from the side of the government, the incompetent handling of the commission, and their fear that fewer and fewer survivors were seen on the streets (Nałkowska, ed. Kirchner, 2000, Part One, 43f). She also remembers that Nałkowska was very keen on collecting detailed information about the camps (55f).

The initiatives of Boguszewska and Kornacki were early attempts to document atrocities, which ran parallel to the extensive efforts of Jewish historians to gather documentation of the Holocaust in the period immediately after the war.[19] The Central Commission often collaborated with the Central Jewish Historical Commission in Poland. It did so, for example, during the viewing and inspection of the Chełmno death camp, as described in "The Man Is Strong" in *Medallions*. Nałkowska's diaries from this period often touch upon a thorny issue of the Polish–Jewish relations. In early May 1945, she received a letter from the Central Jewish Historical Commission, signed by Emil Sommerstein, informing her about brutal attacks on Jewish survivors and asking her for a public appeal in this case (Nałkowska, ed. Kirchner, 2000, Part One, 68f). Kirchner relates that among Nałkowska's papers deposited in the Adam Mickiewicz Museum of Literature in Warsaw, there is a folder with the materials from her work with the commission, which includes a copy of the report from the Jewish pogrom in Rzeszów in April 1945, which she must have saved (Nałkowska, ed. Kirchner, 2000, Part One, 69f). Indeed, in her entry from 18 July 1946, Nałkowska mentions the Kielce pogrom as one of the things tormenting her. There is also her comment on the Jewish exodus from Poland following the pogroms, on 15 August 1946, when she meets two young Jewish men on the train who are talking about people leaving: "So this is how people are leaving us."[20]

In the case of Polish–Jewish relations, history and memory cannot be understood as "static repositories of archival content or unmediated experience, but rather as complex, often conflictual, symbolic, interactional processes" (Brodzki 2007, 100). The past is being written and rewritten according to the needs of the present as this narrative is constantly challenged and revised, but it is equally true to speak of constant claims of the past on the present. Until the late 1980s, public discussion of the Holocaust and Polish–Jewish relations during and after the war was largely limited and falsified by sacrosanct assumptions of Polish martyrology, innocence, and victimization.[21] Only recently, after a long hiatus, has the Holocaust re-entered Polish collective memory as a formative event through which Poles have to define their relationship to key aspects of late modernity such as nationalism, modern ethics, exclusion of otherness, solidarity, and tolerance (Czapliński 2010, 345).[22] Looking at the reception of *Wartime Diaries* and *Medallions* in different times and contexts, we can recognize a range of responses typifying certain characteristic tendencies that cannot be separated from the issue of the larger political manipulation of the Holocaust. Thus, after a brief period of Stalinist censorship that condemned *Medallions* for promoting a specific "moral climate" cultivating "the horrors of the occupation" that "should not poison our life" (Nałkowska, ed. Kirchner, 2000, Part Two), *Medallions* has become entrenched as a mandatory school reading. As a permanent fixture in the Polish curriculum, it has been subjected to two types of appropriation: on the one hand, its representation of the Holocaust can be "polonized" and used to emphasize the suffering of the Polish nation, while on the other hand, it can be "universalized" and used to illustrate such theses as the banality of evil, or the totalitarian instrumentality of the Nazi genocidal machine. Ironically, *Medallions* can also provide support for wilful misreading of Nałkowska's *Wartime Diaries* as not much different from the generalized "norm" of Polish indifference to the fate of the Jews. However, it seems that a careful unfolding of her life writing related to the war and the Holocaust demonstrates the possibility of adopting a stance of active witnessing and constructs an opening for the much-needed cross-generational and cross-cultural dialogue about this history that can bring a promise of transformation. Moving beyond the conundrum of the impossibility and the necessity of Holocaust testimony, Nałkowska directs us away from the far edge of silence, from skepticism or even solipsism, symbolized by Agamben's figure of *Muselmann*, towards realism attached to the belief that we can and must bear this testimony—"bear" in a double sense of producing and being able to hear it.

NOTES

1 Early Gentile eyewitness accounts of the Warsaw ghetto include Czesław Miłosz's poem "Campo di Fiori" and Jerzy Zagórski's "Psalm." Both provide an outside view of the Ghetto Uprising from the "Aryan side." Jerzy Andrzejewski's novella "Wielki Tydzień" (Holy Week), written in April 1943, from his collection *Noc* (Night), published in 1946, is, according to Henryk Grynberg, "the earliest attempt in prose to tackle the moral shock of the Holocaust" (1983, 35). Nałkowska's editor Hanna Kirchner also points to Miron Białoszewski's poem "Jerozolima" about the gates to the ghetto (Kirchner 2000, 107).

2 *Medallions* has been translated into more than twenty languages, including German in 1956, Spanish in 2009, and Dutch in 2011.

3 Kirchner addresses some of these distortions and methodological problems in Opalski's approach, mostly the fact that it is unacceptable to generalize from the author's attitude to an entire society's attitude toward Jewish fellow citizens and their genocide (Kirchner 2000, 106).

4 "People dealt this fate to people" appears in the diary entry from 28 July 1944: "Oh, it's always people—history and war are made always only through people, their differences and their similarities.... People dealt this fate to people. People are everything in the world, and independently of their value or their entitlement—only people determine reality." All subsequent translations from Nałkowska's diaries are mine, but I use Diana Kuprel's version of this sentence.

5 I extend Marianne Hirsch's (1997) usage of second-generation "postmemory" from Holocaust survivors' children to children of bystanders affected by the trauma of Polish–Jewish
co-existence during and after the Holocaust.

6 This term, used by Nałkowska's Polish critics (Marszałek 2003, 194n), can be applied
both to her scrapbook-like technique of writing and to the elegant "sartorial" style of the
clothes for which she was famous.

7 Similarly, Nałkowska's postwar diaries show that, on top of her service in the commission,
she joined such progressive organizations as the League Against Racism, formed in March
1946, a rare example of common Polish and Jewish initiatives to fight anti-Semitism. Its
members were mostly former associates of the Polish Council to Aid Jews (Rada Pom-
ocy Żydom) created by Armia Krajowa (the underground Home Army) in September
1942 (Nałkowska, ed. Kirchner, 2000, Part One, 399). The league's first treasurer was
Irena Sandler, who helped to save twenty-five hundred Jewish children. Nałkowska also
wrote a preface to the last commander of the Ghetto Uprising Marek Edelman's memoir
Getto walczy (The Ghetto Fights, 1945), and an introduction to Michał Borwicz's book
Organizowanie wściekłości (Organized Rage), published by the league in 1947. She maintained close ties to the community of Jewish survivors, supporting the Jewish orphanage
in Otwock and reading from *Medallions* for the Jewish Historical Society (see entries
for 12 November 1945 and 16 June 1951). Given this context, it is understandable why
Hanna Kirchner is so critical of Opalski's accusations of anti-Semitism in Nałkowska's
1913 novel *Węże i róże* (Snakes and Roses), which includes a social and psychological
portrayal of Jewish financial elites (Kirchner 2000, 116). I argue that even if Opalski's
claim that Nałkowska was "colour-blind" and associated mainly with assimilated Jews had
some validity before the war, Nałkowska's witnessing of the Holocaust and her postwar
anti-racist activism suggest otherwise.

8 Shallcross quotes critiques of Nałkowska's use of the adjective "*dziwne*" (strange, odd),
which,

> belonged to the author's entrenched lexical repertoire … in using it, Nałkow-
> ska tended to blur everything.… The word, particularly popular in the Young
> Poland period, can easily obfuscate the meaning of its context and, indeed, even
> sound naïve. In the case of Nałkowska's Holocaust narration, though, we deal
> with a different, quite subtle, and relevant meaning of 'most odd, perplexing'
> as a qualifier for her encounter with … an extreme experience with which she
> empathized *against all odds* and, especially, against an overwhelming sense of
> loss and dehumanization. (2011, 66)

9 One might argue against the thesis of the common fate of Poles and Jews by reminding
the reader of the existential difference between Jews and Poles, as Przemysław Czapliński
does: death was certain for Jews, possible for Poles—that is, every Jewish life was threatened, but not every Polish (2010, 363).

10 Several critics notice Nałkowska's humanism through her links to existentialism
(Marszałek 2003) or personology (Janowska 2007). For example, Magdalena Marszałek
locates the affinities with existentialism in Nałkowska's dramatic view of human existence
as having no foundation and her postulate of conscious self-realization and active living
in the present (2003, 183). There is a poem about Nałkowska written by Czesław Miłosz
(1998) called "In her diary," where he cites her entry from 14 April 1943, in which she
expresses shame and torment at the atrocities happening in the ghetto, ending with her
philosophical musing: "Is the world horrible?… The world is like that, the world is ordinary. What is strange is only my feeling of horror, mine and others like myself." In his
free-verse response to her atheist acceptance of "the world as it is," Miłosz says that "much
courage is needed to recognize the mass crimes of the twentieth century as ordinary," and
adds that "in our asking ourselves where this scream of horror comes from, the defense
of the peculiar place of man [sic] begins."

11 See, for example, entries from 3 March 1944, 18 May 1944, or 16 July 1944.

12 See her entry on 18 April 1942: "Reading is not an escape from the horrors of today's life nor an escape from 'people'. Rather it is experiencing them to the highest degree, it is also finding oneself amidst the horror of the world."

13 Here is her interesting comment on life writing: "What a fascination—someone else's revealed, exposed life—a huge enrichment and intensification of one's own, a phenomenon that brings me closer to something like a discovery: creativity as absorption of other life, a capacity for it. The consciousness widens, strengthens, and deepens through another's drama of being" (15 July 1942).

14 With the exception of one story, "The Cemetery Lady," which is actually based on her diary sketch of an anti-Semitic woman tending the graves near the walls of the Warsaw ghetto.

15 Shallcross (2011) critiques Nałkowska's aestheticizing strategy in describing the human corpses, especially the headless torso of a sailor with a religious tattoo: "Her verdict denied any agency to the sailor, rendering his faith and his corpse entirely powerless," thus suiting Nałkowska's atheism. And yet, the corpse has "survived" as remnant to testify to its abject humanity and to the indignity done to the human body.

16 Henryk Grynberg famously paraphrased Nałkowska's sentence in his 1984 essay "People dealt this fate to Jews," claiming that her sentence erodes the real meaning of the Holocaust by universalizing it as catastrophe of humankind and making it possible to place it among other totalitarian crimes. The victims of the Holocaust were persecuted and died as "Jews" not as "people." In fact, "people" was a category reserved for the perpetrators. According to Grynberg, the Holocaust is a unique event and cannot serve as a metaphor for human suffering and genocide. "People dealt this fate to Jews" is a statement of fact while replacing "Jews" with "people" is an act of interpretation that obscures the historical truth of the event (Grynberg 1990, 43). In his polemic against Grynberg, Marek Zaleski defends Nałkowska's sentence as a liminal statement, uttered as if by the tragic chorus (Zaleski 2000, 95), and he interprets her words precisely as an indictment of the enlightenment metaphysics of violence, where in European culture the Jew has functioned as a figure of the "other" (97). By affirming the Jewish "difference," Grynberg paradoxically reinforces the logic adopted by the Nazis who excluded Jews from the category "people." At the same time, Grynberg's logic may lead to the erasure of the perpetrators' identity as "people"—they were not "people" but Nazis, collaborators, extortionists, kapos, and supporters of the Nazi system (Zaleski 2000, 93). Przemysław Czapliński (2010) adds yet another layer to Nałkowska's sentence, changing "People dealt this fate to people" to "Neighbours dealt this fate to neighbours." He alludes to the publication of Jan Tomasz Gross's *Neighbours* (2000), a book about the 1941 pogrom in Jedwabne, which created the need to confront collective responsibility for the indifference of the majority of the Polish population to the plight of the Jews and for anti-Semitic crimes during and after the Holocaust.

17 A similar case of being transfixed by death is recalled in her postwar diary on 5 October 1945. She clips and retains a photograph of the execution scene from a Warsaw street, published in a Polish paper, saying that she cannot walk away from the expression on the faces of the six men who are about to die: "I don't know what thought, what feeling can compensate for their suffering. One can't live thinking about it. The only thing one can do is to think about it continuously, be there with them, for them, put oneself in their place, relive what each of the five who are still alive must have felt—again and again" (Nałkowska, ed. Kirchner, 2000, Part One, 102).

18 According to Kirchner, the first meeting of the commission took place on 29 March 1945 in Kraków, but Nałkowska was not able to attend because of illness (Nałkowska, ed. Kirchner, 2000, Part One, 44). In December 1949, the commission's name was changed

to the Central Commission for the Investigation of Hitlerite German Crimes in Poland. During the Stalinist era, its activities were cut back, and between 1984 and 1991 it was known as the Central Commission for the Investigation of Hitlerite Crimes in Poland— the Institute of National Remembrance (IPN). The commission continued its work until 1991, when after the fall of communism its name was changed again to the Commission for the Prosecution of Crimes against the Polish Nation (IPN), so as to extend its mandate to include Nazi crimes, communist crimes, and crimes against peace. These name changes suggest in a subtle way how attitudes towards the war and the Holocaust in Poland have been politicized and manipulated over the years to serve the national interests.

19 In her overview of Polish historiography of the Holocaust, Natalia Aleksiun (2004) mentions the Central Jewish Historical Commission, formed in August 1944, which led to the establishment in 1947 of the Jewish Historical Institute, one of the crucial institutions of Holocaust research in Poland. Already, this configuration of the Soviet, Polish, and Jewish investigators present on Holocaust sites foreshadows future politicized interpretations of the Holocaust: its "polonizing" by nationalist interests, its communist "internationalizing" (universalizing), and its "particularizing" as a unique Jewish event.

20 Michael Steinlauf quotes statistics from January 1946 that show 86,000 officially registered Jews in Poland (1997, 46). By August 1946, after the repatriation from the Soviet Union, the number swelled to 244,000, reaching "a postwar peak" (combining those who survived and returned). By 1951, the Jewish population shrank to less than 80,000 (Steinlauf 1997, 52).

21 On the Communist regime's politics towards the Holocaust, see Michael Steinlauf's *Bondage to the Dead: Poland and the Memory of the Holocaust*. In his essay "Wounded Memory" (2000), Jacek Leociak reviews the commemoration of the Warsaw Ghetto Uprising in the Polish postwar press as symptomatic of the process of interpretation and revision of Polish–Jewish relations during the Holocaust that has shaped public memory of these events.

22 Both Aleksiun (2004) and Czapliński (2010) credit Claude Lanzmann's film *Shoah* (1985) for triggering this new wave of discourse, initiated by the publication of Jan Błoński's essay "The Poor Christian Looks at the Ghetto" in 1987, in which Błoński calls for admitting the fact of Polish indifference to the suffering of the Jews and asking for forgiveness. Czapliński suggests that such an admission might heal not only Polish–Jewish relations but also intergenerational relations, especially for younger Poles who feel shame for the concealed acts of wrongdoing, and who have inherited this legacy of "innocence," xenophobia, anti-Semitism, and disdain for others that may have led to indifference during the Holocaust (2010, 351).

WORKS CITED

Agamben, Giorgio. 1999. *Remnants of Auschwitz: The Witness and the Archive*. New York: Zone Books.

Aleksiun, Natalia. 2004. "Polish Historiography of the Holocaust—Between Silence and Public Debate." *German History* 22 (3): 406–32.

Barcikowski, Wacław. 1965. "Fragmenty Wspomnień o Zofii Nałkowskiej" [Fragments of memories of Zofia Nałkowska]. *Wspomnienia o Zofii Nałkowskiej* [Remembering Zofia Nałkowska]. Warszawa: Czytelnik.

Brodzka-Wald, Alina, Dorota Krawczyńska, and Jacek Leociak, eds. 2000. *Literatura polska wobec Zagłady* [Polish literature and the Holocaust]. Warszawa: Żydowski Instytut Historyczny.

Brodzki, Bella. 2007. *Can These Bones Live? Translation, Survival, and Cultural Memory*. Stanford, CA: Stanford University Press.

Butler, Judith. 2005. *Giving an Account of Oneself*. New York: Fordham University Press.

Chare, Nicholas. 2011. *Auschwitz and Afterimages: Abjection, Witnessing and Representation*. London & New York: Taurus.

Czapliński, Przemysław. 2010. "Zagłada—niedokończona narracja polskiej nowoczesności" [The Holocaust—the unfinished narrative of Polish modernity]. In *Ślady obecności* [Traces of presence], edited by Sławomir Buryła and Alina Molisiak, 337–81. Kraków: Universitas.

Davies, Norman. 1981. *God's Playground: A History of Poland. Volume II: 1795 to the Present*. Oxford, UK: Clarendon Press.

Felman, Shoshana, and Dori Laub. 1992. *Testimony: Crises of Witnessing in Literature, Psychoanalysis, and History*. New York: Routledge.

Frank, Arthur W. 1995. *The Wounded Storyteller: Body, Illness, and Ethics*. Chicago and London: University of Chicago Press.

Galant, Arleta. 2010. *Prywatne, publiczne, autobiograficzne: O dziennikach i esejach Jana Lechonia, Zofii Nałkowskiej, Marii Kuncewiczowej i Jerzego Stempowskiego* [Private, public, autobiographical: On the diaries and essays of ...]. Warszawa: Wydawnictwo Dig.

Grynberg, Henryk. 1983. "The Warsaw Ghetto in Polish Literature." *Soviet Jewish Affairs* 13 (2): 33–46.

———. [1984] 1990. *Prawda nieartystyczna* [Inartistic truth]. Katowice: Almapress-Czeladź.

Hirsch, Marianne. 1997. *Family Frames: Photography, Narrative, and Postmemory*. Cambridge, MA: Harvard University Press.

Janowska, Magdalena. 2007. *Postać-człowiek-charakter: Modernistyczna personologia w twórczosci Zofii Nałkowskiej* [Person–character–man: modernist personology in Zofia Nałkowska's works]. Kraków: Universitas.

Kirchner, Hanna. 2000. "Holocaust w dziennikach Zofii Nałkowskiej i Marii Dąbrowskiej" [The Holocaust in the diaries of Zofia Nałkowska and Maria Dąbrowska"]. In *Literatura polska wobec Zagłady*, edited by Alina Brodzka-Wald, Dorota Krawczyńska, and Jacek Leociak, 105–121. Warszawa: Żydowski Instytut Historyczny.

Kristeva, Julia. 1982. *Powers of Horror: An Essay on Abjection*. Translated by Leon S. Roudiez. New York: Columbia University Press.

Leociak, Jacek. 2001. "Aryjskim tramwajem przez warszawskie getto, czyli hermeneutyka pustego miejsca" [On the Aryan streetcar through the Warsaw ghetto, or the hermeneutics of the void]. In *Maski współczesności: o literaturze i kulturze XX wieku* [Masks of modernity: on twentieth-century literature and culture], edited by Lidia Burska and Marek Zaleski, 75 87. Warszawa: IBL.

———. 2000. "Zraniona pamięć (Rocznice powstania w getcie warszawskim w prasie polskiej: 1944–1989)" [Wounded memory: anniversaries of the Warsaw Ghetto Uprising in the Polish press: 1944–1989]. In *Literatura polska wobec Zagłady*, edited by Alina Brodzka-Wald, Dorota Krawczyńska, and Jacek Leociak, 29–49. Warszawa: Żydowski Instytut Historyczny.

Levi, Primo. 1998. *The Drowned and the Saved*. Translated by Raymond Rosenthal. New York: Simon & Schuster.

Marszałek, Magdalena. 2003. *'Życie and papier': Autobiograficzny Project Zofii Nałkowskiej: 'Dzienniki' 1899-1954* ['Life and paper': the autobiographical project of Zofia Nałkowska: 'Diaries' 1899–1954]. Kraków: Universitas.

Miłosz, Czesław. 1998. "In her diary." Translated by the author and Robert Hass. *The American Poetry Review* 27 (6): 6.

Nałkowska, Zofia. 1970. *Dzienniki Czasu Wojny* [Wartime diaries]. Edited by Hanna Kirchner. Warsaw: Czytelnik.

———. 2000. *Dzienniki 1945–1954*. Edited by Hanna Kirchner. Warsaw: Czytelnik.

———. 2000. *Medallions*. Translated by Diana Kuprel. Evanston, IL: Northwestern University Press.

Opalski, Magdalena M. 1999. "The Holocaust in the Diaries of Zofia Nałkowska, Maria Dąbrowska, and Jarosław Iwaszkiewicz." In *Holocaust Chronicles: Individualizing the Holocaust through Diaries and Other Contemporaneous Personal Accounts*, edited by Robert Moses Shapiro, 231–40. Hoboken, NJ: KTAV Publishing House.

Rodak, Paweł. 2011. *Między Zapisem a Literaturą: Dziennik Polskiego Pisarza w XX Wieku* [Between diary record and literature: twentieth-century polish diarists]. Warsaw: Wydawnictwa Uniwersytetu Warszawskiego.

Shallcross, Bożena. 2011. *The Holocaust Object in Polish and Polish-Jewish Culture.* Bloomington & Indianapolis: Indiana University Press.

Steinlauf, Michael C. 1997. *Bondage to the Dead: Poland and the Memory of the Holocaust.* Syracuse, NY: Syracuse University Press.

Zaleski, Marek. 2000. "'Ludzie ludziom' … ? 'Ludzie Żydom' … ?' Świadectwo literatury" ['People to people' … ? 'People to Jews' … ? Testimony of literature]. In *Literatura polska wobec Zagłady*, edited by Alina Brodzka-Wald, Dorota Krawczyńska, and Jacek Leociak, 89–103. Warszawa: Żydowski Instytut Historyczny.

RE-DRESSING WOMEN'S HISTORY IN THE SPECIAL OPERATIONS EXECUTIVE
The Camouflage Project

Lesley Ferris and Mary Tarantino

She said: What is history?
And he said: History is an angel
being blown backwards into the future
—Laurie Anderson, "The Dream Before (for Walter Benjamin)"

INTRODUCTION

On 6 June 2011, Baroness Crawley initiated a debate in the House of Lords in the British Parliament on the lack of recognition for the women who served in the Special Operations Executive (SOE) during World War II. Created by Churchill as a clandestine operation in 1940, the SOE trained agents to go behind enemy lines. For the first time in British history, women were recruited as secret agents, had rigorous and demanding training as couriers, wireless operators, and saboteurs, and served alongside fellow agents and members of the French Resistance in occupied France. Their experiences and the deadly outcome for many agents were effaced by time. Despite their contributions and courage, as Lady Crawley pointed out in her debate, these women have been ignored and forgotten. In her impassioned speech, she stated, "We just cannot let the mist of oblivion creep over the memory of these women" (Crawley 2011). This essay describes our process of creating a memorial to the British women agents who played an important role in supporting the French Resistance. We developed a performance and exhibition we entitled *The Camouflage Project*. Complex issues surround the practices of remembering the war dead, and our essay examines these briefly before we detail our own multidisciplinary "memorial" honouring the women of the SOE.

At the time of the House of Lords debate, a collection of thirty essays entitled *Lest We Forget: Remembrance and Commemoration*, edited by Maggie

Andrews, was published. Sir John Kiszely begins his foreword to this collection as follows: "Remembrance Sunday and Armistice Day ceremonies have, over the past decade, been growing once more in significance as public events; and war memorials remain a key element of the landscape of many of our cities, towns and villages" (2011, 11). The Royal British Legion, founded ninety years ago, is the deputed "National Custodian of Remembrance," and is familiar to the British populace each year when it sells red poppies to support its remembrance efforts (Royal British Legion). The first official Legion Poppy Day was held in November 1921, commemorating the war dead of World War I. The National Memorial Arboretum in Staffordshire opened in 2001, and is the year-round centre in the United Kingdom for remembrance. One of the central charities of the Legion, "The National Memorial Arboretum was conceived as a living tribute to the war time generations of the twentieth century and as a gift to their memory for future generations to reflect upon and enjoy" (National Memorial Arboretum).

Amid this past decade of memorial activity, including the 2007 dedication of the Armed Forces Memorial on the Staffordshire memorial grounds, is a background refrain of "What about the women?" Starting with Boudica, the woman warrior who rose against the Romans (ca. AD 60–66), Debra Marshall, in her essay "Remembering Women: Envisioning More Inclusive War Remembrance in Twenty-First-Century Britain" (2011), provides a brief overview of women's activities in war. Marshall links the efforts of millions of women who contributed to the World War I Women's National Memorial located in York Minster to current-day controversy over a World War II memorial dedicated to women.[1]

In 1997, work began on raising funds for this memorial with a view to having a monument in central London that would equal the 1920 cenotaph dedicated to servicemen, the site of yearly memorial ceremonies. The National Monument to the Women of World War II was unveiled in July 2005 by Queen Elizabeth II. Despite the fact that both memorials are in Whitehall and that they are in close proximity to each other, the cenotaph, Marshall points out, is the only site for the Remembrance Sunday commemorations (2011, 201).[2]

Remembering and honouring both the war dead and the survivors has often been contentious. One of the most recent and recurring debates focuses on the absence of governmental recognition for SOE women agents, as we saw with Lady Crawley's address. Her opening statement asked what steps Her Majesty's government was "taking to recognize the contribution made by women put on active service by the Special Operations Executive in the Second World War" (Crawley 2011). The debate agenda has a particular history: the women were not formally recognized for their service, and information about the women and their fates following the end of the war was minimal and often non-existent. At war's end, no public disclosure about the fate of SOE women was forthcoming. A group of SOE women agents had gone missing, and the postwar British government closed down the Baker Street headquarters of the SOE office. It was only through the efforts of Vera Atkins (1908–2000) and a few insistent SOE staff that an agreement was made to continue Atkins's position and rank so that she could travel to Europe and officially investigate what had happened to the missing agents (Kramer 1996, 50).

A second major effort in the 1950s to acknowledge the SOE women parallels the recent debate in the House of Lords. Relatives of the missing women and press inquiries following trial testimonies of Nazi officials pushed the government for answers. The British government invoked the Official Secrets Act[3] as a matter of course when asked about what happened to the SOE agents. As a result of this official refusal to address the issues, Baroness Irene Ward asked pointed questions in the House of Commons in early 1956. She asked why the SOE files could not be made available. She was told that national security was paramount (Kramer 1996, 224). Ward was insistent, broaching the topic numerous times. After much stalling, the Foreign Office commissioned an official history of the SOE's French (F) Section in 1961. Historian M.R.D. Foot's *SOE in France: An Account of the Work of the British Special Operations Executive in France 1940–44* was published in 1966.

Ward pursued the commissioning of the book to counter authors who wrote and published "unofficial" sensational accounts of certain SOE agents claiming that "unsuitable and insufficiently trained women had been sent into the field, that they were sacrificed as a result of either gross incompetence or betrayal or a combination of both, and the results … were not worth it" (Kramer 1996, 232). Ward, along with many others, hoped that an official account would end the disparagement of women agents while contesting reports that the SOE had no impact on the war effort.

Against this particular background, this essay documents the research and creative process involved in developing and devising *The Camouflage Project*, produced in May 2011. We aimed to highlight the work of those forgotten women agents. In April 1942, Churchill's War Cabinet permitted the SOE to put women in the field, not merely in auxiliary roles in Britain, but also in occupied France. Training women to work behind enemy lines was unprecedented in the British military, and the decision was as secret as the training process. Only the recruiting men agents and trainers knew. The women were sworn to secrecy. The decision was made partly because women could move more freely in France than men of conscripted age. They would be less noticeable, and cover stories would be easier to invent (Kramer 1996, 65). Another factor was simply the need for more agents at a time when the German war machine was clearly dominant on its multiple fronts. At this time, women were forbidden to be combatants in war, and all the agents were officially members of the First Aid Nursing Yeomanry (FANY).[4] They went to work in FANY uniforms while training, and they received honorary commissions in the Women's Auxiliary Air Force (WAAF) before going to France. As Rita Kramer explains, "It was hoped that rank as officers in the regular services would improve their chances to be treated as prisoners of war, and not as spies, if they were captured in the plain clothes they would be wearing in the field" (1996, 66). Despite the SOE efforts in this regard, the women who were arrested faced grim and terrifying prospects as captured agents.

In the following sections, we draw on the multi-vocal nature of *The Camouflage Project*. In many cases, we are co-authors speaking with a single voice (such as in this section), but in other parts it is necessary to introduce a singular voice. Thus, MT (Mary Tarantino) and LF (Lesley Ferris) indicate individual voice and point of view.

THE PROJECT'S GENESIS

LF: About ten years ago, while visiting my parents, I discovered one of my mother's old Book of the Month Club selections that I had never noticed before. The jacket blurb made it sound intriguing and I began to read it. The book was Etta Shiber's 1943 memoir, *Paris-Underground*, which gave an account of her efforts while living in Nazi-occupied Paris with her British companion, Kitty, to help nearly two hundred British soldiers escape occupied France. The Nazis finally arrested both Etta and Kitty. The American Shiber was imprisoned, while Kitty was sent to a camp and never heard of again. The United States had not yet declared war on Germany, and as a US citizen, Shiber's treatment was relatively tolerable and eventually she returned to her home in New York.[5] I found this story compelling and fascinating. What impressed me was the ability of these two amateurs to risk everything to save British soldiers caught behind enemy lines. I thought the story cried out to be turned into a theatre piece, and over the months and years that followed I kept returning to the idea of working on it. Shiber's story initiated a search for other stories in which women played a central but hidden role in the war effort. Other books that had been recently published included Agnes Humbert's *Résistance: Memoirs of Occupied France* (2008), Sarah Helm's *A Life in Secrets: Vera Atkins and the Missing Agents of WWII* (2005), and Nicholas Rankin's *Churchill's Wizards: The British Genius for Deception, 1914–1945* (2008). Mary Tarantino and I started our own two-person reading group sharing our thoughts about the material we were discovering.

We were hooked on the project and dedicated to seeing it come to fruition. In January 2009, the Ohio State University committed itself to providing us with the necessary and considerable resources to create a new work focusing on women in World War II, and particularly those working as agents in France. We also met with key members from the Advanced Computing Center for the

Arts and Design (ACCAD). After much discussion and planning, both agreed to be co-producers, and by fall 2009 the project was set for production in May 2011. *The Camouflage Project* creative team consisted of a group of traditional theatre production personnel: directors, designers, dramaturgs, technicians, and graduate student performers and production assistants. A website was set up to document our process: http://camouflage.osu.edu/. The Ohio State University Department of Theatre's interdisciplinary partner, ACCAD, brought research staff and graduate students to the team.[6] They embarked upon two areas of research for *The Camouflage Project*: 3-D projection mapping and digital fabrication.

During several trips to London, I began to examine the special collections on the SOE, many of which are housed at the Imperial War Museum. I spent hours in the research room calling up box after box of material—from transcripts of the trials that Vera Atkins attended in Europe following the end of the war, to official reports on the status of missing women agents, to a number of interrogations conducted by Atkins and her colleagues of Germans who had arrested SOE agents. I found fascinating material on how the agents were trained. More and more material was being made available to the public. In 2001, the National Archives published *SOE Syllabus: Lessons in Ungentlemanly Warfare, World War II* (Rigden 2001), which became immensely useful in explaining the rigours and challenges of training agents. The following year, Russell Miller edited the volume *Behind the Lines: The Oral History of Special Operations in World War II*, and the voices of several SOE agents—both in the written text and through audio tapes in the archives—were yet another important source.

In April 2009, my notes for a draft paper ("Working Title: The Camouflage Project") distributed to the production team described the goal of the project as devising a new performance work based on "the variety of women who worked for the war effort" including British agents and members of the French Resistance, camouflage artists, and agents who specialized in wireless operation. By fall 2009, we had determined that the project would have three parts, and we began to target grant opportunities. We described the project as follows in several of our grant proposals: "The project goal is to create, organize and execute a three-part interdisciplinary endeavour linked to the theme of secret agents, camouflage, deception and disguise in World War II, specifically the F section (France) of the Special Operations Executive (SOE)." The three parts were the performance, an exhibition, and an international symposium. While we now had a detailed description of the project for our grant proposals, we still needed our story: How were we to tell the story? Which agents would be our focus? How would the exhibition work in relation to the live performance? In order to pursue our research, we continued our joint collaboration on learning more about the agents, but we also divided our focus: I concentrated on finding a way to tell the story in performance, and Mary Tarantino worked on the camouflage artists and developed the concept behind the exhibition.

One book that was crucial to the final shape and focus of the project was Rita Kramer's *Flames in the Field: The Story of Four SOE Agents in Occupied France*. First published in 1995, it had been in process for several years. Kramer came to the topic of her book accidentally when, in the late 1980s, she and her husband were driving on the rural roads of eastern France and came across a troubling and confounding signpost that indicated one direction "To Bar Restaurant" and the other "To Gas Chamber" (1996, 11). Following the latter sign, Kramer discovered a little-known piece of French history that led her to Natzweiler-Struthof, a concentration camp for men prisoners sixty kilometres south of Strasbourg, where four SOE women agents were brutally executed. In the book's preface, Kramer describes her work as "a journey of such complexity that, if I had known then what I know now, I probably would not have begun it—but I would have missed the most fascinating quest of my life" (1996, 4). As Kramer's "fascinating quest" was already ours, we now considered focusing on the women of Natzweiler-Struthof whose stories Kramer captured with such detail and depth.

A RESEARCH JOURNEY

To fully experience and honourably recreate the experiences of the SOE agents, we realized that our investigation would need to be as comprehensive as possible, taking us beyond books, archives, and documentary films. We would need to establish a tangible connection to the places where our subjects worked, lived, and died.

MT: As Lesley Ferris moved forward leading our research into the SOE agents, I embarked upon gathering sources concerned with coding and camouflage. A 2009 London trip pointed me to Bletchley Park (or Station X), a former manor house that was at the heart of code-breaking activity in Britain during World War II.[7] Walking through the various huts revealed rudimentary spaces where decryption teams toiled, operating the wheels on "the bombe" in what have been remembered as hot, smelly, machine-oil-laden conditions. These teams consisted largely of women, conscripted in Britain first in 1941.

Camouflage research led me to the work of Roy Behrens: artist, scholar, and author of hundreds of articles and half a dozen books or more on the subject. His compendium of camouflage, *Camoupedia*, helped bring into focus the intersections of art, perception, psychology, and theatre in the creation and marketing of *The Camouflage Project*. Ferris and I arranged to meet Behrens at his lecture and exhibition "Seagoing Easter Eggs" in Cincinnati (early 2010), which featured the art of dazzle camouflage used by naval forces in America and Britain starting in World War I. Behrens served as an invaluable consultant for *The Camouflage Project* and spoke at our international symposium held during the performance run in June 2011 at Ohio State.

As part of planning for a more extensive research visit in summer 2010, I visited Ottawa's Canadian War Museum (CWM) and the special exhibition *Camouflage: From Battlefield to Catwalk*, sponsored in partnership with London's Imperial War Museum (IWM). By this point in the project development timeline, Ferris and I were clear that our devised performance would require an accompanying pre-performance exhibition to introduce the topics of the SOE, wireless operation and paramilitary training, and disguise by way of "cover stories" manufactured and committed to memory by the agents—very much a form of personal camouflage.

The CWM exhibit, as suggested in the title, broadly encompassed camouflage from its early military development in World War I to art, fashion, and kitsch in the twenty-first century, including Andy Warhol's camouflage prints and pink camouflage bras and panties. I was drawn to the camouflage training films, uniforms, military weapons, and paint techniques of both world wars, which served to at times conceal and at other times confuse the enemy.

We designed and constructed seven exhibit stations to provide context about the SOE, examining agent training sites around England and Scotland, describing weapons and sabotage devices, and providing an overview of the history of camouflage. Marine camouflage, likely designed in World War I, developed the concept of confusion through disruptive camouflage, also known as dazzle. Artist and British naval officer Norman Wilkinson writes about arriving at his theory of dazzle painting for ships: "Since it was impossible to paint a ship so that she could not be seen by a submarine, the extreme opposite was the answer … paint … not for low visibility, but in such a way as to break up her form and thus confuse a submarine officer as to the course on which she was heading" (Wilkinson 1969, 79).

The Ohio State dazzle exhibit station revealed a quirky-shaped and painted dazzle structure, a miniature ship model, and a recreation of a dress for the Dazzle Ball held at the Royal Albert Hall in March 1919 (Figure 2.1). A video loop featured Noreen Riols, one of three individuals we interviewed at length for the production, recollecting SOE women agent training activities.

In July 2010, our research team travelled to England and France to visit collections, gather images from monuments and affiliated buildings, and conduct video interviews. Multiple visits to the Imperial War Museum's *Secret War* permanent gallery exhibit provided a comprehensive understanding of the SOE, particularly the clandestine aspects of training and fieldwork. Artifacts such as wireless transmitters disguised in suitcases, Welrod silencer guns, and

Figure 2.1 *The Camouflage Project* dazzle exhibition and dazzle dress. Courtesy of Matt Hazard.

Fairbairn–Sykes fighting knives flanked the well-known directive set forth by Winston Churchill in the formation of the SOE: to "Set Europe Ablaze" and create subversion and sabotage behind enemy lines. The displays immediately brought to life the urgency and danger the agents faced. The museum's Documents Room rewarded us with images of the SOE women agents—represented in official identity card photos, posed in uniform, but also in relaxed, civilian situations. Another powerful moment came when we held the sketches of the SOE women at the Natzweiler-Struthof concentration camp, drawn from memory by SOE agent Brian Stonehouse (Figures 2.2 and 2.3). In his recorded interview, Stonehouse describes seeing the women at the camp in 1944:

> I got a view of them for about five minutes at the most. They were walking down through the camp. They were four girls. It was a lovely afternoon in July, and [they were in] civilian clothes. And of course, we hadn't seen a girl, a woman in the camp. I couldn't understand what they were doing there. I made a detailed description of what each girl wore. It was absolutely accurate. You could tell that they had been in jail for several months. One girl had this little ribbon in her hair, as sort of a defiant gesture. It was very touching. One of the girls had a fur coat on her arm, and when one of the SS guards walked back up to the camp, he had the fur coat over his arm. (Stonehouse 1987)

Figure 2.2   Ink sketch of Diana Rowden at Natzweiler, by Brian Stonehouse, in a letter from Stonehouse to Vera Atkins, 8 January 1946. Courtesy of the Department of Documents, Imperial War Museum, London (GB62 IWM: Squadron Officer V.V. Atkins, File 8/1/1A).

In addition to archival research, our videography team collected still and moving images of key memorials in London and Paris. The Knightsbridge memorial in London's West End honours members of FANY, redesignated as the Women's Transport Service (WTS) shortly before the onset of World War II. The plaque lists the thirty-nine women who "gave their lives for king and country." Of this group, there were thirteen French (F) Section women agents who did not return. Many died in concentration camps and received posthumous commendations. Of the thirteen, we decided initially to focus on the following agents for *The Camouflage Project*: Andrée Borrel (1919–1944), Croix de Guerre, executed at Natzweiler-Struthof; Noor Inayat Khan (1914–1944), George Cross, Member of the Order of the British Empire, Mentioned in Despatches, and Croix de Guerre with Gold Star, executed at Dachau; Vera Leigh (1903–1944), King's Commendation for Brave Conduct, executed at Natzweiler-Struthof; Diana Rowden (1915–1944), Member of the Order of the British Empire, Croix de Guerre, and Mentioned in Despatches, executed at Natzweiler-Struthof; and Violette Szabó (1921–1945), George Cross, Croix de Guerre, and Médaille de la Résistance, executed at Ravensbrück (Valençay SOE Memorial).

Figure 2.3 Ink sketch of Andrée Borrel at Natzweiler, by Brian Stonehouse, in a letter from Stonehouse to Vera Atkins, 8 January 1946. Courtesy of the Department of Documents, Imperial War Museum, London (GB62 IWM: Squadron Officer V.V. Atkins, File 8/1/1A).

Our group also collected images of the SOE memorial on the Albert Embankment in London. Unveiled in 2009, it features a bust of Violette Szabó, who represents the combined sacrifice of the SOE: "This monument is in honour of all the courageous SOE agents." Along with still images, our videography team captured interviews with three individuals associated with the SOE (Noreen Riols, M.R.D. Foot, and Tania Szabó), whose recollections of the women agents became an integral part of our script. These interview snippets were featured in multiple scenes and transitions throughout the play, characterized as "Those Who Remember."

Noreen Baxter Riols (1926–) is a former SOE "secretary" who completed agent training and was assigned at Beaulieu, 120 kilometres southwest of London. Also called Station B, this was the final training station for agents to learn how to maintain a cover story under interrogation conditions. Riols had a special role in testing the confidentiality of agents preparing to depart for France, and was often present for debriefings upon their return.

Figure 2.4   Noreen Baxter Riols, 2010. Courtesy of Dave Fisher and Janet Parrott.

Figure 2.5   M.R.D. Foot, 2010. Courtesy of Dave Fisher and Janet Parrott.

M.R.D. Foot (1919–2012) fought with the Royal Artillery in France in the later stages of World War II. He referred to himself as the former SOE historian and author of several books on the SOE. Foot's intelligence expertise and familiarity with cryptanalyst Leo Marks provided clarity on the often-fractious relationship of the SOE to MI5 (which oversees national security interests) and MI6 (international security and counter-intelligence).

Tania Szabó (1942–) is the daughter of Etienne, a French Foreign Legion officer who was killed in battle at El Alamein just months after she was born. Her mother, Violette, was executed at Ravensbrück less than three years later. The legacy of her parents' sacrifice was made clear when our research team visited the Jersey War Tunnels, or Hohlgangsanlage 8 (Ho8), an underground hospital that was under construction during the German occupation. At the Szabó permanent exhibit, Tania spoke to us about her parents, pointing out personal artifacts such as family photographs, as well as images of weapons drops and Lysander transports, as she explained Violette's missions to France.

At the conclusion of our interview with M.R.D. Foot, he suggested we visit the Special Forces Club, tucked away on a quiet crescent-shaped street behind a noisy, bustling Harrods department store in Knightsbridge. Founded in 1945

Figure 2.6   Tania Szabó, 2010. Courtesy of Mary Tarantino.

by the men and women who served in the SOE, the club celebrates the "Spirit of Resistance" in its motto and club logo, which features a figure with an open parachute descending into a city engulfed in flames and smoke.[8] The club's cozy interior reveals a modest lobby, leading to a dining area, bar, and library with collections of books, artwork, and other memorabilia. The most powerful moment arrives as one walks slowly up the stairs, where dozens of framed black-and-white headshots of SOE agents look back at the viewer. On the first landing, one cannot help but pause quietly to reflect upon the framed watercolour drawing Brian Stonehouse made of the four Natzweiler-Struthof women many years after the war.

The Camouflage Project research trip concluded with a flight to Strasbourg and a drive to Natzweiler-Struthof—the only concentration camp that was built on French soil—which has approximately fifty sub-camps in its system. The camp "contained a large number of inmates referred to as 'NN' prisoners (Nacht und Nebel Night and Fog). These were primarily members of resistance movements in France, Belgium, the Netherlands and Norway. They lived in seclusion and were forbidden to receive or send correspondence" (Natzweiler). In essence, they were meant to disappear into the night and fog. SOE agents Albert Guérisse, Robert Sheppard, Brian Stonehouse, and Ian Hopper were at the camp in the summer of 1944 when four women walked into the camp under heavy guard. Andrée Borrel, Vera Leigh, Diana Rowden, and French resistance fighter Sonia Olschanezky (who worked with the Juggler sub-circuit in the SOE) were executed shortly after their arrival. The other four agents, who survived the war, gave witness to seeing them.

Today, the Natzweiler-Struthof site encompasses a museum and the European Centre of Deported Resistance Members, which examines in various exhibits the resistance movements that took place across Europe. The camp barracks were demolished in the 1950s, leaving only the kitchen, prison cellblock, and crematorium block. A large stone monument rises more than thirty metres above the ground near the high elevation point of the site, sculpted into the shape of an eternal flame. At the lowest elevation point and opposite the prison cellblock, a cross with two horizontal bars honours the resistance fighters who were executed here.

LF: In her book, Rita Kramer reconstructs the events of 6 July 1944, when the four women entered Natzweiler-Struthof. As I entered the camp in the summer of 2010, with Kramer's book in hand, pages marked with key moments, I felt haunted by history—this particular history. I felt the need to set myself apart from my colleagues, from the others visiting the camp. I had a gnawing compulsion to be alone, solitary, isolated. I needed to be surrounded by empty space as I walked that same path to the blockhouse. The Natzweiler-Struthof visit had a major impact on me—an emotional encounter that was difficult to articulate. Carrying Kramer's book was a solace of sorts, because her experience in many ways paralleled mine. Kramer describes how upon leaving the camp, "we re-entered our own lives" (1996, 2). This feeling of doubleness, a world set apart, outside of one's own day-to-day existence, is something I experienced deeply. The sense of doubleness is very much acknowledged in the world of theatre. In live performance, spectators and actors alike experience existing in two worlds: the imagined world of the play and the "real" lived-in world that returns as soon as the curtain call takes place. How would it be possible to draw on this doubleness in the performance we were developing? How to capture that sense of being present in the challenging moment of the past and then returning to the present?

MT: In stark contrast to the glorious view of forested landscape, the imposing gate, watchtowers, and barbed wire embedded deeply into the mature trees at Natzweiler-Struthof quickly conjure a presence of evil. The real consequences for four women agents who signed on to "Set Europe Ablaze" stared back at me as I walked through the prison cell and on to the medical experiments room and disposal oven, finally catching sight of the remembrance plaque (translated from French): "To the memory of four women British and French paratroopers executed in this camp."

DOUBLE ACT: DIRECTOR'S CONCEPT AND DESIGN APPROACH

LF: Both co-producers wanted to know the actual focus of the project—as we did—and I set out to develop a series of what I called "narrative threads," a montage-type approach to creating a script. I sketched out the threads by hand on numerous occasions, discussed them in weekly meetings with Tarantino and others, and by May 2010 I had typed a simple chart with three titled columns: "Training" (which included recruitment, training, and final debriefing), "Characters" (under which I wrote "Still finalizing" and did include some possible scenes that would highlight the stories of the agents), and "The Camo Artists" (which had a few entries, including "Teaching the Art of Disguise"). While I was developing the narrative threads, I was also thinking about how we could portray the stories visually. In July 2010 I wrote a short paper entitled "Visual Imaging: Camouflage Project" in which I wrote the following: "A metaphor of digging, excavation, exhumation: digging to hide the parachute, clawing into a crawl space to hide, digging for meaning, turning the soil, digging for a grave." The impetus for this image of digging came from accounts I had read of agents having to bury their parachutes as soon as they had landed to obscure the evidence of their landing. I was also inspired by Suzan-Lori Parks's articulation of playwriting: "Since history is a recorded or remembered event, theatre, for me, is the perfect place to 'make' history—that is, because so much of African-American history has been unrecorded, dismembered, washed out, one of my tasks as a playwright is to ... locate the ancestral burial ground, dig for bones, find bones, hear the bones sing, write it down" (1995, 4). While Parks writes this in relation to African-American history, I also connected it to the women agents—their hidden, erased history, and the need to "write it down."

Walter Benjamin provided me with an additional connection to this idea of digging, stating the following:

> He who seeks to approach his own buried past must conduct himself like a man digging. Above all, he must not be afraid to return again and again to the same matter; to scatter it as one scatters earth, to turn it over as one turns over soil. For the "matter itself" is no more than the strata which yield their long-sought secrets only to the most meticulous examination. That is to say, they yield those images that, severed from all earlier associations, reside as treasures in the sober rooms of our later insights—like torsos in a collector's gallery. (1999, 576)

Benjamin's text adds two other important elements that were central to the developing concept. First is the link between digging and layering—the ways in which digging reveals layers, strata, hidden treasure. Second is the suggestion of "return(ing) again and again to the same matter"—this notion of recurrence, reiteration, repetition, and replication is central to excavating history. We have to keep at it, expose that which is hidden, let the bones sing. Theatre is, of course, the art form of repetition, of doubling, of ghosts—both literally and metaphorically

Once this conceptual framework started to take shape, the narrative threads of the story started to come into focus. The threads now linked to the ways in which we would dramatically tell the story. The three threads are as follows: "Those Who Survived" (the figures who were involved in recruiting and training the agents, as well as agents who survived), "Those Who Were Executed" (those agents who were killed in their service to the war effort), and "Those Who Remember" (those who are connected to the SOE in the current day). The dramatic technique for each was different to help distinguish the threads from each other as well as to give the sense of weaving and linking the threads. "Those Who Survived" was created as a series of first-person monologues delivered directly to the audience; the second thread used dramatic dialogue; and the final took the form of video interviews of three contemporary figures intimately connected to the SOE.

As we expanded and developed the narrative and the ways in which the stories could be performed, we also worked on the actual space of storytelling itself. Two key aspects developed. First, we felt it was important to have a non-traditional theatre space—one that could contain the actual stage and the exhibition space. The multi-layered nature of the work demanded that we step outside the norm. We reimagined the stage as a multi-sited space, not neatly bifurcated into performance and exhibition, but with numerous overlapping areas. Second, within this multi-sited space we used identically shaped rectangular boxes, each approximately the size of a door. These boxes served multiple purposes: as props for tables and benches, as projection screens, as prison cells, as coffins, and as display cases for the exhibition.

MT: My early role as production designer, creating a visual framework for the project, was later fleshed out by colleagues in scenic, costume, sound, video, and media design. Responding to Ferris's idea of an overlapping space of performance, audience, and exhibition, I was simultaneously visualizing a prevailing sense of confinement that would add tension and forced intimacy to the action, while accomplishing a flexible design. This also allowed me to plan for how light would be a major design element to establish location and mood, and aid in the transition between scenes.

Reflecting on the research and our evolving scene list, elements of confinement abounded. A Lysander transport plane departing from Tangmere or Tempsford airfields carrying SOE agents and supplies was reported to be cold and very much confining. Agent interrogations in a small, windowless room with a single bright overhead light bulb evoke a sense of claustrophobia. The notion of confinement suggested a rectilinear space: controlled, inorganic, inflexible, and unyielding.

In applying confinement to the production design, we came up with a scene design that took the form of a cube featuring lengths of silver aluminum truss on vertical and horizontal axes, framing the performance space for a 7 m x 7 m x 5 m enclosure. The cube structure would also function as the apparatus for mounting lighting, projection, and sound equipment, creating the impression of a ceiling hovering over the action. The multi-purpose portable boxes had a cool white colour treatment that was repeated in the design of additional fixed prop and costume storage cabinets, situated in view and to the immediate left and right of the performance cube. Making these normally offstage cabinets accessible and in full sight for the audience meant the performance ensemble would likewise be visually present in virtually all scenes. When not involved in a particular scene, actors would be placed just outside the performance area, observing, or at a cabinet retrieving a prop for an upcoming scene. This strategy emphasized the concept of doubling, deliberately showing each participant as both actor and character. Likewise, the two prop cabinets were situated so that they served a double purpose—as functional storage (as noted above), and as projection surfaces. Additional flat and three-dimensional projection surfaces were flown in and/or placed within the cube for various scenes. This use of the props is an example of the layering we wished to highlight.

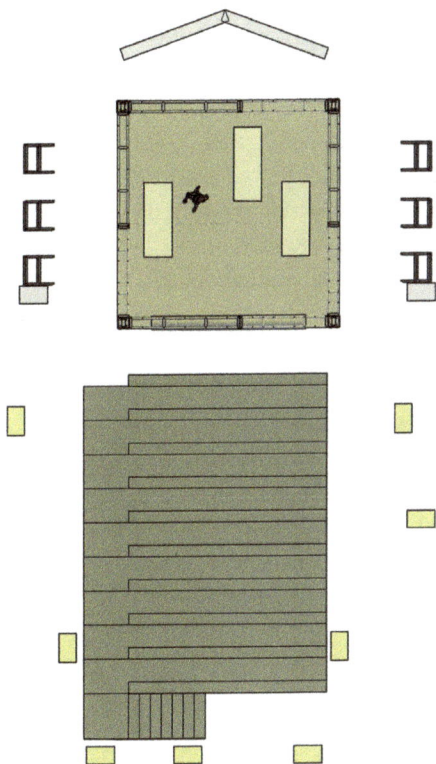

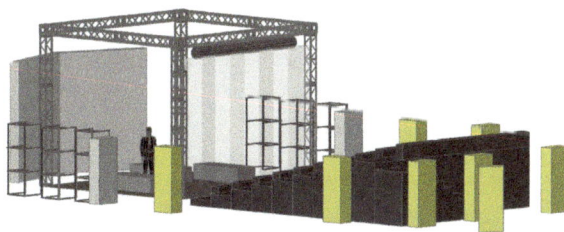

Figures 2.7a and 2.7b   Plan and isometric views of the stage, truss, audience risers, and exhibit stations for *The Camouflage Project*. Courtesy of the Department of Theatre at the Ohio State University.

In coordinating the exhibit design, boxes similar in dimension and colour treatment were constructed to house most of the seven exhibition stations, distributed around the audience seating area. Several stations responded directly to the theme of women agents. One exhibit box functioned as a memorial, a sort of wall of honour, displaying each agent's picture, code name, and short biography. Another exhibit displayed a large French circuit map illustrating the Prosper circuit and others active between 1941 and 1944. War posters decorated another exhibit box. A Remembrance Day poppy wreath emphasized the ambiguous element of formal war memorials. Devices of sabotage, defence, and deception used by SOE and British commandos completed the exhibit, including a recreation of an explosive rat, a modified wooden smoking pipe concealing a secret message, a British Sten Mk. II gun replica, and a Fairbairn-Sykes knife.

Another exhibit box, constructed of clear Plexiglas, was covered in vinyl letters and numerals, depicting an overview of cryptology, specifically codes and ciphers: Morse code "dits" and "dahs," the Playfair cipher and binary code, and an image and short biography of Leo Marks, an expert cryptanalyst who was assigned to the SOE. Marks made a special agreement with SOE agent Noor Inayat Khan, instructing her to secretly embed a string of eighteen dummy letters at the beginning of her message to signal that she had been captured. Khan did manage to convey that information, but did not survive the war—she was executed at Dachau.

To complete the idea of *The Camouflage Project* as a multi-sited space, the cube stage, exhibit, and audience seating were reconfigured on the stage area of the department's traditional proscenium stage. Special risers for 120 patrons were constructed, surrounded on one end by the exhibition, and on the other by the performance space. Patrons were rerouted into the theatre by way of a side stage area normally used for storage. Subscribers and others were confronted with a confined, maze-like journey from the lobby to the exhibit, and then, finally, to the seating area—an experience of confinement from start to finish.

DEVISING AND DEVELOPMENT

LF: In developing the piece, I organized a short work-in-progress showing on 1 September 2010 at Theatro Technis in north London. Seven students performed, while the others served as designers and technicians. This small-scale experiment was immensely helpful in providing me with a testing ground for creating new work with students and trying out different methods of storytelling. Three aspects from this workshop carried over into the final performances nine months later: the significance and dramatic use of period popular music, the use of tap dancing to dramatize Morse code training, and the use of a parachute in the final moments of the performance.

The devising process went into full scale in late September with a graduate seminar focused on the history of the war and the SOE. There were three main assignments: select a period song and articulate a rationale for including it in the production; research a key figure from the SOE or camouflage practice and write a first-person monologue in the voice of that person; and stage a short scene in collaboration with lighting students.

MT: Students used aspects of my research visits to Trinity College and Bletchley Park as they created first-person monologues for Leo Marks and Julian Trevelyan. I shared images from our summer research travel and my own study of the intersections of art, cryptology, and forms of camouflage used to distract the enemy—aircraft, factories, and (of great importance for the women) personal camouflage.

At the end of the fall term, the student devising team collaborated with students from a digital and physical lighting course and created visual media, text, and movement scenarios involving women agent training, "passing" in a French café, and camouflaging a rail track with explosives. These scenarios were presented to the public at *The Camouflage Project* campus launch in December 2010.

LF: In the winter quarter, Jeanine Thompson, movement and new works specialist, joined the performance team. We then decided to focus on the women who were executed at Natzweiler-Struthof: Andrée Borrel, Vera Leigh, Diana Rowden, and Sonia Olschanezky. For a long time, Sonia could not be identified because she was a member of the French Resistance working with the SOE, and, as such, was not trained by the SOE. For some time, her identity was confused with that of Noor Inayat Khan, an SOE wireless operator who was also missing at the end of the war. Focusing on these five women, and the confusion over Sonia and Noor, gave *The Camouflage Project* its needed focus as we moved ahead with developing the script. A draft script was completed by early March 2011, and formal rehearsals began later that month. The script went through many revisions before the production opened on 12 May 2011.

KEY PERFORMANCE MOMENTS

The play begins in an abrupt series of four rapid-fire mock interrogation scenes. A woman agent is isolated in a pool of overhead light. The man who is interrogating her lurks in the shadows, asking questions aggressively in an effort to get her to blow her cover story. This sequence repeats at an ever-quickening pace until each of the four interrogations is completed.

"Those Who Remember" is comprised of integrated media sequences that reveal the voice and image of our three interview subjects: Noreen Riols, M.R.D. Foot, and Tania Szabó. These sequences often function as transitional scenes—as the video and audio are projected onto a downstage translucent screen, stage

Figure 2.8   Mock interrogation scene. Courtesy of Matt Hazard.

boxes may be rearranged, actors may change costumes, and other projection surfaces may be set up. In one sequence ("Those Who Remember"—M.R.D. Foot), the voice of M.R.D. Foot recalls Vera Atkins as "the brains of Buckmaster's 'F' Independent French Section.… She'd paid particular attention to the women and gave them extra careful briefing."[9] As he speaks, images of the four Natzweiler-Struthof women appear, ending with a fifth image of Noor Inayat Khan, the agent mistakenly thought to have been executed there. This was done in part to establish the confusion faced by Atkins following the war, as she sought to determine the fate of her missing agents who did not return to England, and the further confusion in identifying Noor Inayat Khan and Sonia Olschanezky. During this sequence, the actor playing Vera Atkins appears downstage centre, sternly gazing at the audience.

Agent training included mandatory parachute jumps. In this integrated media and stage movement sequence, Agent Borrel completes her nighttime jump. At the start of her guided descent from the Lysander, an animation of an unfurling parachute is projected behind the actor, opening simultaneously with her physical movement. As she floats to the ground and completes her landing,

Figure 2.9   "Those Who Remember"—M.R.D. Foot. Courtesy of Matt Hazard.

Figure 2.10   Agent Andrée Borrel's parachute jump. Courtesy of Matt Hazard.

the ensemble disperses. The focus of the animation shifts from the parachute to the agent's point of view. Throughout the rest of the animation, the audience shares the agent's viewpoint as she looks out on the horizon and then down onto a field at night. A full moon appears in the distance as the fields below grow closer and loom larger.

The scenes in "Those Who Survived" are presented as direct-address monologues. Actors are revealed in isolated beams of light that confine them, mimicking the scenic design. At centre, Vera Atkins asserts, "But what did all my girls have in common? Bravery." Agent Henri Déricourt (far right) coyly states, "I did not take any money! Well … not much anyway." Brian Stonehouse (second from left) recounts agent training: "It was all a bit schoolboyish, an adventure. Combat training was quite fun, actually." Journalist Jean Overton Fuller (far left), who was friends with Agent Khan, recalls, "The title of my book is 'Madeleine'—Noor's cover name in France.… It was my friendship with Noor that propelled me to seek the truth about what happened to her. It took me years." Finally, camouflage artist Julian Trevelyan (second from right) declares, "Camouflage was once an instinct in the natural world.… Camouflage is an art, a craft, a science. It is visual warfare."

Agents were taught survival, self-defence, communication, and coding techniques. In the camouflage-training scene, the instructor gives the agents a lecture on the application of camouflage in nature, and in naval manoeuvres, aided by projections on the upstage wall, designed to replicate an old-fashioned slide

Figure 2.11   "Those Who Survived." Courtesy of Matt Hazard.

Figure 2.12   Training: Camouflage. Courtesy of Matt Hazard.

Figure 2.13   "Those Who Remember"—Tania Szabó. Courtesy of Matt Hazard.

show on a pull-down screen. He refers to the importance of personal camouflage as well as techniques used to disguise factories. He points to a factory model (at left) onto which 3-D projection mapping features an animation involving military vehicles driving down a road, which then transitions into a camouflage paint treatment, obscuring the details of the factory's shape and contours.

In the final "Those Who Remember" scene, the projected image and voice of Tania Szabó fills the stage. At the same time, the actor boxes, portrayed in a vertical orientation as prison cells, are very slowly lowered to the stage deck in a horizontal alignment, resembling coffins. Tania recalls Vera Atkins's affection for her agents: "She was always very protective of them.... When they didn't come back … she decided she would go to town on this and went to Nuremberg.... She wanted to do it for the families of these girls … because those families were in agony."

The *Camouflage Project*'s final scene is best described in the stage directions:

The Ensemble begins to sing: When the Lights Go On Again, *a cappella. The back door opens with a blinding light . . . the parachute is pulled out of the door, brought to the center of the cube, opened up by the Ensemble [which holds on to] its circular shape, then they raise it in the air, whoosh, it rises and slowly descends. The four women walk underneath it as it falls, and it rests on the*

Figure 2.14   "We Remember: Poppies." Courtesy of Matt Hazard.

*four coffin boxes. The four women [each] take a poppy and lay it on the box.
The stage is slowly covered with images of red poppies, starting at the back wall,
covering the shroud, and moving forward towards the audience.*

CONCLUSION

The research we began in earnest in 2009 to prepare for this project had an enormous impact on us, both as individuals and as theatre artists coming to terms with the long shadow of the twentieth century: a shadow of silence and secrets that at times did its best to obscure, and in some cases make invisible, much of the material we hoped to encounter. Our investigations can in some ways be compared to those of a forensic anthropologist who works with a team of specialists to identify skeletal remains and assess the circumstances of the person's death. Our digging revealed to us multi-threaded narratives, occasions for knowing, while simultaneously exposing the rifts of what can only be described as oblivion—that which is forever lost and beyond us.

We began this essay discussing a recent call for a memorial to the SOE women. Recognition of women in relation to war has a long and troubling past. As Debra Marshall explains in her essay on a "more inclusive" memorial strategy, "British women have moved from participating in war remembrance, largely as mourners of men, to claiming recognition for their own contributions" (2011, 202). Public acknowledgement, however, is slow. Marshall continues: "It was only in 2000, more than half a century after the end of the Second World War, that the Women's Land Army … joined other veterans in the annual Remembrance Sunday parade past the Cenotaph for the first time." Yet, acts of remembrance have the ability to move beyond these ritualized public events or the placing of an engraved stone. In a letter to Vera Atkins, Rita Kramer solicited her help as she contemplated embarking on her book: "I would like to write a book about them. About who they were and what they did. I think they deserve to be remembered. History, after all, is what we choose to remember. I cannot think of anything I would rather learn about and write about than their stories, which must eventually become one story, the way the stories of Achilles and Agamemnon and Ulysses become one story. Would you help me …?" (1996, 2–3)

Kramer's book is indeed a memorial to the women. And this essay and *The Camouflage Project* it documents are also memorials. "History is what we choose to remember." And sometimes we cannot help but remember—indeed, we are forced to remember. Our encounter with the stories of the SOE women evokes Walter Benjamin's angel of history: "History is an angel being blown backwards into the future" (Anderson 1989). Like Benjamin, like Rita Kramer, we were blown backwards into history so we could move forward into the future.

ABOUT THE CAMOUFLAGE PROJECT

The Camouflage Project: A Devised Performance/Exhibition was conceived by Lesley Ferris and Mary Tarantino. The world premiere was 12–27 May 2011 on the Thurber Stage of the Drake Performance and Events Center in Columbus, Ohio, and was produced by the Ohio State University's Department of Theatre and Advanced Computing Center for the Arts and Design with support from the Mershon Center for International Security Studies, the College of Arts and Sciences, and the Coca-Cola Critical Difference for Women grant. The creative team was as follows: Lesley Ferris and Jeanine Thompson, co-directors; Dan Gray, scenic designer; Kristine Kearney, costume designer; Mary Tarantino, lighting designer and exhibition designer; Lowri Sion, sound designer; Janet Parrott and JR Gualtieri, video designers; Chris Zinkon, technical director; Eric Mayer, production stage manager; Jim Knapp, production system engineer; Vita Berezina-Blackburn, 3-D animation production pipeline design and supervision; Matthew Lewis, digital fabrication; Chelsea Phillips, dramaturg; Elizabeth Harelick, assistant dramaturg; Francesca Spedalieri, assistant director. Performance team: Alex Boyles, Ashley Kobza, Jirye Lee, Tory Matsos, Kevin McClatchy, Emily Mills, Moopi Mothibeli, Mahmoud Osman, Charlesanne Rabensburg, Ibsen Santos, Alison Vasquez, and Aaron Zook.

NOTES

1   Marshall explains that 32,000 members of the public subscribed to the national appeal for a memorial that "was described at the time as the world's first war memorial to women." The memorial, dedicated by Queen Elizabeth in 1925, listed the names of 1,465 women from the British Empire who died as a result of their participation in the war effort (2011, 198).

2   The *Lest We Forget* volume of essays does not mention the Special Operations Executive.

3   The Official Secrets Act, amended several times, set out penalties for divulging sensitive information to an enemy, or for acting carelessly with sensitive information.

4   In 1907, the First Aid Nursing Yeomanry was organized as the first women's voluntary corps in Britain. Their initial work was relegated to nursing, but later they were elevated with official recognition as an army volunteer transport unit.

5   Shiber returned to the United States as a result of an arranged trade between the Germans and the US government. Shiber was exchanged for a German spy who had been placed in custody by the Americans prior to their entering the war in December 1941.

6   See ACCAD's website detailing their research process: http://accad.osu.edu/researchmain/gallery/project_gallery/camouflage.html.

7   One recent acknowledgement of women's role in World War II was the mystery miniseries *The Bletchley Circle*, produced for ITV in 2012, which featured four code breakers from Bletchley Park.

8   In 2004, the Natural History Museum in London unveiled a life-sized plaque of Spirit of Resistance. The citation includes a dedication to the men and women of the SOE and explains the museum's connection: "From 1942 to 1945, SOE Station XVB, known as the Demonstration Room, occupied three sealed galleries in this part of the National History

Museum. Here, specialised military equipment was displayed for briefing British and Allied staff and SOE field agents."

9   All quotations in the following section are from the final script of *The Camouflage Project* (Ferris and Tarantino 2011).

WORKS CITED

Anderson, Laurie. 1989. "The Dream Before (for Walter Benjamin)." *Strange Angels*. Warner Brothers. CD.

Andrews, Maggie, ed. 2011. *Lest We Forget: Remembrance & Commemoration*. With Charles Bagot Jewitt and Nigel Hunt. Stroud, Gloucestershire: History Press.

Behrens, Roy. 2009. *Camoupedia: A Compendium of Research on Art, Architecture, and Camouflage*. Iowa: Boblink Books.

Benjamin, Walter. 1999. *Selected Writings 1927–1934*. Edited by Marcus Paul Bullock, Michael William Jennings, Howards Eiland, and Gary Smith. Cambridge, MA: Harvard UP.

Crawley, Baroness. 6 June 2011. "Women: Special Operations Executive—Question for Short Debate." House of Lords. http://www.theyworkforyou.com.

Ferris, Lesley, and Mary Tarantino. 2011. *The Camouflage Project: Script*. MS. Collaboratively written with Alex Boyles, Phil Garrett, Elizabeth Harelik, Ashley Kobza, Tory Matsos, Kevin McClatchy, Moopi Mothibeli, Chelsea Phillips, Charlesanne Rabensburg, Ibsen Santos, Francesca Spedalieri, and Aaron Zook. Columbus, OH: Ohio State University.

Foot, M.R.D. [1966] 2004. *SOE in France: An Account of the Work of the British Special Operations Executive in France 1940–1944*. New York: Frank Cass Publishers.

Helm, Sarah. 2005. *A Life in Secrets: Vera Atkins and the Missing Agents of WWII*. New York: Nan A. Talese.

Humbert, Agnes. 2008. *Résistance: Memoirs of Occupied France*. Translated by Barbara Mellor. London: Bloomsbury.

Kiszely, Sir John. 2011. "Foreword: Lest We Forget." In *Lest We Forget: Remembrance & Commemoration*, edited by Maggie Andrews, 11–12. Stroud, Gloucestershire: History Press.

Kramer, Rita. 1996. *Flames in the Field: The Story of Four SOE Agents in Occupied France*. London: Penguin.

Marks, Leo. 1998. *Between Silk and Cyanide: The Story of the SOE's Code War*. London: Harper Collins.

Marshall, Debra. 2011. "Remembering Women: Envisioning More Inclusive War Remembrance in Twenty-First Century Britain." In *Lest We Forget: Remembrance & Commemoration*, edited by Maggie Andrews, 197–202. Stroud, Gloucestershire: History Press.

Miller, Russell. 2004. *Behind the Lines: The Oral History of the Special Operations in World War II*. New York: Penguin Group.

National Memorial Arboretum. http://www.thenma.org.uk/index.aspx.

Natzweiler (Struthof). http://www.edwardvictor.com/Holocaust/Natzweiler.htm.

Parks, Suzan-Lori. 1995. "Possession." *The America Play, and Other Works*. New York: Theatre Communications Group.

Rankin, Nicholas. 2008. *Churchill's Wizards: The British Genius for Deception 1914–1945*. London: Faber and Faber.

Rigden, Dennis, ed. 2001. *SOE Syllabus: Lessons in Ungentlemanly Warfare, World War II*. Richmond, Surrey: National Archives.

Royal British Legion. http://www.britishlegion.org.uk.

Shiber, Etta. 1943. *Paris-Underground*. With Anne and Paul Dupre. New York: Charles Scribner and Sons.

Stonehouse, Brian. July 1987. "Interview: Brian Stonehouse." Imperial War Museum. CD.

Valençay SOE Memorial. http://en.wikipedia.org/wiki/Valençay_SOE_Memorial.

Wilkinson, Norman. 1969. *A Brush with Life*. London: Seeley.

TWO SISTERS
Contrary Lives

Charmian Brinson and Julia Winckler

Women's lives, to a greater degree than men's, are frequently lived in the shadows, leaving little imprint. Such traces as there are—for example, in the form of private records, family photographs, and personal documents—must be sought out and identified. This essay explores the lives and memories of two ordinary women, German sisters, from a historical perspective by drawing on such fragments, and sets out to recreate and reflect the sisters' key memories in artistic form. Our chapter frames that history within our own process as our collaboration took shape. It draws, in particular, on archival source material that Julia Winckler gathered for *Two Sisters* (2004), a multimedia photographic exhibition shown on the Isle of Man and in France, which explored some of the wartime experiences and memories of Viktoria and Martha Probst. Viktoria Probst is Julia's maternal grandmother, and Martha is her great-aunt. Combining of archival photographs and contemporary photographs taken by Julia on location with documents, objects, and sound, this exhibition rediscovered and reconstructed the very different experiences of two sisters separated by and entangled in events far beyond their control: World War II.

We seek to represent multiple viewpoints: those of the two sisters, both in wartime and beyond, and our own. Charmian Brinson is a cultural historian with a specialism in women's exile and internment, and Julia is an artist and lecturer with a long interest in life narratives, historiography, and memory. We first met in 2002, when Julia approached Charmian with questions about women's internment on the Isle of Man during World War II. Julia, undertaking archival research for the *Two Sisters* exhibition, was about to travel to the Isle of Man to photograph locations of former internment camps. Charmian shared her extensive internment material with Julia, also putting her in touch with Johanna Lichtenstern, a Jewish refugee from Berlin and a former internee on the Isle of Man. Yvonne Cresswell, curator of Social History at Manx National Heritage

Museum in Douglas, Isle of Man, invited Julia to exhibit the finished project in the museum gallery in 2004, and Charmian gave a talk on the opening night of the *Two Sisters* exhibition. For Charmian, this was the first occasion on which she had found herself in the actual location of the former alien internment camps. Since then, Charmian and Julia have worked on several internment-related projects together, exploring the role of the artist as witness. The present paper builds on Charmian's extensive research and numerous publications in the field of German exile studies, which are combined here with Julia's artistic approach, drawing on hidden histories and private memories.

The first part of this essay maps out the two sisters' biographies, juxtaposing key events in their lives between 1933 and 1945. In the second part of this essay, we move on to describe the *Two Sisters* exhibition and the curatorial strategies, which employed a set of photographic techniques to visualize, reconstruct, and question processes of recollection and memory. Julia confronted the complexity of family stories and contrasted the sisters' life narratives, which brought to light many parallels but also highlighted significant tensions.

In order to bring together important biographical information, we have drawn on a range of sources: Viktoria Probst is now 100 years old, and over the past sixteen years has agreed on numerous occasions to let Julia record conversations with her, while Martha's life narrative is mediated by and based on Julia's childhood memories and the recollections of older family members. Martha died in 1976; information about her has been received through indirect testimony, and some biographical details cannot be reconstructed with certainty. Viktoria's wartime memories remain selective. A small repertoire of anecdotes has been retold frequently, but on closer investigation some of them contain inconsistencies. When confronted with specific questions, photographs, or documents, Viktoria has been more able to recall details, and occasional flashes of memory, in the form of specific smells, sounds, and visual memories, have occurred. The more we have listened and learned, the more complex the retelling of their story has become.

Our archival source material can loosely be divided into the following four categories:

1) *Informal personal life narratives*: recorded interviews with Viktoria, which carry huge testimonial, historical, and emotional value, but which, due to their subjective nature, also have significant limitations, as other factors (e.g., omission, repression, and forgetting) come into play; a short unpublished memoir that Viktoria wrote ten years ago; tape recordings that Martha made in the 1960s and '70s; letters and postcards; personal photographs; memory documents (such as an embroidered memento handkerchief with each corner

representing the various phases of Martha's captivity); and books in Martha's library.

2) *Official documents, both personal and public*: a German identity card and employment documents, and a family register from the sisters' personal archives, which are supplemented by documents such as newspaper clippings and British Home Office documents held in public archives in Britain and Germany.

3) *Indirect testimony*: recorded accounts by others, such as Viktoria's daughter, who also knew Martha well.

4) Finally, we draw on *contemporary research and historical representations*: up-to-date historical knowledge and research, independent of the two women's narratives, which is verifiable and essential to frame their story and to provide anchors and signposts. This demands and provides a nuanced reading of the women's biographical narratives while emphasizing the importance of a historical and political context, which frames their subjective experiences.

Up to a certain point, life narratives and their reconstructions are readily traceable, though some biographical details and life stages can be brought to mind less easily than others, especially when the associated memories are painful or ambivalent. Working on this essay, we attempted to elucidate the more difficult biographical details by asking Viktoria further questions, but frequently this only raised more questions and uncertainties. In the end, we found it necessary to draw on additional testimonial accounts and contemporary academic knowledge about World War II, Nazi Germany, and wartime Britain in order to supplement our information. Discussing the potential of archival research, Peter Muir writes that "the archives provide a further reserve, an index or 'habitation' for the social and political significance of history, even though those that now view the archive will see only an artefact or phantom of the events and processes (social, political and historical) implied in the depictions" (2010, 58). French historian Pierre Nora uses a powerful visual metaphor for these kinds of archival remains: "Indeed, it is this very push and pull that produces *lieux de mémoire* moments in history torn away from the movement of history, then returned; no longer quite life, not yet death, like shells on the shore when the sea of living memory has receded" (1989, 12). These insights inform our investigations.

The theoretical underpinning of this chapter, and of the *Two Sisters* exhibition, is based on the work of cultural historian Aleida Assmann. In her essay "Between History and Memory," Assmann discusses the significance of personal, collective, and cultural forms of memory in mediating and remembering, as well as forgetting, past experiences. She draws a useful distinction between episodic memory, "what has been experienced," and semantic memory, which is based on "what we have read or learned" (Assmann 1999, 27; authors' translation). We draw primarily on semantic memory, which, as Marianne Hirsch states, is "mediated not through recollection but through an imaginative investment and creation" (1997, 7). This semantic memory, or postmemory, as Hirsch prefers to call it, has the ability to transport us into a past that predates our own, through the exploration of archival material such as photographs, documents, and objects.

1933: GERMANY BECOMES A TOTALITARIAN STATE

Traditionally, women's progression through life has tended to be determined as much by chance as by choice; their life options have more often than not been severely limited. The economic and political upheavals of the twentieth century undoubtedly restricted women's choices still further, while at the same time, paradoxically, opening up unexpected avenues. The two sisters forming the subject of this essay happened to be young at a time of great turbulence in European history: the aftermath of World War I, the assumption of power by the National Socialists in Germany, and the advent of World War II. Unemployment, a desperately serious problem in the 1930s, was the factor that initially separated the sisters, with Martha being compelled to accept an offer of employment in England. Their separation was made permanent by the onset of war. This essay focuses, both in historical and in artistic terms, on the time in their lives that they perhaps experienced most intensely: wartime.

On 30 January 1933, when Adolf Hitler became chancellor of Germany, the sheer speed of events would have made it hard to foresee what the final outcome would be. He and his National Socialist German Workers' Party, founded in 1919, had shot to power within a terrifyingly short period of time: their share of seats in the Reichstag had progressed from a mere twelve in 1928 to a startling 230 in July 1932 (though their electoral support would decline slightly by the end of that same year) (Willett 1978, 248, 258). President Paul von Hindenburg and ex-Chancellor Franz von Papen offered Hitler the chancellorship, believing that between the two of them they would be able to control the troublesome man and his party. But in this they proved grievously mistaken, not least because Hitler immediately began to do away with the democratic systems by which he himself had come to power, and to establish a totalitarian regime in their place. In order to eliminate the opposition, Hitler and his party suspended key basic rights, and by April 1933, the Nazis had set up the Secret State Police Office. With the ushering in of the Third Reich, the scene was set for the death and dislocation of millions, both within Germany and well beyond its borders.

Figure 3.1   Martha and Viktoria, 1932, from *Two Sisters*.

TWO SISTERS: SETTING OUT

A fading grey page, in an album held together by a piece of brown string, contains a small photograph: "Martha and Viktoria 1932:"[1] Two stylish young women stand in front of a tall haystack at harvest time. Martha, on the left, with shoulder-length brown hair, a white summer dress, in a masculine pose, hands on her black belt, flat shoes, cigarette in her mouth. Viktoria, with a short, blonde bob, white blouse with bow tie, long black skirt, and high heels, reaches over to light Martha's cigarette. They look out of place in this rural landscape, which they were soon to leave.

Martha and Viktoria, whose lives would follow opposing trajectories—partly by chance, partly by choice—were aged twenty-one and seventeen, respectively, in the following critical year of 1933. They had lived in the small German town of Elze, situated near Hanover, the family consisting of four siblings and their mother who had been widowed during World War I. Thus, warfare had already left its mark on the family. Widowhood brought poverty with it, and for financial reasons Viktoria had spent her early years in nearby Mahlum with a childless aunt and uncle. At the age of three, she had walked the three kilometres there with Martha and Hermann, an older brother, for a visit, unaware that her mother would decide she should stay in Mahlum due to the family's financial plight. She did not rejoin her mother and siblings until the age of ten, when, experiencing homesickness, she returned to Elze. Martha, the second-eldest of the four children, had completed an apprenticeship as a milliner, but, in the harsh economic climate prevailing in the last years of the Weimar Republic, was unable to find work. In early 1933, she responded to a job advertisement in a Hanover newspaper. Her application was successful and she emigrated to England that same year to work as a nanny near London.

Since Martha's motives appear to have been wholly or largely economic, her emigration cannot be equated with that of the political and racial victims of Nazism who were beginning to flee from the Reich at this time. Indeed, it was only somewhat later in her life in Britain—at the time of her internment as an "enemy alien," and above all in her marriage to Hugo Hecker, a Jewish refugee—that her life path would intersect with the tens of thousands of refugees seeking asylum in Britain.

The Britain in which Martha arrived in 1933 was, like Germany, burdened with high unemployment. Generally speaking, workers from abroad were permitted to take jobs only in fields in which there was a labour shortage, such as domestic service. While it is fairly well known that Jewish refugees frequently arrived in Britain in the guise of domestic servants, whether or not they had any experience in domestic work, it is less well known that large numbers of non-Jewish, non-refugee girls from Germany—among them Martha Probst— also found domestic employment in Britain during the 1930s (Barnes 2005, 122–23).

In the winter of 1932–33, Martha's younger sister Viktoria moved to Hanover. There she worked as an assistant to a German Jewish radiologist, Dr. Calm, co-founder of the Radiological Society of Lower Saxony, Bremen, and Sachsen-Anhalt. Attacks on Jews had begun soon after Hitler's assumption of power, with the Nazi boycott of Jewish businesses taking place on 1 April 1933. On 7 April, the "Law for the Restoration of the Professional Civil Service" had been passed, whereby "non-Aryans" were excluded from positions in the German Civil Service (including school teachers and university lecturers). Similar legislation curtailed or prohibited the activity of Jews in other professions, including the medical profession. Viktoria has recalled how, on arriving for work one morning, she discovered a Star of David and a swastika daubed on the walls of her employer's house. As she set about removing the paint, she was accosted by two members of the Gestapo and ordered to accompany them to their headquarters, where she was reprimanded.

Viktoria continued to work for Dr. Calm until 1935, in which year, despite his eminence in his field, he was dismissed from his hospital post as a consultant radiologist. He also lost more and more of his patients until only his Jewish patients remained. Viktoria remembers that there was no longer sufficient work to justify employing her as his assistant. It is, however, far more likely that Dr. Calm was forced to let Viktoria go following the infamous Nuremberg Laws of September 1935, and particularly the "Law for the Protection of German Blood and German Honour," which prohibited the employment of "Aryan" women under the age of forty-five in Jewish households. In late 1937, Dr. Calm and his wife emigrated to Britain, representing two of the perhaps eighty thousand racial and political refugees from Hitler's Germany to settle there either temporarily or permanently. Viktoria stayed in touch with the Calms until their emigration, and also occasionally met up with their cleaning lady, Mrs. Bergmann, whom she had befriended. Following the Calms's departure, Mrs. Bergmann would describe to Viktoria how she had seen Gestapo officials working in the Calms's home, cataloguing and packing their belongings into crates over several days. The Calms had to pay shipping costs, but Mrs. Bergmann later learned that their crates never arrived in England, having been confiscated by the Nazis.

In 1934, Viktoria met Kurt Otto, an engineering student, whom she married in 1935. Their son was born later that year in Oldenburg, where they had moved after Kurt was dismissed from his engineering course at the University of Hanover in 1934. He had allegedly been seen at a left-wing demonstration and was arrested by the police but released after two days. A family friend had removed any books from his home that could have been incriminating. Interestingly, there is a photograph of him in a Marine "Korps" uniform in one of the family albums, dated 1934 by Viktoria. When asked why Kurt appeared in an SA uniform, she explained that, in an attempt to conform and fit in, and in the hope of being able to finish his university course, Kurt had briefly joined the newly formed "Korps," a subsection of the SA Marine "Sturms," which had created motor, aviation, equestrian, and marine subsections. However, his affiliation did not result in him being readmitted to university, and according to Viktoria, he soon left the "Korps."

In Oldenburg, the small family was primarily dependent on the financial support of Kurt's parents, who would send them twenty marks weekly, and Kurt's irregular income as a physiotherapist. (In an attempt to find a new source of income, he had taken a short physiotherapy course and Dr. Calm had furnished him with references for local doctors.) To help make ends meet, Viktoria occasionally accepted work as a typist in a private school and completed a course in stenography. Between 1937 and 1938, she also worked as a typist for the Gauleitung (the National Socialist-led regional administration) of Weser-Ems in Oldenburg, compiling lists of newly signed up party members. In 1938, Kurt had finally found work as an engineer with the recently "Aryanized" firm DEKA (Deutsche Kabelwerke) and moved to Fürstenwalde, near Berlin.[2] Viktoria followed with their son some months later, and over the next few years she would carry out the traditional role of housewife and mother. Despite the fact that Kurt had been unable to return to university to obtain his engineering qualifications, he quickly progressed at DEKA, where he worked in the research and development department, patenting new forms of cable insulation.

Martha, on the other hand, remained in England, visiting her family in Germany only once in the pre-war period, in 1936. Viktoria recalls that Martha had refused to adopt the official "Heil Hitler" salute and expressed her concern at the changes she observed in German society. In 1938, she left her employment as a nanny and became a housekeeper for Dr. Stronach, a popular veterinary surgeon in Mansfield in Nottinghamshire, a market town some 190 kilometres north of London. After obtaining her driving licence in March 1939, she also served as Dr. Stronach's driver, taking him to and from his professional appointments. She is known to have enjoyed small-town life and to have made the most of her leisure time (among other things, she was a great reader). However, Viktoria recollects having heard that when the war broke out in September 1939, everything changed for her sister. Many local residents who had been very friendly with Martha started to distance themselves from her. Martha and Viktoria would not see each other again until several years after the war, in 1950.

VIKTORIA IN BERLIN

After Martha's emigration to Britain, and especially starting in 1939, when the sisters were living in countries at war with one another, Martha and Viktoria's lives followed opposing paths. Of the two sisters, it was Viktoria who, superficially at least, lived the more conventional life: she had remained in Germany, had married young, and had given birth to her first child in 1935.

In May 1939, Kurt was drafted into the army and spent six weeks in Prenzlau, Brandenburg, receiving military training. After four weeks, he was allowed to come home for a weekend, and told Viktoria how he disliked the camp. The heavy boots, the rough treatment, and the harassment and teasing of intellectuals, with whom he had aligned himself, were difficult to cope with. By this time, he was a lance corporal (*Gefreiter*). Aside from brief Sunday visits between June and August, he was not allowed home, and on the outbreak of war, he was sent directly to the eastern front. Kurt was part of the German forces invading Poland in early September 1939. Some distressing photographs came to light when Julia looked through family albums with her grandmother Viktoria, which revealed some uncomfortable truths about her grandfather, Kurt.

Roland Barthes observes the ability of particular photographs to provide direct "material connection[s] to the past" (1981, 88), which result in immediate, deep, and personal connections between viewer and photograph. He likened this photographic moment (or *punctum*) to something that pricks through the surface of the image, revealing what is there, and stings the viewer in an act of recognition. Jacques Derrida describes elements of the archive as carrying trauma, which can cut into us when we uncover something painful or difficult (1995, 14). Several haunting photographs of burnt-out houses and tanks on Polish streets have survived in two pages of an album. On the back of one such photograph, Julia found some handwritten annotations by Kurt: "2 September 1939: to the right of this farm building the regiment in Poland was located between the first and the second of September."[3] Two other photographs carry the typed captions "21 September. Burned out houses in Malkinia" and "Destroyed house in Ostrów-Mazowiecka." These photographs work in stark contrast to, and sit oddly next to, other photographs in the album, such as photographs of family outings: a boat trip, a family picnic in the forest. It is unclear to us whether Kurt took these photographs himself, who it was that put them into the album, and why they were included. Viktoria herself cannot remember. In a postcard dated 9 September 1939, Kurt wrote to his parents: "We continued to drive on a bit yesterday, and are resting today. We are all well and hope that you are too. I haven't yet received any post from you." The focus here on everyday matters is mirrored in a letter from Viktoria to her parents-in-law, dated 23 September 1939. After reporting that Kurt had described in a letter to her how he had "felt strange when the first Polish grenades arrived," and expressing concern for his welfare, she moves on to say that she had made peach jam and blackberry jam and would make more the following week. By the time of her next letter to her parents-in-law, dated 26 October 1939, Kurt had already moved to the western front and was in the Saar region, on the border between France and Germany. Viktoria informs them that Kurt has described his work as "tiring and dangerous." She worries that one day he might find himself in French captivity. She then proceeds to describe her life in Fürstenwalde and lists her four-year-old son's birthday wishes: a barrel, a tank, and a soldier's car. She thinks that it would be more important for the boy to receive socks and a shirt, and wishes for a pair of stockings for herself. In addition, she thanks her in-laws for the money, chocolate, and biscuits they had sent her, items that were evidently in short supply.

Kurt did not return to his family until June 1940, by which time he had been made a corporal (*Unteroffizier*), owing to his status as a professional engineer. Viktoria recalls that back at DEKA, he had to train schoolteachers to become air-raid wardens. Because of Kurt's technical abilities, DEKA considered him indispensable, and had successfully claimed him back for essential work. From the start of the war, DEKA's workforce had also included slave labourers, including French and Polish prisoners of war whom Kurt would sometimes mention to Viktoria.

Among Viktoria's wartime documents is her 1941 identity card. The photograph stapled to the card shows a serious and Germanic-looking Viktoria, hair in braids, wearing a white blouse. The identity card bears several stamps of the German Reich, with its ominous swastika and black eagle. Next to the photograph, there are inked fingerprints of her left and right index finger.

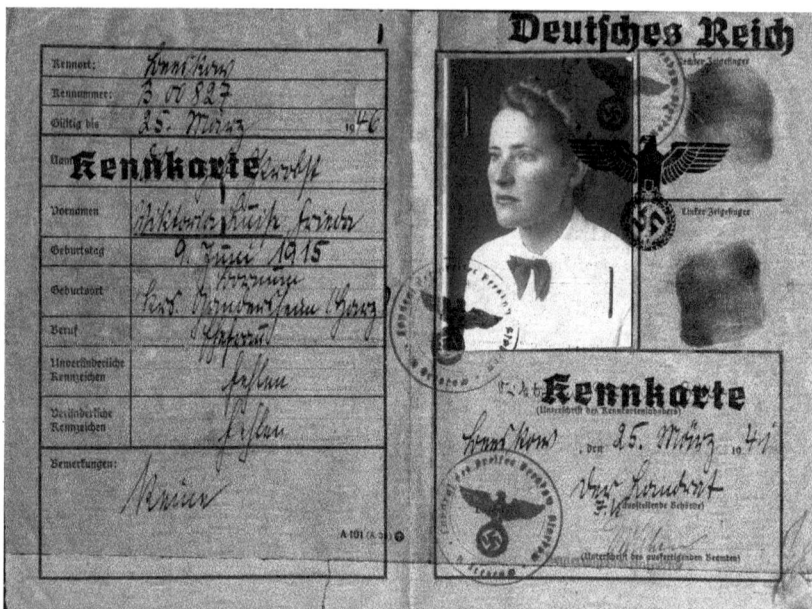

Figure 3.2   Viktoria's identity card, 1941, from *Two Sisters*.

There is something undeniably sinister about this card, which can be seen to stand for Nazi officiousness, brutality, and racial laws of inclusion and exclusion. The "Aryan" Viktoria was safe, protected by her identity card. On the other side of the racial divide, however, starting just a few months later (in September 1941), all German Jews from the age of six would be required to wear a yellow star in public, which they had to purchase themselves and sew onto their clothes. On 20 January 1942, six days before the birth of Viktoria's second child in Fürstenwalde, the Nazi regime declared the "final solution" at the Wannsee Conference, in a lakeside setting on the other side of Berlin. This "solution" led to the deportation of most Jews in Nazi-occupied Europe to death camps. The first gassings took place at Auschwitz on 23 June 1942.

Personal difficulties between Viktoria and Kurt led to a temporary separation in 1943. Viktoria had very little of her own money, so in late September 1943, in order to be financially independent from her husband, she made the difficult decision to send the two children to Kurt's parents and to rent a room for herself in central Berlin. A letter addressed to her two small children survives, dated 30 September 1943. In it, Viktoria writes that she has sent them some sweets to make up for her absence, and promises to visit the children soon. She assures her son (now nearly eight) that he is now a "big boy," and exhorts him to play with his sister (who is now twenty months old). She asks both children to obey their grandparents.

The fact that she was by herself in Berlin meant that Viktoria was able to take up a post as a typist for the Central German Railway Authority in its technical department near the *Landwehrkanal*. She worked there between October 1943 and the spring of 1944. Viktoria was one of more than 190,000 German women who, by late 1943, had been recruited by the authority as part of the war effort, to make up for the loss of men and to ensure the maintenance of the German railway infrastructure. She has described her work as that of a typist and secretary working in a large office. One of her responsibilities was to check whether orders for specific components, such as special new braking systems, had been delivered. If the supervisor was not available, she would have to meet with representatives from manufacturers and suppliers who would frequently try to sell her their new products. She also recalls how it was bitterly cold during the winter, and how she would have to warm up her hands and fingers by holding them close to a toaster that she had brought to work especially for this purpose, because the office windows were frequently broken in bombing raids.

Civilian slave labourers and prisoners of war had also been put to work for the authority. Viktoria remembers seeing Italian slave labourers at work clearing rubble after air raids (following Italy's capitulation, Germany's former allies had become enemies), and describes how, having noticed the conditions in which they lived and worked, she would sometimes leave food out for them. She also recalls their dishevelled uniforms and huddled gait. Journalist Ursula von Kardorff offers another eyewitness account, commenting on the large groups of Russian prisoners who were ordered to clear the debris in the streets as Berlin was destroyed from the air in December 1943. These prisoners, she recalls, were "not to be treated as humans" (Kardorff 1962, 99).

When she was not working, Viktoria's energies went into a constant search for provisions, as there was little food. What was available was rationed. At the same time, people were buying and selling on the black market, which was thriving. Viktoria was well aware that some restaurants in Berlin were still offering a wide choice of food, while for many Berliners life had become a battle for a daily meal. She received coupons to buy clothes, but these, too, became harder to obtain. Viktoria travelled to work by underground train from the Nollendorfplatz, where she had rented a bed-sitting room from another tenant. She describes living in constant fear of bombing, which usually took place at night. There was an air-raid shelter in the building where she lived on Ansbacher Strasse 40, and she frequently took refuge there. On weekends, it was safer to leave Berlin, so she often travelled back to Fürstenwalde or to Nienburg, where her children were living. Later, as more bombs fell and whole streets were destroyed, Viktoria recollects being able to sense the fear of other Berliners. She often had to shield her face from the smoke with a wet scarf, and eventually lost her bed-sitting room when her own house was bombed. She recalls moving

Figure 3.3   Viktoria's daughter in Berlin, 1944, from *Two Sisters*.

around often in Berlin, but by the spring of 1944, she had brought her children back to Fürstenwalde following a reconciliation between her and her husband, and she gave up her work for the German Central Railway Authority.

There is a photograph from 1944 in which Viktoria's daughter, by then a toddler, pushes a cart with a teddy bear in front of her. She appears to be walking by the river. In the new layered image, created for the *Two Sisters* project, the Central Railway Authority's Berlin headquarters are barely visible in the background. Blended in on the left, there emerges a faint map of Berlin and an image of a train ticket for a return journey. At the top right, there is an image of a timetable at the Anhalter Bahnhof, and a faint map of Berlin in the background. This was one of three railway stations in Berlin from which more than fifty-five thousand Jewish Berliners were deported in a total of 122 rail transports. These transports, ordered by the Reich Transport Ministry, were carried out by the railway authority.

Raul Hilberg writes that house raids tended to take place in the early morning hours, and that Jewish citizens were often taken away before the morning traffic to avoid attention. Windowless lorries were used to transport people to the stations, from which the windowless train carriages would depart for the camps (Hilberg 1996, 237). Viktoria has never mentioned witnessing or knowing of these transports. The references she makes to German Jewish citizens pertain only to the time period before 1939 and after 1945. However, Hilberg contends that even without witnessing such transports, the non-Jewish population would have had to notice the progressive disappearance of the Jews from their midst (1996, 237).

After more than five years of working as an engineer for DEKA in Berlin, Kurt was recalled to active service in the late spring of 1944, and was summoned to join an artillery regiment based on the eastern front. Before he left, he reportedly told his wife of his conviction that the war had been lost for Germany at the Battle of Stalingrad, and that he would desert from the army at the first opportunity, should he be able to head west. After only a short time at the eastern front, Kurt went missing at the Polish–Russian border near Grodno on 22 July. He had worked in reconnaissance and, according to a letter from one of the regimental lieutenants, he had been sent alone to deliver a message to a nearby regiment. He was presumed dead. The letter explained further that the German Army had suffered heavy losses and had been retreating in the face of a strong Russian advance.

In Kurt's last letter to Viktoria, on 17 July 1944, he had (presciently) urged her to take herself and the two children out of an ever more war-torn Berlin. Finally, in February 1945, Viktoria succeeded by means of a train journey lasting five days in getting the three of them to Hanover and then to Elze, where they would stay in her mother's home for a year. They travelled with the fiancée of Viktoria's brother, who had been staying with them for a few months, having previously been displaced from Breslau. On their journey, they saw large numbers of injured and bandaged soldiers, a tangible sign of Germany's forthcoming defeat.

MARTHA IN BRITAIN

When war broke out in September 1939, Martha found herself stranded in Britain as an "enemy alien." The previous month, in view of the impending war, the German embassy in London had advised all its nationals resident in Britain to return home. Martha's continuing stay in Britain, therefore, seems likely to have been a matter of choice. In fact, her life would not have seemed very different in the so-called "phoney war" period (the first months of the war), other than the fact that she would have had to appear in front of a tribunal for classification. She, like the majority of aliens, was initially put into the "C" category, indicating that she posed no threat to British security, and was subject to various relatively minor restrictions. All that changed, however, in mid-1940, when the German Army swept across Europe, occupying one country after another, and when it seemed a real possibility that Britain, too, would be invaded and occupied. Whereas prior to that only a small number of particularly suspect aliens had been interned, the British government now introduced a policy of mass alien internment, imprisoning around twenty-five thousand men and four thousand women, with Martha among them.

Generally speaking, category "C" women enemy aliens like Martha remained exempt from internment, a measure that was reserved for women in the suspect "A" and "B" categories (unlike the more sweeping measures applied to men). However, Home Office documents reveal that on some unspecified date, Martha was reclassified as "A," indicating that she was then deemed to pose the highest level of security risk.[4] Martha would later explain to her niece that her reclassification had come about as a result of her "left-leaning" political views. In the absence of any documentary evidence, however, one may speculate that Martha, who was neither a racial nor a political refugee, may also have had difficulty in producing convincing proof of her loyalty to Britain, leading to this unfortunate re-categorization.

As a direct result of this, on 15 June 1940, Martha was arrested and taken to Holloway Prison, a large women's prison in north London, where some of the women internees were held pending their transportation to the Isle of Man. Holloway proved to be a formative and unprecedented experience for its refugee inmates, who were not only startled by contact with the standard prisoners but

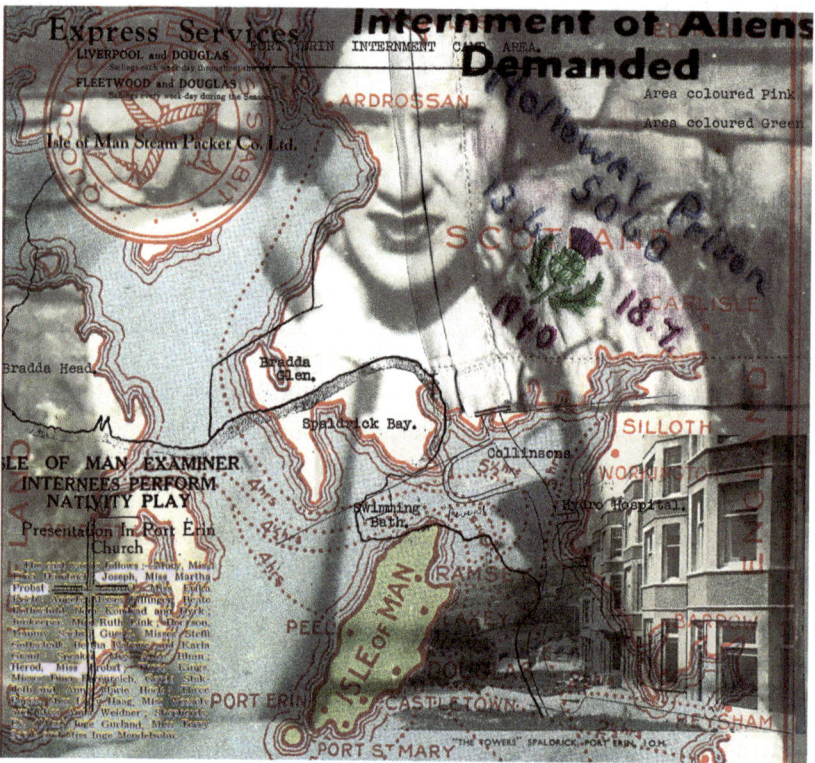

Figure 3.4   Martha's handkerchief, 1940–41, from *Two Sisters*.

were also subjected to one indignity after another: strip searches on arrival, for example, or an open-door ruling on using the lavatory. Those few accounts that have survived of the (generally brief) Holloway experience also recall the initial solitary confinement, the lack of clean clothing or personal possessions of any kind, the uncomfortable prison beds, the screams from adjacent cells, and the general uncertainty and fear. On the other hand, such accounts all emphasize the support gained from the presence of other women in the same situation.[5] This was a point that would also be made many times over in reports of internment in Rushen Camp, the women's camp on the Isle of Man comprising the two small holiday resorts of Port Erin and Port St. Mary that was Martha's next destination. On the island, in the enforced idleness of internment, Martha embroidered the stations of her detention onto a memento handkerchief, with each corner representing one of the various phases of her captivity.

In the archives of Manx National Heritage Museum in Douglas, Isle of Man, Julia found Martha's identity card from the internment period. While the cards of all men internees have unfortunately been lost, most of the women's cards have been preserved. Martha's card, dated 18 July 1940, includes a photograph clipped to the card with two staples: her hair is covered by a scarf, her eyes are

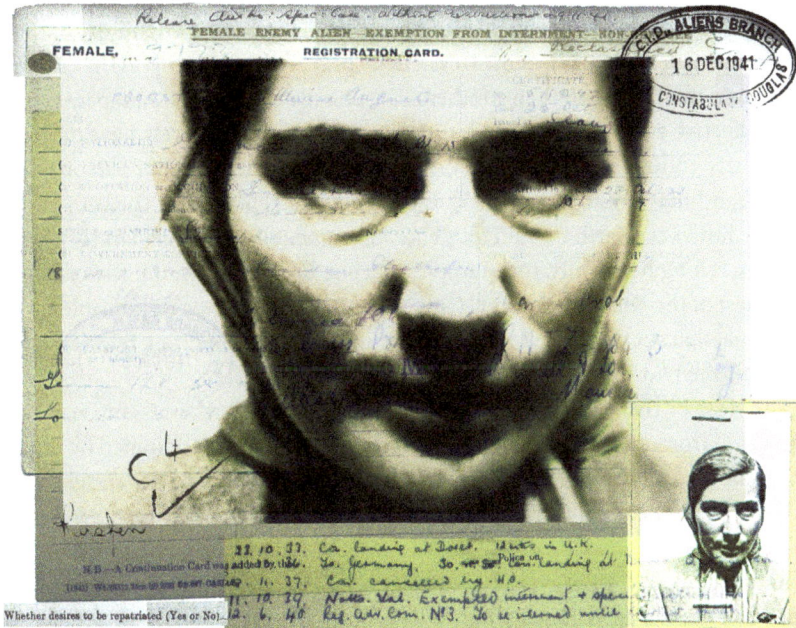

Figure 3.5   Martha's identity card, 1940, from *Two Sisters*.

averted from the camera, and she looks apprehensive and tired. It was taken on the day she arrived on the Isle of Man from Holloway Prison, which happened to be her thirtieth birthday. She was to be interned at Port Erin in Rushen women's camp for eighteen months.

Superficially, at least, there could scarcely have been a greater difference between imprisonment in Holloway Prison and internment on the Isle of Man. The women's internment camp, on the southern peninsula of the island, was situated in exceptionally beautiful surroundings, the internees being accommodated in the hotels and boarding houses that had previously served the Manx holiday trade. Moreover, the summer of 1940 was a particularly fine one and the women were able to avail themselves of the beaches and sporting facilities that Port Erin and the neighbouring Port St. Mary had to offer (Brinson 2003). After an initial period of semi-chaos, the internees also had a wide range of educational and cultural activities at their disposal. Martha was a keen reader, for instance, and it is likely that she took advantage of the camp library.

The local newspaper, the *Isle of Man Examiner*, which regularly wrote about the cultural activities in Rushen Camp, reported that at Christmas 1940, Martha took part in a nativity play by and for fellow internees, held at the local Methodist church.[6] In the British Newspaper Archive, where Charmian came across this article, she learned that Martha played the part of Herod and that fellow actors included Inge Mendelsohn, known to have been a friend of Martha's, and Inge Gurland, the headmistress of one of the schools set up in the camp for children interned with their mothers. Despite the undoubted therapeutic value of collective activity of this kind, such diversions would scarcely have disguised the surrounding barbed wire that signified the internees' lack of personal freedom, and that would have served as a permanent reminder of the war. In later years, however, Martha would recall her internment in Rushen in largely positive terms, telling her family, for example, that she had stayed on the Isle of Man as a "guest of the King of England" (since the Home Office was responsible for the internees' accommodation and board). Significantly, she never referred to the month she had spent prior to that in Holloway Prison.

Most of the four thousand women detained in Rushen Camp had been released from internment by mid-1941, a process that was facilitated by the fact that the majority of them were refugees from Nazi oppression (and should therefore not have been categorized as "A" or "B" enemy aliens in the first place). This, of course, was a group to which the "Aryan" Martha did not belong, which is why her internment continued until December 1941, when she, too, was reclassified as "C" once again. Following her release, she made for London, where she initially worked in a food-processing factory but soon transferred to a munitions factory, thereby effectively aligning herself with the British war effort. Unfortunately, no documentary evidence survives of Martha's life between 1942 and the end of the war. Martha, however, would later relate to her sister that she had also worked as a munitions lorry driver. She would already have come into close contact with members of the Jewish refugee community while in internment.

In her later marriage to Hugo Hecker, a Jewish refugee of Polish-Austrian descent, and in their joint decision to remain in Britain after the war, Martha can possibly be said to have joined the Jewish refugee community by choice. Hugo's parents had been German-speaking Jews from Galicia and Silesia, and eminent business people in Strumień, a small town less than forty kilometres west of Auschwitz. Hugo had moved to Vienna in the 1920s, where he had worked for Fox Films and later became managing director of KIBA (in the 1930s, a socialist, state-owned film distribution company). He had escaped from Vienna to Prague in 1938, and from there to England via Switzerland in July 1939. Two of his nieces, Erika and Lilly, had arrived in England on a *Kindertransport* that same month from Prague, and Herbert and Arthur, two of his brothers, were also able to save their own lives (one in a camp in Russia, one in an internment camp in Mauritius). Apart from these four, however, Hugo lost all other family members in the Holocaust.

Within Julia's family, it was always thought that Martha had met Hugo while both were interned on the Isle of Man. Occasions on which internees could meet members of the opposite sex that they were not related to, or at the very least engaged to, however, were few and far between. It is more likely that their meeting took place in London after Martha's release (Hugo, as a Jewish refugee, having been released before her) through mutual friends from the internment period. These friends, to whom they remained close for the rest of their lives, included Carl Wehner—a journalist who enjoyed the dubious distinction of having been interned by the British in both world wars—and his wife Johanna. The Wehners were ultimately transferred to the Married Camp on the Island, remaining in internment until late 1943.

At some point after his release, Hugo took up residence in Westbourne Court, in London W2, a block of flats in Paddington, near the railway station. It is not certain when Hugo and Martha met, nor precisely when Martha joined Hugo in Westbourne Court (although her first driving licence renewal document indicates that she had already done so by 1946). During the war, this block had been vacated by many of its original British inhabitants, who sought to escape the regular bombing of the station and railway lines. Its wartime tenants had included a considerable number of German-speaking refugees, attracted by the reduced rents but also by its location—its proximity to the Austrian Centre in nearby Westbourne Terrace. The Austrian Centre was a significant social and cultural meeting place for Austrian refugees, boasting a membership of around thirty-five hundred at its height. Founded in 1939, it finally closed its doors in 1947. Under surveillance by the British authorities because of the strong

Communist influence prevailing there, the centre performed a very valuable service for its politicized and non-politicized members alike. It offered a substantial program of music, lectures, theatre, courses, and amenities of all kinds to the refugee population. A restaurant served authentic Austrian dishes, even under British wartime rationing, and a well-stocked library lent out books in German, English, and other languages at a rate of one penny per book per week (Bearman et al. 2008, 11). A young poet worked as a librarian there for a while: the later celebrated writer Erich Fried. Because of Martha's fondness for literature, it is no surprise that among her effects after her death in 1976 were two books from the Austrian Centre library, which the centre had sold off upon closure.

THE POSTWAR YEARS: 1945–1950

The chaos that characterized the last months and the end of the war was followed by the chaos of the immediate postwar period, particularly in defeated Germany. Martha and Viktoria had not had any communication with one another since the onset of war; neither knew where the other was, nor, indeed, whether the other was still alive. Each had been thinking about the other and had hoped the other was safe. In the months immediately following the war, communications remained poor, but eventually Martha was able to track her family down in Elze via the British Army. When she learned that Viktoria was bedridden with a serious lung infection, Martha offered to send her penicillin. Widowed at twenty-nine, with two small children, Viktoria took more than a year to recover. In England, Martha was also stricken with lung disease, in her case with tuberculosis. She later attributed her chronic lung problems to her work in the munitions industry and exposure to dangerous chemicals. She, too, needed a year to recover, and was hospitalized outside London, at Ashford, Kent. It would be five years before the sisters would meet again, in 1950, when Martha, who had by then become a naturalized British citizen, would visit Germany accompanied by her new husband, Hugo.

Everyone had experienced great losses. Viktoria had lost her husband in the war, as well as a young nephew who, at the age of seventeen, had been drafted into the German Army in the final months of war. Martha's husband Hugo had lost his parents, three sisters, a brother, all but one of his sisters-in-law, all of his brothers-in-law, and many nieces and nephews in the Holocaust. In the last letter Hugo had received from his parents, in early September 1939, they had shared their fears and described the ever more distressing living conditions in Nazi-occupied Poland. At the end of October 1939, all Jewish men aged sixteen to seventy in Strumień were taken to a nearby men's camp (in Nisko). A few months later, women were also taken away to a camp in Skoczów. Due to its proximity, it is most likely that they were all later murdered in Auschwitz. Another sister-in-law was murdered near Vienna. When, in 1946, Herbert Hecker, one of Hugo's surviving brothers, wrote to Hugo in England, he described how he had gone to look for the family "all over Poland," but could not find a single family member alive.[7]

Significantly, such traumatic subject matter remained largely undiscussed by the two sisters after the war. Viktoria maintains that she never spoke to Hugo about his family's terrible fate, nor did she speak about her husband's position during wartime, or her own family's involvement. Following the war and her widowhood, Viktoria visited England frequently and made many Jewish friends from within Martha and Hugo's circle. She would stay with her sister and brother-in-law at Westbourne Court and carry out tailoring alterations for the refugee residents who, for years after the war, and long after the closure of the nearby Austrian Centre, still inhabited the modest west-London residential block.

THE FRAMEWORK FOR THE EXHIBITION *TWO SISTERS*

When starting work on the photographic project *Two Sisters* in 2002, Julia wanted to contextualize the archival source materials and explore the historical, political, and cultural processes through which they had originated. At the same time, as this was to be an art exhibition, she had to make aesthetic choices and think of imaginative ways of presenting her great-aunt and grandmother's wartime experiences so that their relevance to the present would become visible. A critical engagement with the present, while situating these traces and fragments historically, sets in motion a dialectical process whereby the present informs the past and the past informs the present. Semantic memory is unstable, like quicksand, and the constellations can change with the acquisition of new knowledge. In order to treat this delicate subject matter respectfully, she grappled with the question, faced by all contemporary artists dealing with this historical period, of how to approach the terrible legacy of the Holocaust.

For decades, Theodor W. Adorno's 1949 dictum that "to write a poem after Auschwitz is barbaric" (Adorno 1967, 34) has triggered debates about the ethics and aesthetics of art and representation after Auschwitz. Although he later revised his statement, writing that "perennial suffering has as much right to expression as a tortured man has to scream" (Adorno 1973, 62), this still leaves us with vital questions: Do we have the right to make work about the experiences of other people? Who gets to speak for whom? How can we, as artists and historians, represent the personal experiences and memories that others share with us? How can the fugitive quality of our own and others' memories be substantiated or compensated for through archival research? In Elie Wiesel's words, how can we avoid "Trivializing Memory" (1990, 166)? In *NachBilder des Holocaust* (Afterimages of the Holocaust), Inge Stephan and Alexandra Tacke explore artistic and literary projects in which writers and artists have drawn on archival material (from public and personal collections), and discuss some of the difficulties inherent in the engagement with memory work and the enactment of memory. At the heart of their inquiry is how and with what means artists memorialize and historicize the past—how they work with it (Stephan and Tacke 2007, 12). Referencing James E. Young, they remind us that to "engage in memory work is to remember a memory, to experience the past second hand" (8).[8] Memory work is further complicated, they explain, because "processes and acts of remembrance are a combination of recalling and forgetting, of remembrance and repression" (7).[9] They highlight the theme of repression and withholding or concealing of information as a key problem in intergenerational memory work (28). Because of these inherent problems and shortcomings, it is vital to keep alive debates about the past. In the last part of this chapter, we move on to describe how Julia approached the *Two Sisters* project with these concerns and questions in mind.

RECONSTRUCTING LIVES AND ENGAGING WITH THE PAST: THE *TWO SISTERS* PROJECT

As a child, Julia had often visited her great-aunt Martha in her Sussex home, to which she had retired following Hugo's death in 1964, and had become familiar with her wartime stories. With a grant from the Canada Arts Council, she chose an approach that was to raise questions and include multiple readings. Julia developed a visual framework to anchor the project: employing a variety of photographic techniques, she combined contemporary images with archival material. In order to reflect on the fugitive and layered nature of memory, and to open the material up for a range of critical readings, she chose a fragmented approach, rather than developing one linear body of work. Julia understood early on that it would be necessary to use more than one photographic technique to allow for a multiplicity of voices and experiences. Moreover, as the subject area was both delicate and complex, it became evident that the wartime experiences of the two women could not be presented in a comprehensive way.

The project fell into four closely interconnected parts, the first engaging with family documents from the pre-war and wartime years and situating personal events within their broader historical framework. For Part One—the historical section entitled *Two Sisters 1932–1945*—material from the family archive (letters, documents, photographs) was interwoven, layered, and blended with newspaper clippings, maps, and other historical material into collages. This moved the referents from the purely personal and created connections with simultaneous political events. This juxtaposition exposed the simultaneity of the sisters' everyday experiences on the one hand, and the brutal and catastrophic political developments in Germany on the other.

Julia searched for traces on location to secure some of the historical evidence available in archives, and to photograph and record what was still visible in the architecture and landscape of particular spaces and places, such as the location of the former women's camp at Port Erin, Isle of Man. Pierre Nora's *lieux de mémoire*, "created by a play of memory and history, an interaction of the two factors" (1989, 14), informed this site-specific search for traces. Martha's embroidered handkerchief, to take one striking example, serves as the surface onto which contemporary images of the Isle of Man were projected, thereby merging past and present. This formed the second part of the exhibition.

While carrying out research in Berlin for the third part of the exhibition, Julia started taking photographs from streetcars and trains. This was an important development, as it reflected, on one level, Julia's grandmother's employment at the railway, and on a second level, the synchronous deportations of Jews and others. Julia went to all of the railway stations in Berlin from which Jews had been deported, visiting Grunewald station together with the painter Barbara Loftus, whose grandparents and uncle had been deported from Berlin to Auschwitz, where they were murdered.

Julia based the final part of the exhibition on the period from the end of the war to the present day. The photographic techniques for each part reflected her mediated access to the past, resulting in, quite literally, less focused and layered historical images. The present was expressed in a series of documentary images: a portrait of Viktoria and a series of photographs of Martha's precious belongings. Julia also selected personal objects that had belonged to Martha and Viktoria for display. Martha's favourite and slightly battered red slippers, for example, were suggestive of a past life. And the handkerchief upon which she embroidered the sites of her internment was evocative in a personal sense, but also constitutes a significant historical artefact.

Working on the exhibition layout at Manx National Heritage Museum together with curator Yvonne Cresswell, Julia decided that all four photographic parts would be displayed in the gallery space so that, depending on the direction followed through the exhibition, visitors were offered a different temporal pathway: one led from past to present and another pointed from present to past. Of course, it was also possible to revisit and re-enter the exhibition choosing the other route, and visitors explored the different feelings and emotions this evoked. Some of the older visitors remembered the time when "the aliens" had stayed on the island. Referring, usually with affection, to the internees, they shared stories, and several described how their parents' hotels and boarding houses had been turned into accommodation for them from 1940 onward.

Figure 3.6   View of exhibition layout at Manx National Heritage Museum.

With technical support from digital artist Nerea Martinez de Lecea, Julia made a twenty-minute looped sound piece, which she included at the very heart of the exhibition to further highlight the fragmentary nature of memory and experience. Exhibition visitors were able to hear the sound from anywhere in the gallery. The sound piece played back extracts from postwar letters, which Martha and Viktoria frequently wrote to each other. In these, the sisters share news about the family, and reflect on life, love, and relationships. Interviews with Viktoria were combined with tape recordings by Martha, which Julia had discovered in an old biscuit tin. A third sound element, the sea, was added: water can be seen both as separating and linking the two women throughout World War II. Julia also added a poignant recording of "Kinds Wiegele," a Yiddish song recorded by the German Jewish refugee Johanna Lichtenstern (née Metzger), who was interned at the same time as Martha (though probably not known to her personally). Johanna had given Julia and Charmian this song about a Jewish mother trying to comfort her little boy. Neither mother nor child is safe, living in a world of persecution and fear. It is a well-known lullaby by Polish composer Mordechai Gebirtig. This recording adds an additional historical dimension as Johanna Lichtenstern, a classically trained singer, had been forced to emigrate to England from Berlin in 1939, a year after Viktoria had moved there.

CONCLUSION

In this essay, we have attempted to show that despite their shared background, the sisters' life trajectories would lead them in contrary directions. By confronting and juxtaposing their biographical narratives and interweaving them with contemporary photocollages, we have drawn out tensions and contradictions, and have made visible relationships that had not been evident in the women's own narratives.

We were interested in how, in the postwar period, the two sisters reconstructed and talked about their lives. What did they emphasize, and what did they omit from their narratives? Having been in opposing countries during the war, how did they remake their personal lives, and how did they recount these to each other? Some clues can be found in the recorded interviews and present-day conversations with Viktoria, and in Martha's letters, tape recordings, and recollections. While oral interviews and personal recollections are of course crucial, they are, as discussed earlier, subject to significant limitations. It could be argued that it was easier and less problematic for Martha to recollect her wartime memories. She openly talked about her time as an "enemy alien." In England, she aligned herself with the Jewish refugee community—both during internment and later in her marriage to Hugo. Before and during the war years, she was openly critical of the Nazi regime. Although she missed Germany, she took on British citizenship and identified herself as British. Martha never returned to live in Germany. She identified strongly with the refugees from Germany and retained a general distrust of Germans and Germany. It is interesting to note that she was much more vocal in her critiques than Hugo, who would not talk about the loss of his family with any of Martha's German relatives.

Viktoria, the younger sister, has remained in Germany throughout her life, and, at the age of 100, still lives in Nienburg, in the former house of her parents-in-law. It has been, and continues to be, difficult and complicated for Viktoria to talk about her wartime experiences. Everyday activities (from writing about jam-making to listing her son's birthday wishes in 1939) are foregrounded to a much greater extent in Viktoria's recollections than the horrors of World War II. When asked to recall those years, her narrative becomes intermixed with self-justification and the need to reconstruct the narrative of her life in a way that makes sense, and is acceptable, to her now. This seems to have been an almost inevitable psychological outcome—one that is by no means unique to Viktoria. Under German fascism, all democratic structures were destroyed; Nazi laws and Nazi language permeated all levels of society. Yet, when the Allied troops finally arrived, the Germans were quick to realign themselves, and any remaining support for the Nazi regime eroded immediately (Kershaw 2011). Claudia Koonz describes how perpetrators "rationalized their participation in Nazi schemes for genocide and repression by divorcing what they did from who they were" (1987, 42). Why Germans became perpetrators or bystanders, and why so few helped others or resisted the regime remains an essential question. Why Viktoria opted for "outward compliance" cannot be established (Karl Jaspers, quoted in Koonz 1987, xxxiv). What choices would others—would we—have made in similar circumstances?

Shortly after the war, Viktoria, who had never been political, joined the Anglo-German Club and began to take English lessons. Psychologically, it was important to forget the time of National Socialism, and to put it behind her. There is another photograph of the two sisters from 1971, taken on one of Martha's last visits to Germany, nearly forty years after the photograph of the two young women next to the haystack in the German countryside was taken. In this later photograph, they are holding hands beside a lake, boats in full sail visible behind them. Martha is again wearing a white dress, and Viktoria is wearing a white top and black skirt. The war, which still lay ahead of them when the 1932 photograph was taken, has now receded far into the background. But the imprint war made on their lives, although not visible in the photograph, is huge. From the strands and traces of their life narratives—as they continue to exist in a range of archival documents—a complicated picture of these two women's war experiences emerges. Some of the surviving archival documents (in particular the wartime photographs and letters) have revealed contradictions, omissions, and repressed memories. However, each archival document has also opened up new possibilities for re-entering their lives. It should be added that Viktoria recently read an earlier version of this essay, and found the experience a forceful one. While the initial research for the exhibition in 2002 had already drawn her back to the war years, our renewed and probing questions for this essay led her to comment that this time, the process "went even deeper."

By participating in the German Army's invasion of Poland in 1939, Viktoria's husband became part of the war machine that would facilitate the subsequent humiliation, imprisonment, and murder of Jewish communities there, including Martha's husband's family. In this light, it is perhaps all the more remarkable that the two sisters, separated by war, grew close again in the years following the Holocaust, and were able to support one another until Martha's death.

NOTES

1   All photographs are from author Julia Winckler's private collection.
2   Between April 1933 and April 1938, two-thirds of Jewish-owned businesses in Germany were "Aryanized." Jewish workers and managers were dismissed and businesses transferred to non-Jewish Germans, who were able to purchase them at prices officially fixed well below market value. Following the pogroms on Jewish businesses in November 1938, the expropriation of Jewish-owned businesses was accentuated.

3   All quotations from the correspondence of the Probst sisters and their family members are from letters in the private collection of Anke Winckler.

4   National Archives, Kew, London, HO 396/272.

5   For example, Elisabeth Janstein, "Der Weg ins Gefängnis von Holloway," in Frederick Baker, ed., *Europa erlesen: London*, Klagenfurt: Wiser, 2001; Erna Nelki, "Autobiographie einer politischen Emigrantin" in Gisela Dischner, ed., *Eine stumme Generation berichtet: Frauen der dreißiger und vierziger Jahre*, Frankfurt a. M.: Fischer, 1982. For a semi-fictional account, see Ruth Borchard, *We are Strangers Here: An "Enemy Alien" in Prison in 1940* (London: Vallentine Mitchell, 2008).

6   See "Rushen Internees Perform Nativity Play," *Isle of Man Examiner*, 3 January 1941, p. 6.

7   Among Martha's estate are many of her husband's family documents, including his parents' last letter to him from September 1939, and his brother Herbert's first letter after the war.

8   "Erinnerungsarbeit wird zur Erinnerung an die Erinnerung, eine Vergangenheit aus zweiter Hand," quotation from James E. Young, *At Memory's Edge: After-images of the Holocaust in Contemporary Art and Architecture* (New Haven/London: Yale Press, 2000).

9   "Erinnerungsprozesse als eine Kombination aus Erinnern und Vergessen, Eingedenken und Verdrängen."

WORKS CITED

Adorno, Theodor W. [1955] 1967. "An Essay on Cultural Criticism and Society." *Prisms*. London: Neville Spearman.

———. 1973. *Negative Dialectics*. Routledge: London.

Assmann, Aleida, and Ute Frevert, eds. 1999. "Zwischen Geschichte und Gedächtnis." *Geschichtsvergessenheit, Geschichtsversessenheit: Vom Umgang mit deutschen Vergangenheiten*. Stuttgart: DVA.

Barnes, James J., and Patience P. Barnes. 2005. *Nazis in Pre-War London 1930–1939: The Fate and Role of German Party Members and British Sympathizers*. Brighton/Portland: Sussex Academic Press.

Barthes, Roland. 1981. *Camera Lucida: Reflections on Photography*. New York: Hill and Wang.

Bearman, Marietta, Charmian Brinson, Richard Dove, Anthony Grenville and Jennifer Taylor. 2008. *Out of Austria: The Austrian Centre in London in World War II*. London/New York: Tauris Academic Studies.

Brinson, Charmian. 2003. "'In the exile of internment' or 'Von Versuchen aus einer Not eine Tugend zu machen'. German-speaking women interned by the British during the Second World War." In *Politics and Culture in Twentieth-Century Germany*, edited by William Niven and James Jordan, 63–87. Rochester, NY: Camden House.

Derrida, Jacques, and Eric Prenovitz. 1995. "Archive Fever: A Freudian Impression." *Diacritics* 25 (2): 9–63.

Hilberg, Raul. 1996. *Täter, Opfer, Zuschauer: Die Vernichtung der Juden 1933–1945*. Frankfurt a M.: Fischer.

Hirsch, Marianne. 1997. *Family Frames: Photography, Narrative and Postmemory*. Cambridge, MA/London: Harvard University Press.

Kardorff, Ursula von. 1962. *Berliner Aufzeichnungen: Aus den Jahren 1942–1945*. München: Biederstein.

Kershaw, Ian. 2011. *The End: The Defiance and Destruction of Hitler's Germany, 1944–1945*. New York: Penguin.

Koonz, Claudia. 1987. *Mothers in the Fatherland*. London: Jonathan Cape.

Muir, Peter. 2010. *Shimon Attie's Writing on the Wall: History, Memory, Aesthetics*. Farnham: Ashgate.

Nora, Pierre. 1989. "Between Memory and History: les Lieux de Mémoire." In *Representations*, no. 26, Special Issue: Memory and Counter-Memory.

Probst Family Letters. 1933–1945. TS. Private collection of Anke Winckler.

"Rushen Internees Perform Nativity Play." *Isle of Man Examiner*. 3 January 1941.

Stephan, Inge, and Alexandra Tacke, eds. 2007. *Nachbilder des Holocaust*. Cologne: Böhlau.

Wiesel, Elie. 1990. *From the Kingdom of Memory*. New York: Summit Books.

Willett, John. 1978. *The New Sobriety: Art and Politics in the Weimar Period, 1917–1933*. London: Thames and Hudson.

FROM PLANTER'S DAUGHTER TO IMPERIAL SOLDIER AND SERVANT IN BRITAIN'S WAR

Patrick Taylor

During World War II, the British government mobilized women in the Caribbean to contribute to the war effort through organizations such as the St. John Ambulance Association and its affiliated Brigade, and the British Army's Auxiliary Territorial Service (ATS). The women in the St. John Ambulance Association were organized on a local basis and received training in first aid and nursing. One of their primary duties was to attend to wounded sailors who sought refuge from the war at sea on islands such as Barbados. In contrast, the ATS was tightly integrated into the broader British war effort. Some Caribbean ATS recruits were trained and posted to local ATS organizations, others were sent to Canada for training and then on to the United States to provide support to the British mission there, and some were sent to Britain for training and posted there. Although their duties were often of a clerical nature and excluded combat roles, ATS volunteers found themselves in the theatre of war, working as drivers, radar operators, aircraft spotters, searchlight operators, and the like, and many lost their lives in the process ("A.T.S. Remembered").

Marguerite Doreen Payne joined the St. John Ambulance Brigade Overseas in 1940 in Barbados, and was recruited to the ATS in 1943. She was sent to the Canadian Women's Army Corps (CWAC) training camp in Kitchener, Ontario, for "basic military training" and then assigned to the British Joint Services Mission offices in Washington, DC. Following the war, she settled in the Washington area permanently, working first for the British and then the Australian embassy. She married an American citizen, though she remained a British subject, never becoming an American citizen herself. After she retired, she wrote several short memoirs, including one based on her experiences in the ATS entitled *For the Duration: The ATS Come to Washington*. It was distributed in a photocopied typescript with an accompanying "Pictoral Record" to selected friends and family.

Marguerite, or Doreen, as family and friends knew her, was my aunt and godmother, and although she lived in the United States and I in Barbados (and subsequently Canada), I always felt I had a special relationship with her. Doreen was the second-eldest of eight children, four girls and four boys. She and her twin brother had both settled in the United States as young adults, after first spending some time in Canada, whereas the rest of the sisters had remained in the Caribbean until a later migration wave took my mother, Grace, to Canada and their eldest sister, Joan, to England.[1] Their father had been the manager of a series of plantations of moderate size, but did not own the properties he worked. His large household was supported by an extended family network, and my cousins, my sister, and I had grown up with many family stories about life on the plantations of our parents' childhood.

I was particularly intrigued to discover that Doreen was finding time in her retirement years to write about her life growing up in Barbados. Among embassy officials and staff in Washington, she had often met with the question that immigrants become so used to hearing: "Where are you from?" Born neither in Britain nor Australia but in Barbados, she had the additional burden of explaining how it was that she could be white and West Indian at the same time. To respond to this, she had to address an additional wrinkle. In his study of the development of early Barbadian white identity in *White Creole Culture, Politics and Identity during the Age of Abolition*, David Lambert observes that in the late eighteenth century and early nineteenth century, Barbadian whites were often on the defensive in their dealings with English reformers, for whom Barbados represented "an aberrant colonial space requiring metropolitan intervention" (2005, 142). In response, the Barbadian plantocratic elite emphasized its Englishness, stressed the uniqueness of the Caribbean situation, and argued that the "paternalistic 'good master' cared for 'his' enslaved workforce and could win their respect and loyalty" (65). Similar attitudes towards Caribbean whites greeted Doreen in the embassies of twentieth-century Washington, and she was keen to explain from her perspective what life was "really like" for her as a young person growing up in Barbados in the early twentieth century. One way to do this was by writing.

Doreen was legendary in the family because of some of the "strange" ways in which she behaved. According to one story, she would bang on the walls of her house in Silver Spring, just outside of Washington, to disrupt the secret microphones she believed had been hidden there to monitor her. It is said that she would not speak to neighbours, especially African American neighbours, and would not stop her car at stop signs for fear of being mugged. The fact that she had written a manuscript about her family and her life as a child growing up on a plantation in Barbados, and, moreover, that she carried the manuscript around in her car so that no one could steal it from her house, added to the mystery surrounding her. Could her apparent paranoia be attributed to the nature of her work for the British Army Staff, Ordnance, during World War II? Or was it a legacy of the Cold War in Washington's embassy life? Was her resistance to her black neighbours a measure of the change brought about by the civil rights movement and the failure of white America to embrace them? Or was she haunted by her plantation past and its racial legacy?

Over the years, I became more interested in family history, and on a few occasions when I visited, she showed me some of her work, including an essay on the ATS, of which she gave me a copy. My own scholarly interests in the Caribbean have largely focused on the literary, religious, and cultural context of nationalist and post-nationalist thought in the region. Doreen's writing, however, tapped into a different aspect of the Caribbean—the colonial Caribbean, which shaped her, and also shaped me, at some level, but which was rapidly disappearing as I was coming of age in Barbados in the 1960s. Barbados won its independence from Britain in 1966, without the violent struggle that accompanied the anti-colonial movement in many other parts of the globe, but not without a workers' rebellion and the upsurge of an active, organized labour movement, which became the backbone for the rise of the "coloured" and "black" elites that would, with national independence, assume political power if not economic control (Beckles 1990; Hoyos 1978).

I approached Doreen's writings, therefore, with considerable ambivalence. I knew her, but I did not really know her. I knew about the colonial experience, but I knew it through the lens of a different history. I had visited plantations in Barbados and on other islands, including one plantation she had grown up on, but I had never lived on one. I heard about World War II from Barbadian teachers who had been in it, and I knew that distant relatives had even lost their lives in it. Close family members had been in the reserves and the St. John Ambulance Brigade, but I did not understand what that meant if they were not engaged actively in warfare. Reading Doreen's work, therefore, would be an important learning experience.

Nevertheless, I feared that if I were to use any of my aunt's work in my own writing I would risk betraying it, suspecting that hers would be a romanticized version of white Barbadian life. I am reminded of the comments that the Dominican scholar Silvio Torres-Saillant makes about his father, whose erudition in the classics, the Bible, Shakespeare, and even the Lake Poets was in large part responsible for the young Silvio's interest in intellectual endeavours: "Not atypically for his generation, my father evinced a neglectful regard for the implications of his uncritical embrace of the view that equated humanity with the West" (Torres-Saillant 2006, 57). There is a sense in which all writing is betrayal, and this may be true particularly of the memoir, not merely because the reader brings his or her own being to the reading, but also because memoir is a construction of the self, and by virtue of that self-selecting. But was my concern perhaps that the writing would betray me? I concur, in any case, with the words of Martinican psychiatrist and political activist Frantz Fanon, who concludes after writing his own searing examination of the black self in the white colonial world, "Was my freedom not given to me then in order to build the world of the You?" (1967, 232).

Doreen's ATS memoir is a highly scripted narrative that tells us something of the impact of the war on British colonies, the possibilities opened by war for social mobility and migration, and the definition, nature, and limits of women's work and women's agency in a time of war. World War II was a major social leveller, in that it brought women of different backgrounds into active service with men in support of Britain's national enterprise. Ruth Pierson argues, however, that in the Canadian case, although women were needed and utilized in the war effort, their participation remained under the control of men. After the war, the emancipatory promise of women in uniform was displaced by a return to "the principles of male economic primacy in the public sphere and male headship in the private" (Pierson 1986, 216). How far was Doreen, as an individual, able to break out of the gender stereotypes and roles assigned to women of her generation? Beyond the gender issue, what is to be made of the colonial context in which the agency of women such as Doreen defined itself? In their study of West Indian women in the ATS, Ben Bousquet and Colin Douglas demonstrate the extent to which racial constructs and policies limited the participation of women from Britain's colonies: British "racism and sexism jockeyed with each other to determine the basis on which black women should be excluded from the forces" (1991, 1). What is the significance of the fact that participation in the war effort as expressed in Doreen's narrative is limited to white women, and where in Doreen's narrative are women of colour to be found?

These questions are all the more pertinent in Doreen's writing about her life because of the nature of the white planter family in which she was raised. The family was not wealthy, like some landowning white planter and merchant families in Barbados who maintained strong ties to England. Nor was it poor, like the descendants of white indentured workers, many Scottish and Irish in origin, who also lived on the island. Most Barbadian whites maintained a strong sense of their identity as white and English, and, as such, saw themselves as culturally and racially superior to the majority of the population who were descendants of enslaved Africans. However, white Barbadians also manifested a spirit of independence going back to the early days of the colony, when, in 1639, Barbadian settlers established their own democratic, parliamentary system of governance within a British colonial order, albeit limited to wealthy, white men. Ironically, claiming their Englishness and refusing what the governor of the time described as "a slavery" that would give "lordship to a Parliament in which we have no representatives," they staked allegiance to the King and took up arms against

Oliver Cromwell's Commonwealth forces in 1651 (Hoyos 1978, 28). After a siege of the island and several battles, articles of agreement were signed with England, asserting, among other things, that the island would be allowed to trade freely and there would be no taxes without the consent of an elected assembly.

Over time there developed new social and cultural patterns peculiar to the colony—patterns that would be fundamentally influenced by the development of an enduring plantation economy beginning in the late seventeenth century. Although England was the primary beneficiary of the vast profits of the plantation system and the Atlantic trade that came with it, the shift to industrial capitalism and the accompanying humanitarian movement subsequently set the English against West Indian planter society (Williams 1964, 154). If white Barbadians were all too eager to defend their Englishness, this was partly because the taint of slavery was all too real.

The legacies of slavery were present in the very institution of the plantation on which Doreen grew up. Slavery had formally ended in 1834, but it nevertheless remained the historical basis for her family's social privilege. The women in the family were not taught to cook or keep up the house as it was expected that there would be others to do this work. Instead, it was understood that they were to be educated, and it is not surprising that they would all end up as salaried employees for some or all of their lives. However, none of them would have the opportunity of a post-secondary education, a privilege that only the eldest brother would earn. The family was not without its own inner contradictions. A spinster aunt, my great-aunt "Bebs," who lived in and assisted with the household and was committed to the Moravian faith in contrast to the mainly Anglican family, is supposed to have burned some old plantation documents that she found because slavery was unchristian. That same aunt adopted a child, Myrta, who was older than Doreen and her brothers and sisters and who also helped out in the house. Although Myrta was, in biological terms, their first cousin, in social terms she was the daughter of an uncle and a woman whom he did not or could not marry because of her racially defined status: she was not white. Strangely, however, Myrta became one of the family's main emotional and spiritual guides, and was, in fact, my own mother's godmother. As adults, the brothers and sisters and their families would regularly visit Myrta in her small house, with its attached village shop that catered mainly to black villagers.

Years ago, I asked Myrta, to whom I was also close, to tell me more about the family. She responded with a quiet laugh and suggested that it might not be a good thing to dig too deeply as you never knew what you might find. Doreen made a commitment to telling the story of how she grew up in Barbados and then gained entry into the United States during World War II by joining the British Army, but she ended up writing memoirs about her experience as a middle-class white woman. In her refusal to dig more deeply, there would be many silences and omissions, particularly around issues of race, colour, and the construction of whiteness. If there were things you knew but could not talk about, the past was nevertheless real, and the tragedy is that the ghost from that past would return in her work as it would in Barbadian life, for it had not been put to rest.

Arguing against tendencies in Caribbean historiography to reduce white women to victims, Hilary Beckles has observed that a gender analysis must take seriously the role and agency of white women in the colonial enterprise (1998, 6–7). Doreen's narrative is about an enterprising woman unobtrusively breaking out of some of the limits placed on her as a woman, but it is also about the construction of whiteness in Barbados, and therein lies its own creative mythology, deception, and, ultimately, betrayal. Silent on its colonial context, a context determined by the racial constructs of plantation society and the peculiarly colonial Barbadian hypersensitivity to whiteness, this nostalgic text is haunted by the ghosts of slavery and colonialism, which continue to roam Barbados today. Beneath the trials and opportunities of Doreen's venture into the world of men's work and men's wars lies an expression of loss that some contemporary theorists have called "post-colonial melancholia," a loss that haunts not only Barbados but also the wider post-colonial world (Cheng 2001; Khanna 2003; Gilroy 2005).

THE ST. JOHN AMBULANCE BRIGADE: "I COULD SPLINT A BROKEN BONE AND APPLY GENERAL FIRST AID"

It was not until I encountered Doreen's memoir that I realized how close World War II had come to what I always thought of as distant, tropical Barbados—a place too far from the depredations of Old Europe to be of significance in the war. True, the cenotaph at my school listed the men and boys who had lost their lives in two world wars, and there was an annual Remembrance Day parade. As a child, I had heard that the submarine net in Carlisle Bay had been breached during the war and that a merchant ship, the *Cornwallis*, had been sunk by a German U-boat. Indeed, today tourists and locals alike snorkel and scuba dive around the old wreck to see the corals and watch the fish at play. I also knew that my father had joined the reserves but had not seen action, and that my mother, along with two of her three sisters, Doreen and Joan, were proud of the first-aid training they received when they joined the St. John Ambulance Brigade. But what did they actually do?

Doreen writes that she and her sisters diligently took the required courses in first aid and home nursing, naively thinking that they were ready for any contingency. What they did not know was that with the entry of the United States into the war, and the value of oil, bauxite, and other goods transiting the region, 263 ships would be sunk in the Caribbean Sea by the end of 1942 (Allen

2001, 4). (In contrast, Commander Karl M. Hasslinger [1996] states that 400 merchant ships were sunk in the Caribbean area, with a loss of only 17 U-boats). When the wounded were expected to arrive on the island, Doreen, like other members of the St. John Ambulance Brigade, would request time off from her regular work as a secretary, ride her bike across town to her home, change into a white uniform and cap, and find her way to wherever survivors from a U-boat attack were expected to land. She states, "When I arrived on the scene the first time, I was totally inexperienced, unprepared for human suffering, and more afraid than the wretched oil covered survivors themselves. I could splint a broken bone and apply general first aid, which I did, but I felt inadequate when it came to rendering encouragement to survivors of such an ordeal at sea, who regarded us as angels of mercy, because of our white uniform and youth!" (Allen 2001, 4).

These women were proud of their contribution to the war effort, and their work was regarded as very valuable. Like other volunteers, my mother received a royal certificate of appreciation at the end of the war, which she kept in her possession and which has come down to me. It reads, "in recognition of devoted service to the cause of humanity during the second world war 1939–1945" and is signed "George R.I, Sovereign Head, Order of St. John of Jerusalem" (George VI), and "Elizabeth R., President, British Red Cross Society" (the Queen Mother). Yet, there can be little doubt about the gendered structure of the St. John Ambulance Brigade. Dr. Harold Skeete was one of the physicians who taught the women their first aid. Their roles were clearly limited, defined entirely in relation to the patriarchal medical and military hierarchies of the day. Two photographs of Dr. Skeete's group in the memoir, dated 1940 and 1941, respectively, illustrate this most clearly. Sisters Doreen, Joan, and Grace pose in their nursing clothes along with the other members of the brigade. Perfectly centred in the first photograph (Figure 4.1) are two men in suits. One of these suited men is also in the

Figure 4.1   St. John Ambulance Brigade, Barbados Branch, 1940 (Allen 2001, 8).

Figure 4.2   St. John Ambulance Brigade, Barbados Branch, 1941 (Allen 2001, 8).

second photograph (Figure 4.2), and though he is not directly in the centre in this image, he certainly stands out among the women.

THE AUXILIARY TERRITORIAL SERVICE: "OURS NOT TO WONDER WHY, OURS BUT TO DO OR DIE"

The British Army sent a woman, known only as Subaltern Carter, to recruit ATS volunteers in Barbados. Doreen writes that Carter treated the volunteers who left Sewell Airport in Barbados sitting on benches aboard a Royal Air Force plane "as if we were a group of school children to be herded and escorted on a tour of foreign lands" (Allen 2001, 7). Stopping unexpectedly in various Caribbean islands, then in Miami, before taking the train to Washington to receive their assignments and then on to Toronto for training, the thirty recruits quickly learned the meaning of army life: "blind obedience or acceptance of a given situation with no questions asked and natural curiosity submerged" (10). From Toronto, the Barbadian ATS recruits were sent for basic training with the Canadian Women's Army Corps in Kitchener, Ontario. Doreen's narrative emphasizes repeatedly the place of obedience and discipline in every aspect of army life—from making a bed and shining shoes to marching with a respirator and gas mask. Even if "cycles and stomachs were upset (causing wonderings about immaculate conceptions)," duty came before personal comfort, as Subaltern Carter reminded the women, saying, "ours not to wonder why, ours but to do or die" (22). Doreen writes, with a touch of irony and sense of humour, "I began to understand a little more about the esprit de corps of an army's tightly-wound human machine, disciplined, well-fed, trained to split-second reaction on command. We were becoming soldiers in every sense of the word, except armed combat, although we were destined for the asphalt jungle" (31). Doreen's use of the word "soldier" here is particularly significant: the term was reserved for men because only they were permitted to engage in actual combat, even if many of them did the same non-combatant work as the women (Pierson 1986, 120).

The ATS, the CWAC, and the related Navy and Air Force services in Britain and Canada provided a parallel military space in which women could find a place for themselves as soldiers among soldiers, working to support the war effort. In a letter published in the local newspaper, *The Barbados Advocate*, Doreen and one of her fellow ATS recruits, Peggy Gooding, thanked supporters, many of them women, for raising funds and providing woollen garments for the trip to North America. "We leave Barbados full of enthusiasm for our work," the letter states, and "feel it a great privilege to take an active part in the War effort of the Empire" (Allen 2001). Unlike in World War I, when such organizations did not exist, women were recognized as trained and disciplined members of the armed forces rather than as mere aids. They now had their own training centre and their commanding officers were also women.

Yet, the "machine" that Doreen describes remained heavily gendered, and her sensitivity to this emerges in several anecdotes. In a classic case of the man doctor/woman patient relationship, she relates that on arrival at the CWAC barracks in Toronto, the new recruits had to go for medical examinations: "Four or five stark-born-naked girls lined up in a row in the Infirmary, their nudity covered by white hospital gowns opening down the front which they clutched like security blankets; a young goodlooking Royal Navy physician walking down the line, examining ear, nose and throat, then, open-gown like a flasher, no time for blushing, while he examined heart lungs and stomach and then on to the next girl" (Allen 2001, 23). Perhaps the humour with which Doreen relates this and similar incidents indicates an aspect of resistance in the narrative to the structures of army power, and it is evident that the young recruits resented the intrusion that accompanied the experience itself.

In another anecdote, Doreen relates that she and two other ATS trainees decided to hitchhike from Kitchener to Guelph one Sunday. After walking a considerable distance, they were picked up by a lieutenant in the Royal Canadian Air Force who, on discovering that they had not asked for formal permission to leave camp, turned his car in the opposite direction and drove them back to the base in Kitchener. The lieutenant was later overheard at an officers' club "regaling his friends with a story of having picked up three British ATS recruits, a red head, a blond and a brunette, who were hitchhiking to Guelph" and who "'didn't even know that they were AWOL'" (Allen 2001, 40). Doreen insists that the women learned "to be disciplined and self-confident individuals" (41), but she also admits that she hated having to salute her authorities, including the lieutenant who returned them to the base and reported them for being "absent without official leave." For his part, when he left them, he returned their salute "and drove away grinning like a Cheshire Cat" (39). Pierson observes that servicewomen were always in a subordinate relationship to servicemen: "The CWAC officer, non-commissioned officer, or private was junior to her male Army counterpart. And while male Army officers and NCOs always enjoyed power of command over CWAC personnel junior to them, CWAC officers and NCOs could exercise power of command over junior male Army officers or male other ranks only under exceptional circumstances" (Pierson 1986, 122).

Commenting on some of the women's responses to basic training, Doreen writes, "Some called it boot camp, some called it basic training, some hated it, some took it in stride. One or two dropped out. One girl was discharged for undisclosed reasons; one girl with absolutely no guile in her was discovered to be a petty kleptomaniac.... One girl who was pregnant disappeared; we heard that she had been billeted with a local family" (Allen 2001, 41). Doreen does not judge these responses. Instead, she looks back "with happy memories" and "appreciation and thankfulness for the kindness, courteousness and profession- alism of the Canadian Women's Army Corps" (41–42). Pierson argues that the differential treatment of men and women in the Canadian Army existed not only in terms of organizational structure, employment opportunities, earnings, and benefits, but also in relation to representations of sexuality and disease. Drawing on the dualistic "virgin/whore" imagery in Western patriarchal thought, she states that it was women who were blamed for any sexual misdemeanour and even the spread of venereal disease. This was despite the fact that the vast major- ity of putative fathers of "out of wedlock" pregnancies were servicemen, and that the incidence of venereal disease was higher among servicemen than service- women (Pierson 1986, 172–73). In a highly personal and memorable essay on her foray into the archives of the CWAC, Pierson tells how she uncovered an army brochure describing two "women" whom the men soldiers had to avoid: "Gonnie" and "Syph," two "skimpily skirted, garishly lipsticked, cigarette-smok- ing 'gals.'" "Merely for a woman to enter the male domain of the military," writes Pierson, "was to call her 'purity' into question" (173). Once "cases, few though they were, of VD and pregnancy 'out of wedlock' surfaced, members of the Canadian Women's Army Corps became the objects of a vicious 'whispering campaign' impugning their morality" (Pierson 2007, 496–97).[2] In Britain in 1941, similarly disparaging remarks about encouraging promiscuity had been made when the Essential Work Order was introduced to force employers to hire women to replace the men who had gone to war, and when, later that year, conscription of women into the armed forces became a necessity (Bousquet and Douglas 1991, 22).

Doreen's Victorian sensibility did not permit her to raise such matters directly in her own narrative, but to her credit, the women of the ATS and

Figure 4.3   British Army Staff, Ordnance, Washington, DC (Allen 2001).

Figure 4.4   Civilian secretaries, Ordnance, Washington, DC (Allen 2001).

the CWAC emerge, in contrast, with humanity and propriety, as women who take control over their lives in an unpretentious way, further marking her own writing's resistance to patriarchal misrepresentations. A similar sense of accomplishment can be found in many of the narratives of CWAC veterans recorded for posterity by the "Memory Project" (Historica Canada), and in the interviews of West Indian women in the ATS and related organizations conducted by Bousquet and Douglas. Doreen's manuscript includes a photograph of the "British Army Staff, Ordnance" in Washington: five ATS servicewomen in uniform stand or sit alongside five servicemen in uniform in postures of relative equality, albeit with an accompanying man as commanding officer and two of the women, one of them her, seated gracefully on the floor (Figure 4.3). This image stands in direct contrast to another with four women in civilian dress, whom she describes as "civilian secretaries on our staff" (Figure 4.4). The clear message is that servicewomen were not "secretaries."

WAR AS ADVENTURE: "PICKING APPLES AT MISS FIELDS"

For Doreen, one of the most notable aspects of basic training was immersion into the world of manual labour. A photo accompanying descriptions of training activities on the ATS base in Kitchener captures her all in smiles as she poses in work clothes, a cleaning brush and pail in hand (Figure 4.5). She relates, "I peeled dozens of potatoes, wielded a mean broom, mopped floors and swilled latrines, the only consolation being that every recruit had to take her turn too" (Allen 2001, 30). Only the women "servants," all of who[m] were black or mixed, would have done such work in her planter father's household. "Growing up in Barbados," she writes with an apparent mix of regret and nostalgia, "there was no chance to acquire any household skills, everything was unobtrusively done for us—it was a way of life, gone with the wind" (23). All of the ATS recruits in her photographs appear to be white, and, as such, beneficiaries of the privilege of whiteness, despite their various class backgrounds.

Another form of manual labour that Doreen experienced in Canada was fruit picking. There is a photo of a smiling uniformed recruit picking apples at "Miss Fields" in Milton, not far from Kitchener (Figure 4.6). "Canadian farmers," Doreen writes, "often invited one or two of us, or even a group of us, at a time to spend Saturday, Sunday or a Bank Holiday with them and help with their apple picking—which we found great fun" (33). Doreen writes that she and her Barbadian friends "looked on basic training as an adventure" (Allen 2001, 32). Bousquet and Douglas observe similarly that war "was an adventure" for Marjorie Griffiths, one of their ATS interviewees from Barbados who had been sent to England. "That is not to say," they continue, "that she was not aware of the serious side of the conflict, and what the fighting was about. But her overwhelming

Figure 4.5   Doreen Payne. Activities on the ATS base in Kitchener, Ontario (Allen 2001, 34).

Figure 4.6   Doreen picking apples at Miss Fields, Milton, Ontario (Allen 2001, 36).

memory was of being able to meet people, and see places she would not have come across had it not been for the war" (Bousquet and Douglas 1991, 111). Likewise, Pierson writes that for Canadian servicewomen, "the second strongest motive after patriotism" for joining the CWAC was "the urge for travel and adventure" (1986, 111). Despite the discipline, the routines, and the work, army life could be exciting for the women who participated in the ATS. According to Bousquet and Douglas, all of the women they interviewed shared "patriotism, a willingness to embark on new adventures, and an above average standard of education" (1991, 126). In this respect, Doreen's memoir often reads like a romantic travelogue. At the stopover in Santo Domingo, where, as she notes, Columbus, Cortés, Balboa, and Drake, among others, had previously set foot, they were "serenaded by a group of young Dominicans" late one night in the hotel courtyard, a "romantic salute" by these Dominican men that would leave the young women "with happy memories of that old colonial capital" (Allen 2001, 13–14). At another stop, this time in Nassau, the new recruits danced in the hotel lobby "with young RAF and US air force officers who were on leave" (15). If the endless rows of parked cars in Miami made the city look from the aircraft as if it were paved with silver rather than gold (16), the journey from Miami to Washington by train was sobering. Washington provided a different kind of adventure, for it was there that the recruits were fitted with uniforms and assigned to their future war employment. Yet, Doreen comments that this "city of strangers," a "shrine to the past" and "hope of the future," caught and held her interest (20). From Washington to Toronto, the train passed through Niagara Falls, but the recruits would have to wait for some free time to actually see what they could only hear from the train as a distant rumble.

Canada existed in the minds of the recruits primarily as a series of romantic images, and as Doreen travelled on the train, she thought of stories she had read with her father of "the Great Northwest Territories, the Yukon, the Rockies, Wolfe and Quebec, of Saskatoon, Saskatchewan, home of a childhood pen-pal, of red-coated Mounties romanticized by Nelson Eddy and Jeanette MacDonald" (Allen 2001, 22). While the recruits waited in Toronto for space to open at the CWAC base in Kitchener, Doreen found an opportunity to really experience Niagara Falls. Joined by her twin brother, Torrence, and a friend, both of whom were studying at McGill University in Montreal, Doreen and another ATS recruit took the *Cayuga* from Toronto to Port Dalhousie to see the falls, which she describes as "breathtaking," and ride below them on the *Maid of the Mist* (25). Was the fact that her twin brother had won a scholarship to McGill and had volunteered with the Royal Canadian Medical Corps a factor in her decision to join the ATS as a way of getting away from Barbados? She writes, "I don't know if Torrence realized how much his visits meant to me—a stranger in a strange land—and how much I appreciated his kindness" (25).

Doreen's travel romance continued on the CWAC base, where basic training was complemented by lectures, concerts, plays, and bridge, as well as "casual sing-alongs around the piano or around a campfire toasting marshmallows" (Allen 2001, 32). Even the failed hitchhiking trip is coded as an adventure, and all the more so when Doreen describes how she told the wary lieutenant that they were heading to Guelph because it "was the home of John McCrae, a soldier in World War I who wrote a famous poem about Flanders fields where the poppies blow, shortly before he was killed at Ypres" (38–39).

If the photo of a uniformed recruit "ready for route march—tin hat, gas mask and respirator" (Figure 4.7) first strikes the reader with the seriousness of basic training, on second glance it becomes an exotic pose, a fitting symbol of an exciting adventure. Nevertheless, although there is a certain amount of "glamour" to Doreen's portrayal of life in the ATS, she does not present the recruits as

Figure 4.7   "Ready for route march—tin hat, gas mask and respirator" (Allen 2001, 35).

"glamour girls" in the way that the Canadian campaign to recruit women did. Canadian Army publicity sought to glamorize women in the army, in some cases using images of women in the CWAC with "good looks" wearing respirators or engaged in other military activities. This glamorization of women, which even included encouraging CWAC women to pose for pin-ups, was a type of forced "femininity," argues Pierson, meant in part to assuage Canadian concern about women's loss of femininity in the army (1986, 142–48).

The photograph of Doreen and Torrence in uniform on the steps of the Cairo Hotel in Washington, where she was billeted for the remainder of the war, stands in contrast (Figure 4.8). Although Doreen is blinking in the photograph, she includes it in the manuscript, presumably to show her closeness to her twin brother. The photograph marks her equality with her brother, both of them volunteers in the services, and elicits a different aspect of the romance of war: dignity bestowed on participants, both men and women, by the military uniform itself.

Figure 4.8   Doreen and Torrence Payne (twins), Cairo Hotel, Washington, DC (Allen 2001).

Life was far less romantic for the many thousands of Barbadians and other Caribbean migrants, both men and women, who travelled to Panama, the United States, the United Kingdom, and, subsequently, Canada in the twentieth century. Many early immigrant women found employment as domestic workers, though some were also nurses. These were the real workers, the black women who left their children with their mothers or aunts to head north in search of a better life, hopeful that their families might follow them later. Emigration helped to reduce the problem of Barbados' very high population density. Already by 1844, the population of the small island of 267 square kilometres was 122,200 (460 people per square kilometre). The population increased to 182,900 by 1891. Migration (and, to a lesser extent, an influenza epidemic) resulted in a subsequent population decline to 156,800 by 1921 (Roberts 1955, 245–46). Despite increased emigration beginning in the 1950s, however, the population had risen again to 230,000 by 1956 (860 people per square kilometre) (Lowenthal 1957, 447), putting even greater pressure on emigration in subsequent years. In addition to addressing the problem of population density, Barbadian emigration was also of significant benefit to the island because of the remittances immigrants sent back to family on the island. Nevertheless, many immigrants found themselves facing harsh working conditions and severe discrimination in host countries (Ebanks, George, and Nobbe 1979, 448).

While emigration from the Caribbean increased, there was a parallel movement of seasonal migrant workers, largely men, who worked on fruit farms in Florida and, in subsequent years, tended tobacco fields and picked fruit in southern Ontario. Under the Caribbean Seasonal Agricultural Workers Program (1966), migrant workers from Barbados, Jamaica, and Trinidad were systematically recruited for Canadian farms (Lowenthal 1957, 488; Parr 1985, 103; Gibb, n.d., 1–28). Short-term contract workers returned home for the winter and had fewer rights than their immigrant compatriots. They could earn more than they could in their home country, but working conditions were harsh and their legal status as migrant labour placed severe restrictions on their mobility and civic rights. Is it possible that Barbadian migrant workers who came after the war picked fruit on some of the same farms frequented by the women of the ATS?

Today, Milton, Ontario, is a thriving town surrounded by farms and orchards. Many of these are open to the public, who arrive by the thousands on weekends to pick vegetables and fruit, or just to be entertained, throughout the summer and fall. My family has participated in this activity since my children were young, picking strawberries, apples, or other fruits or vegetables. On one occasion, Doreen's older sister, Joan, joined us, little aware of her sister's connection to the area. The ATS may no longer be there, but the migrant workers remain, working out of sight in the orchards, or, less often, visible loading up fruit stands for the visitors from the city (Toronto).

THE UNSPOKEN: IMAGE AS ARCHIVAL TRACE

There are few references to ethnicity or race in Doreen's narrative. In a rare moment, as she is concluding her manuscript and emphasizing some of the positive aspects of basic military training, she states that recruits emerged "capable of standing up to be counted, of walking through any crowd anywhere unobtrusively and without fear, able to get along with other nationalities (from the colonial Caribbean alone there were recruits of French, Spanish, Chinese, Portuguese and English descent), and aware of our Allies" (Allen 2001, 41). There is also mention of women at the CWAC training camp from different parts of Canada, including Doreen's roommate, who was from Prince Edward Island, but nothing on their ethnicity. The complex demographic makeup of the Kitchener-Waterloo area is barely discussed. Noting that the area was first set aside by the British Crown for "Six Nation Indians," she states that the land was sold and then settled in the nineteenth century by Pennsylvanian Mennonites and "skilled craftsmen, tradesmen, farmers, artisans and agricultural labourers, who left Germany in great numbers in the nineteenth century" (28). Two neighbouring towns, Berlin and Waterloo, sprouted up, and Berlin became a significant industrial centre by the end of the nineteenth century. During World War I, Berlin was renamed Kitchener, after Field Marshal Horatio H. Kitchener, British Secretary of State for War. Doreen makes no comment on the significance of this symbolic war and the fact that a World War II training camp was located in an area largely populated by persons of German descent. It is noteworthy, however, that unlike in the case of World War I, Canadian authorities generally did not see German Canadian residents and citizens as a serious threat during World War II. Nevertheless, an estimated 850 out of a total population of 600,000 Canadian residents and citizens of German origin were interned across Canada, and thousands more had to report to police on a regular basis (Keyserlingk 1984, 17–18; Bailey, n.d.).

It is even more notable that there are no direct references to persons of African descent anywhere in Doreen's written manuscript. The population of the island of Barbados in the 1946 census was 193,680 (Ebanks, George, and Nobbe 1979, 432), a very large number for such a small island. Of this population, 5 percent was "white," and the remaining 95 percent was "black" or "coloured" (Lowenthal 1957, 467). Yet, the vast majority of members of the St. John Ambulance Brigade in Doreen's groups, as depicted in her photos from 1940 and 1941, were white, as were all of the Barbadian ATS recruits for Washington. To some extent, this reflected an enduring Barbadian social structure where white Barbadian women had access to areas of charitable or social involvement and channels of social mobility, however limited, whereas black women were restricted to working their family land, marketing, tending sugar cane fields, or performing domestic chores for the middle and upper classes. More to the point, however, especially in the case of the ATS, was the fact that for some time, the policy of the British Army was to restrict ATS recruitment to white women. This institutionalized British colour bar was only lifted in 1943, after a black Bermudian was mistakenly accepted, and by the end of the war "more than half of the six hundred West Indians serving with the ATS were black" (Healy 2000, 76–77). The situation was similar in Canada. The CWAC, with which Doreen and her fellow ATS recruits were trained, was largely white. According to the policy of the women's services in Canada, an applicant had to be "a British subject, of white race." The CWAC only changed this policy in 1942, when the first recruit of First Nations descent was admitted (Pierson 1986, 113).

Bousquet and Douglas argue that British military authorities "latched on to the American colour bar to justify their own racism" (1991, 50). They observe that whereas "colonial racism was pompous and duplicitous, its Jim Crow equivalent was blunt and violent" (61). In a letter to the War Office in 1943, the Colonial Office stated that any recruitment process should "preserve the principle of non-discrimination against persons of colour" (152). In the case of the ATS, the Colonial Office was concerned that accepting only white women would lead to objections and provoke disturbances in the colonies. In response, the War Office reminded the Colonial Office that they had agreed earlier that "no one wanted to import large numbers of coloured personnel, either for industry or the Services." However, the War Office was willing to accept "suitable European women from the Colonies for enrolment into the A.T.S" (153–54). It insisted that this policy was necessary because some ATS recruits would be sent to work in the British Mission in Washington, and American whites would not work alongside blacks (157–58). British policy was informed by the type of race thinking characterized by Major General Arthur Dowler's "Notes on Relations with Coloured Troops," where "coloured men" were deemed not to possess "the white man's ability to think and to act to a plan" (164). A compromise was agreed on whereby white and black women could be recruited to Caribbean-based organizations such as the Jamaican ATS and the Trinidadian ATS. However, only white West Indian women could be recruited for the ATS stationed in the United States. As for Britain, when Bermudian recruit L. Curtis turned out to be black rather than white, and fearing that it was too late to reject her without eliciting an unfavourable backlash, the War Office had to revisit its duplicitous race-based recruitment policy. In any case, racial integration existed already among British troops, and some of the British ATS were women of colour (97–99). Eventually, a limited number of black and white recruits from the West Indies were permitted to join the ATS in Britain regardless of race or colour.[3]

In the end, three hundred ATS recruits of different racial backgrounds were trained and stationed in the Caribbean, and one hundred in Britain. Two hundred white recruits were stationed in Washington (Bousquet and Douglas 1991, 2).

Bousquet and Douglas argue that even the white Caribbean recruits met with discrimination and were promoted less frequently than their British counterparts (103–4). Other West Indian women of colour would subsequently be accepted into different services in small numbers, including the Women's Auxiliary Air Force. One of Bousquet and Douglas's interviewees, Lilian Bader, states, "you have to remember that by that time [1944] all the racism of the Germans had been exposed and the British weren't in a position to do anything other than show that they were treating their coloured troops well" (140). Sometimes, however, they were not treated as well as they felt they should have been, and some have reported that they were assigned demeaning tasks or underpaid (114–15). Michael Healy's study of Britain's anxiety over its Caribbean Regiment, which was supposed to be the primary vehicle of deployment for Caribbean men who volunteered during World War II, illustrates the extent to which the racial legacy of imperial Britain continued to have a debilitating impact during the war. Because black West Indians as a group were often perceived to be disruptive and unreliable, and because they wanted to fight as equals, with the same pay and opportunities for commissions as their British counterparts, army field commanders refused to deploy the Caribbean Regiment. The Caribbean Regiment was so restricted that it never saw action, even though it was posted first to Italy and then Egypt. Nevertheless, an estimated ten thousand black West Indian volunteers, supported by government officials, private companies, and local associations, went to Britain to enlist in the army, the navy, and the air force individually once the colour bar in each service was lifted (in 1939 for the army and navy, and in 1940 for the air force). Separate from the men in the Caribbean Regiment and deployed across the different services, they were not seen as a threat and were integrated on an equal basis (Healy 2000, 76). One of the most well known and distinguished of these men was Errol Walton Barrow, who joined the Royal Air Force in 1940, and subsequently became the premier of Barbados, led the country to independence in 1966, and was the nation's first prime minister.

Although Doreen's war narrative occludes the deep history of the plantation and its racialized, colonial context, there is one photo that appears in the early pages of the manuscript that contains an important "trace" (Kadar 2005, 224) that puts in question the absence of racial discourse in the memoir. In the photograph of the St. John Ambulance Brigade, Barbados Branch, dated 1940 (Figure 4.1), one, and only one, of the nineteen women nurses appears to be a woman of African descent. In the second photo, dated 1941 (Figure 4.2), there appear to be no women of African descent. Why did Doreen include both photos in the memoir? If the memoir ignores the presence of race as a key social construct in colonial Barbadian society, the 1941 photo of the St. John Ambulance Brigade serves to purge whiteness of its racial interlocutor. The move from planter's daughter to imperial soldier and servant in Britain's war can be read to some extent through a master narrative of war as grand equalizer. Women were systematically included in the war effort, basic training and army discipline broke through class lines, and the unity of the war effort took precedence over markers of social difference. But the virtual absence of persons of colour in the memoir and its attendant images, and the superimposition of quaint images of white women at work in a context of war, marks the narrative as a colonial romance, the tragedy of which lies in its re-inscription of what Lambert calls a peculiarly Barbadian "white supremacist discourse" (2005, 61–65), but one that cannot be divorced from its British counterpart.

When England went to war in 1938, the governor of Barbados supposedly sent a cable to London, stating, in the memorable words of novelist George Lamming's narrator, "Go brave big England for Little England is behind you" (Lamming 1991, 223). Bousquet and Douglas state that the majority of the ATS recruits from the Caribbean were middle-class Anglophiles (1991, 109–10). In her study of New Zealand settler culture, Radhika Mohanram argues that the white settler subject is "peculiarly located" between indigenous and metropolitan society, "their bodies" functioning "at the intersection of degeneration and white supremacy" (2007, 132). As Lambert has shown in the Barbadian case, the enduring idea of Barbados as "Little England" served as a constant assertion of whiteness in the ongoing "anxiety-ridden" negotiation that characterized the relationship between a slave-based plantation society and an industrializing British society (2005, 163–64). Similarly, Karl Watson argues that the Barbadian elite perpetuated the myth that Barbados was more British than the British in the face of an ongoing creolization of English culture on the island (1979, 41). In a more recent study of the 2007 Barbados Bicentenary of the Abolition of the Slave Trade, Watson observes that "the Barbadian public did not seem to be remarkably enthused by the commemoration," adding that many were admittedly consumed by the Cricket World Cup in Barbados that year (2009, 188). Yet slavery, he argues, continues "to haunt present day Barbados" (181).

Many post-colonial cultural critics influenced by psychoanalysis, and particularly by Sigmund Freud's essay "Mourning and Melancholia," have addressed the idea of slavery and colonialism as ghostly presences haunting an anxiety-ridden white identity. "The past haunts the present," states Mohanram, and the repressed returns in Michel de Certeau's words as a "mnemic trace" (Mohanram 2007, 141). Paul Gilroy identifies "postimperial melancholia" as a key problem for contemporary multicultural Britain. The nation's attachment to the glory of World War II and the defeat of the Nazis is a way of disguising "the guilt-ridden loathing and depression that have come to characterize Britain's xenophobic responses to the strangers who have intruded upon it more recently" (Gilroy 2005, 90). The country's future, Gilroy argues, depends on its ability to confront "the repressed and buried knowledge of the cruelty and injustice … of imperial administration" and acknowledge the "hidden, shameful store of imperial horrors" (94). Mohanram and Gilroy both draw on the work of psychoanalysts Alexander and Margarete Mitscherlich, who argue that a melancholic postwar Germany warded off "a collective process of mourning" that would have involved working through the evil of the Nazi regime in which they were complicit (quoted in Gilroy 2005, 98; Mohanram 2007, 131–32). To single out Germany and ignore the West's colonial legacy, however, would be to fail to recognize the systemic and discursive links between Nazism and Europe's imperial past (Arendt 2001, 440; Césaire 1972, 13–14).

Focusing on the US context, Anne Cheng argues that white American identity operates in a similarly melancholic way. If in melancholia "the subject sustains itself through the ghostly emptiness of a lost other," racialization is produced by a "white national ideal, which is sustained by the exclusion-yet-retention of racialized others" (Cheng 2001, 10). The result is that racialized others also become melancholically caught in an ambivalent relationship to whiteness. Cheng argues that melancholia can be used as a critical tool "precisely because it theoretically accounts for the guilt and the denial of guilt, the blending of shame and omnipotence in the racist imaginary" (2001, 12). Such a tool can lead to understanding and thereby transform the grief of racial injury into an ethically or politically based grievance.

Ranjana Khanna also sees melancholia as a tool for understanding loss, and suggests it forms the basis of a critical consciousness of colonialism. Freud himself, she argues, came to an understanding of the limits of the modern nation state when, as a Jew, he had to flee Germany. The act of mourning, as a form of assimilation into the modern nation, gives way in his writing to the fact of melancholia, as a splitting, distancing, and critique of the nation (Khanna 2003, 64–65). Strongly informed by feminist theory, Khanna argues that Freud's own vision of (white) woman as a "dark continent" can be linked to colonial concepts of Africa and a gendered concept of the primitive. Paradoxically, however, this conflation results in "the total erasure of black women" (48). For Khanna, as for Cheng, the ghosts of colonialism continue to haunt the present, not only in the metropolitan state, but also in the post-colonial nation, which has likewise failed to represent women. As such, spectral traces "problematize the rather romantically conceived spirit of the nation" and demand a critical response (272). "If the archive appears by some to be a national monument and thus a collective memory," Khanna writes, "it can also be a home for the unhomely and the unbeautiful: the phantoms from limbo patrum" (268).

My own journey to Canada with my sister and mother more than twenty years after Doreen's was prefigured by hers, and, to a lesser extent, by Torrence's. Although my family was part of a larger migratory movement that brought thousands of Barbadians to Canada in the 1960s and 1970s, we were indebted to Doreen and Torrence for initiating a type of serial migration within the family. In this respect, Doreen's story is my story—yet in many respects, it is not. Doreen's war memoir presents a white Barbadian woman's spirited attempt to break out of an island mentality and move beyond the roles assigned to women of her colour and social status. Yet it remains a romance of empire, its appeal to whiteness a mark of its post-colonial melancholia. Doreen's narrative is haunted by the spectral presence of a plantation experience that, however much she refuses to let it, must disclose itself. Who is the single woman of colour in the 1940 photograph (Figure 4.1), and what anxiety might she have provoked that another photograph without her is added to the manuscript (Figure 4.2)?[4] Given the nature of Doreen's discourse, why did she even include the first photo, the only representation of a person of African descent anywhere in the manuscript? Doreen's sister, Marjorie, was too young to join the St. John Ambulance Brigade or the ATS, and never migrated from the island. Her memoir is unwritten, but something she said to me may provide an answer to these questions. On a drive in 2003 to visit some parts of the island she remembered from childhood, she told my cousins and me another story about the family: her grandmother, our great-grandmother, was a woman of mixed European and African descent who was born "out of wedlock."[5]

The story of women's involvement in World War II has been subordinated historically to that of the men who fought valiantly for their countries, many of them losing their lives in the process. There has been increasing recognition, however, of the importance of the women who participated in the St. John Ambulance Brigade, the ATS, the CWAC, and similar organizations, and their stories are being told. Today, the CWAC Knollwood training camp in Kitchener, Ontario, has been transformed into two adjoining city parks on East Avenue: Knollwood Park and the Kitchener Memorial Auditorium Complex (The Aud). The CWAC's place in Kitchener's history, and in world affairs more generally, is virtually invisible. However, fronting a small Royal Canadian Army Cadet Corps building adjoining The Aud, there stands a memorial dedicated to the CWAC training centre, commemorating by name the women of the CWAC who died while on active duty during World War II. On the memorial is a bronze statue of a uniformed servicewoman, appropriately entitled *Stepping Out* (Figure 4.9). It is the work of sculptor Colonel André Gauthier, and was unveiled in 2001. Today, the memorial encourages people to ponder the active role of women in World War II—heirs to the tradition of Athena, Greek warrior goddess of wisdom and symbol of the CWAC, whose figure adorns the memorial (Figure 4.10). On a recent visit, some of Doreen's nieces and nephews, several great-nieces, and two great-great nephews—some of them Barbadians, most of them Canadians—assembled at the memorial to remember Doreen's contribution to

Figure 4.9 *Stepping Out* (2001), by Colonel André Gauthier. Photo by author, October 2011.

Figure 4.10 *Proudly They Served*. Close-up of one panel of the *Stepping Out* memorial showing the CWAC's Athena symbol. Photo by author, October 2011.

the ATS and to their own personal journeys. So many stories as yet untold lie hidden within that soldier's image.

NOTES

1 All four sisters had passed away before I began this project.
2 See also Pierson 1986, 206–9; Dundas and Durflinger, n.d.
3 The Imperial War Museum has a useful online archival image gallery of Jamaican and Trinidadian ATS servicewomen at work: www.iwm.org.uk.
4 Interestingly, Doreen's sister, Joan, had her own copies of the photos and questioned Doreen's dates when she read a draft of this chapter. While 1941 is written on the back of Joan's copy of the second photo (Figure 4.2), there is no date on the back of the first photo (Figure 4.1), and Joan wondered if it was taken in 1942 rather than 1940.
5 Her younger brother, when asked about this some years later, said he knew of the claim but could not verify whether it was true.

WORKS CITED

Allen, M.D. 2001. *For the Duration: The ATS Come to Washington.* TS. Private Collection.

Arendt, Hannah. 2001. *The Origins of Totalitarianism.* New York: Harcourt.

"A.T.S. Remembered," http://www.atsremembered.org.uk.

Bailey, Alexandra. n.d. "German Internment during the First and Second World Wars." Edmonton: University of Alberta, Centre for Constitutional Studies, http://www.law.ualberta.ca/centres/ccs/issues/germaninternment.php.

Beckles, Hilary. 1990. *A History of Barbados: From Amerindian Settlement to Nation-State.* Cambridge: Cambridge University Press.

———. 1998. "White Women and a West India Fortune: Gender and Wealth during Slavery." In *The White Minority in the Caribbean,* edited by Howard Johnson and Karl Watson, 1–16. Kingston/Princeton: Ian Randle/Markus Wiener.

Bousquet, Ben, and Colin Douglas. 1991. *West Indian Women at War: British Racism in World War II.* London: Lawrence & Wishart.

Césaire, Aimé. 1972. *Discourse on Colonialism.* Translated by Joan Pinkham. New York: Monthly Review.

Cheng, Anne Anlin. 2001. *The Melancholy of Race: Psychoanalysis, Assimilation and Hidden Grief.* New York: Oxford University Press.

Dundas, Barbara, and Serge Durflinger. n.d. "The Canadian Women's Army Corps, 1841–1946." *Dispatches: Backgrounders in Canadian Military History.* Ottawa: Canadian War Museum Online Educational Resources, http://www.warmuseum.ca.

Ebanks, G., P.M. George, and C.E. Nobbe. 1979. "Emigration from Barbados, 1951–1970." *Social and Economic Studies* 28 (2): 431–49.

Fanon, Frantz. 1967. *Black Skin, White Masks.* Translated by Charles Lam Markmann. New York: Grove Press.

Gibb, Heather. n.d. "Farmworkers from Afar: Results from an International Study of Seasonal Farmworkers from Mexico and the Caribbean Working on Ontario Farms." *North South Institute,* http://www.nsi-ins.ca/english/research/progress/13.asp.

Gilroy, Paul. 2005. *Postcolonial Melancholia.* New York: Columbia University Press.

Hasslinger, Karl M. 1996. "The U-Boat War in the Caribbean: Opportunities Lost." Paper submitted to the Department of Operations, Naval War College. Newport, RI, http://www.dtic.mil/docs/citations/ADA297938.

Healy, Michael S. 2000. "Colour, Climate, and Combat: The Caribbean Regiment in the Second World War." *International History Review* 22 (1): 65–85.

Historica Canada. "The Memory Project," http://www.thememoryproject.com.

Hoyos, F.A. 1978. *Barbados: A History from Amerindians to Independence*. London: Macmillan Caribbean.

Kadar, Marlene. 2005. "The Devouring—Traces of Roma in the Holocaust: No Tattoo, Sterilized Body, Gypsy Girl." In *Tracing the Autobiographical*, edited by Marlene Kadar, Linda Warley, Jeanne Perreault, and Susanna Egan, 223–46. Waterloo, ON: Wilfrid Laurier University Press.

Keyserlingk, Robert H. 1984. "The Canadian Government's Attitude Towards Germans and German Canadians in World War Two." *Canadian Ethnic Studies/Études ethniques au Canada* 16 (1): 16–28.

Khanna, Ranjana. 2003. *Dark Continents: Psychoanalysis and Colonialism*. Durham: Duke University Press.

Lambert, David. 2005. *White Creole Culture, Politics and Identity during the Age of Abolition*. Cambridge: Cambridge University Press.

Lamming, George. 1991. *In the Castle of My Skin*. Ann Arbor: University of Michigan Press.

Lowenthal, David. 1957. "The Population of Barbados." *Social and Economic Studies* 6 (4): 445–501.

Mohanram, Radhika. 2007. *Imperial White: Race, Diaspora and the British Empire*. Minneapolis: University of Minnesota Press.

Parr, Joy. 1985. "Hired Men: Ontario Agricultural Wage Labour in Historical Perspective." *Labour* 15: 91–103.

Pierson, Ruth Roach. 1986. *"They're Still Women After All": The Second World War and Canadian Womanhood*. Toronto: McClelland & Stewart.

———. 2007. "Archival Research as Refuge, Penance, and Revenge." *Queen's Quarterly* 114 (4): 491–99.

Roberts, G.W. 1955. "Emigration from the Island of Barbados." *Social and Economic Studies* 4 (3): 245–88.

Torres-Saillant, Silvio. 2006. *An Intellectual History of the Caribbean*. New York: Palgrave Macmillan.

Watson, Karl. 1979. *The Civilised Island of Barbados: A Social History 1750–1816*. Ellerton, Barbados: Caribbean Graphic Production.

———. 2009. "Barbados and the Bicentenary of the Abolition of the Slave Trade." *Slavery & Abolition* 30 (2): 179–95.

Williams, Eric. 1964. *Capitalism and Slavery*. London: Andre Deutsch.

RESISTING HOLOCAUST MEMORY
Recuperating a Compromised Life

Marlene Kadar

This chapter is a meditation in progress on a primarily interdisciplinary archival biographical research project that takes as its starting point the unsavoury life of Hermine Braunsteiner, a former concentration camp guard, whose story is constructed from auto/biographical fragments, news media sources, and, more recently, historical and legal documents. It has three parts: the first is a short theoretical defence of the subject; the second is a short version of the journey of following Hermine; and the third is a theoretical introduction to some of the conundrums and ambiguities such a project invites or requires, demonstrating the ways that various actors, readers, institutions, and cultures may be said to resist remembering even as remembering is, by its very nature, carried from my limited point of view as someone who is caught between the two poles of resisting and following. However, this state has helped me tolerate the incommensurable aspects of traumatic subjects (Lyotard, trans. Bennington and Massumi, 1984) and the unfinished work of remembering Hermine, the betrayed, undecidable subject of my study.

A DEFENCE

The subtitle of this presentation is "Recuperating a Compromised Life," in part as an answer to the response we see to certain kinds of feminist recuperation in this era, and in part to trouble the contradictions that wisely hamper our so-called "working through" the historical memory of one of Hitler's guards whose guilt has been established by a court of law, yet whose life still is a human one. Allan Meek proposes that historical trauma is found not in memory traces but in what is forgotten in the texts of academic critique, psychoanalysis, critical theory, and other activities. Nor can historical traumas be verified by empirical research; the requirement is to read the text of Hermine's life against the grain in order to demonstrate contradictions and difficulties in certainty as an intellectual option. Yet, as with all aporias, the way must be tried. Meek references Derrida: "The rapidity with which 9/11 was spoken of as a 'traumatic event' effectively negated a deeper reflection on and more gradual working-through of its political significance" (Meek 2010, 4–5). But to every time there is a season, and it may be that the time is *still* not right to consider the deeper questions Meek anticipates, including the question of the ordinary killer about whom we have been cautioned since Hannah Arendt's satiric essay "We Refugees" in 1943. I have tried to represent the in-between, unfixed, constantly changing middle ground on which I have encountered Hermine because it seems the only way to adapt to new grey-zone knowledge when, as Omer Bartov has stressed, "the historiographies of the victims and perpetrators rarely overlap" (2000, 118). But, as Joanne Sayner responds, their histories certainly do (2007, 312).

I do not in any way want to suggest that the events of the Holocaust deserve forgiveness. What I want to explore is the possibility that the tender, poignant ambiguities of life writing (life writing writ large) "complicate and dissemble the victim/perpetrator dichotomy in ways that encourage us to think through alternatives" to what Jill Scott (2010) calls "blame and hatred," even while it is clear where culpability lies.

In his autobiography, when discussing the analyst's role in interpretation, Sigmund Freud writes that "the *fundamental rule of psychoanalysis* [is] bringing into consciousness of the repressed material which [*sic*] was held back by resistances. Uncovering the resistance … is the first step towards overcoming it. Thus the work of analysis involves an *art of interpretation*, the successful handling of which may require tact and practice but which is not hard to acquire" (Freud, trans. Strachey, 1952, 45). Using this as a metaphor for our subject, I suggest there is repressed material in the stories we tell ourselves about evildoers and "the enemy among us," about their difference from us, about our national purity and/or safe borders, and about humanity. Hermine Braunsteiner's life is instructive because it may help uncover personal, historical, national, archival, and political resistances to her story in our reception of it and what it emblematizes. To uncover these things, we need to hone our skills at thick interpretation, and this will require tact and practice—which may lead to an outcome of "forgetting without amnesia and forgiving without erasing memory" (Whitehead 2009, 156).[1]

FOLLOWING HERMINE: THE JOURNEY

Hermine Braunsteiner was a concentration camp guard who, having worked double shifts at the Ravensbrück (near Furstenberg, Germany) and Majdanek (Lublin, Poland) concentration camps during the Holocaust, fled Austria after the war. She was arrested in New York City in 1973 and extradited the same year to Germany, where she was convicted of war crimes for a second time.[2] After a trial that lasted nearly six years, she and seven other Majdanek guards were found guilty of "collaborative murder in 1,181 cases and being an accessory to murder in 705 cases" (Wiesenthal, n.d.). In 1981, Hermine received two consecutive life sentences. In 1996, for reasons of poor health (she was diabetic), Hermine was released from a prison in Mühlheim by an act of reprieve signed by Prime Minister Johannes Rau. She went on to live a quiet life in an attractive seniors' townhouse residence in Bochum-Linden, Germany, supported by *Stille Hilfe* (Silent Help), a pro-Nazi front group in Munich. That group, which enjoyed official "non-profit club" (*Vereine*) status, had been founded by Heinrich Himmler's daughter, Gudrun Himmler Burwitz, to provide financial assistance for aged Nazis in their retirement years.[3] Between her birth in Vienna on 16 July 1919 as Hermine Braunsteiner and her death in Bochum-Linden in 1999 as Mrs. Hermine Ryan, many details of her life went unnoticed, though they pique our attention now.[4] Even when she was "found out" and extradited, the attention soon died down. There was no fuss made when she died, and her husband seemed to disappear from view as soon as she had passed away. We know his last address in Bochum-Linden, Germany, but that is all.

We do not know very much about Hermine Braunsteiner's early life in Vienna, but some facts were disclosed during various testimonies and trials. Hermine was raised Roman Catholic in the Nineteenth District of Vienna. Her father, Friedrich Braunsteiner, was a butcher; her mother, Maria Ann Knodn Braunsteiner, was a homemaker who took in laundry.[5] There is some confusion about Hermine's real name. Her birth name was Braunsteiner, not Braunstein[6] (the name under which she disembarked at Pier 21 in Halifax), and not Braunsdorfer, as it appeared in 1955–56 Austrian police reports.[7] Braunsdorfer circulated for a few years, but it seems to have been a "simple" typographical error. Such are the accidents and coincidences of archival research on a difficult and elusive subject: "muffings" (Erving Goffman's term for mislabellings) and errors regularly interrupt the journey.

Like many women concentration camp guards, Hermine wanted to be a nurse (a "Blue Sister").[8] She would later recount that because it was impossible to secure such a position in the depressed Austrian economy of her youth, she had made a career choice that enabled a decent (if low) living wage for young women who wanted to work outside the home during the Reich's formative years.[9] According to Jack Morrison (2000), in 1944, a twenty-five-year-old unmarried overseer could earn 185 reichsmarks per month, whereas an unskilled textile worker earned approximately 76. Hermine was recruited to camp work from the floor of the Henkel factory in Berlin, where we can assume she earned a minimum wage.

Hermine was one of at least 3,950 wardresses/matrons who "managed the hotel"[10]—that is, the Ravensbrück camp—between 1939 and 1945 (Schwarz 1994, 32; Brown 2002, 9). Ravensbrück's first prisoners arrived on 18 May 1939: 860 German and 7 Austrian women. On 29 May, 400 Roma women arrived from Austria. On 28 September, the first Polish women arrived. By late 1939, the camp population was 2,290; by the end of 1942, it was 10,800. By 1944, 70,000 had been added to the numbers and placed in one of Ravensbrück's thirty satellite camps. As of 1944, the main camp held 26,700 women prisoners, with a few thousand girls in Uckermark, the detention camp for youth/minors at the back corner of the site. In total, 132,000 women and children were incarcerated at Ravensbrück: 26,000 were Jewish, the major nationality was Polish, and roughly 92,000 died by starvation, execution, or overwork. Guards exterminated as many as possible in the final months of the war, including 130 babies and pregnant women.

New arrivals at Ravensbrück were instructed to address their supervisors as *Frau Oberaufseherin*, and never by a birth or married name, on pain of death. As a result, an accidental catalogue of nicknames and sobriquets developed. Years later, these names were revealed in their fullness and "translated" when former prisoners recognized their jailers on the street or during the war crimes trials, the most important of which was the 1975–81 Majdanek trial in Düsseldorf, where Hermine (Braunsteiner) Ryan was one of sixteen defendants. One of only eight found guilty, she was the only one to get a life sentence. She was identified in the courtroom as "Die Stutte von Ravensbrück" (the "Old" Mare from Ravensbrück)—in Polish, "Kobyla" (Mare). A Polish-speaking friend cautions, however, that "Kobyla" has another meaning that is less polite than "female horse."[11] Hermine's comrade Hildegard Lächert ("Bloody Brigitte," or "Krwawa Brygida" in Polish) got twelve years; Irma Grese ("the Beautiful Beast" or "the Beast of Belsen") was convicted of crimes against humanity and executed on Friday, 13 December 1945, when she was twenty-two years old (at Hameln).

The earliest English-language sources about Hermine are neither readily available nor necessarily scholarly. Among them are two journalistic articles: one in the *Washington Post* (Ross 1972), and a fuller piece by Dorothy Rabinowitz in *Commentary* (October 1976). These are complemented by a series of short news items, including various updates in the *Toronto Star* (1971–74), largely because Braunsteiner had the singular distinction of being the first person to be denaturalized in the United States for lying on her visa application (made in Halifax) and then extradited to Germany on the premise that she had likely committed horrible crimes in a concentration camp. One Majdanek witness, Hanna Mierzewska, testified that Hermine and Hildegard Lächert were the worst, the "most brutal," of the guards, and would use anything to beat them, including a whip and a riding crop (Majdanek Archives 1964). In a Majdanek protocol, "Protokół przesłuchania świadka," taken in 1964 from survivor Danuta Brzosko-Mędryk,

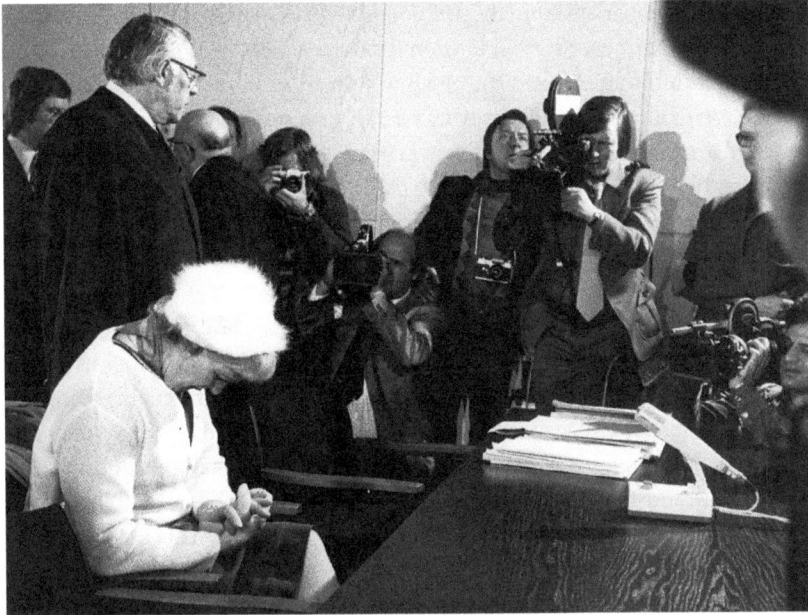

Figure 5.1 Atrocity trial, 26 November 1975: "Hermine Ryan-Braunsteiner, one of the main defendants in the trial of former guards of a concentration camp in Poland, accused of the murder of one quarter of a million Jewish prisoners." Photograph: Keystone/Stringer. Hulton Archive/Getty Images. Used with permission.

a Warsaw dentist, special attention is once again given to Hildegard Lächert and Hermine Braunsteiner. Brzosko-Mędryk writes, "From the same time period [1943] and from field five I also remember Auseherin [sic] Braunsteiner. I personally saw her come to the women's field with a dog, a huge German Shepherd, and she would bait him against the working prisoners whom he would bite, causing pain" (Majdanek Archives 1964).

For the purposes of denaturalization, the US State Department had only to prove that Braunsteiner had lied on her application for a visa and citizenship; for the purposes of extradition, it had only to establish "probable cause" to believe that she had committed the crimes of which she had been accused. They did not have to prove, many years after the fact, that she had stomped old women to death (wearing iron boots) or hanged a fourteen-year-old girl as a lesson to other prisoners not to lie or steal food. The short version of the story goes like this: Braunsteiner was prosecuted for lying on her visa application, and was then extradited to Germany, the US court having found sufficient evidence to sustain the German charges and that the charges were extraditable offences.[12]

Braunsteiner had applied for an immigration visa to the United States when she was thirty-nine years old. She did so at the American consulate in Halifax, where she disembarked from the *Maasdam*, a vessel operated by Holland America, a signatory transportation line, on 23 October 1958. There had been occasional mention that she had travelled by ship from Europe to Halifax, but no details were offered. Some survivors wrongly surmised that Braunsteiner had married an American soldier in Austria soon after her first release from prison, between 1948 and 1950. But Hermine had not married in Europe at all. It took me five years to figure out what really happened, partly because Canada could not help: there was no record of Hermine Braunsteiner in the immigration files kept in the National Archives of Canada (now Library and Archives Canada) (although there are reliable immigration summaries of other immigrants in those archives), and I was unable to procure any of the long versions of personal documents—visa, passport, marriage documents, ship manifests—from the Vital Statistics Office in Halifax. As unbelievable as it may seem today, most of Canada's immigration files from the postwar period had been destroyed.[13] Hermine Braunsteiner had not been dead for fifty years, so I needed permission from her husband to procure more revealing documents. This turned out not to be possible: although I searched graveyards in Bochum-Linden and phone directories and obituaries in New York, Russell Ryan had disappeared from any public record. I had no interest in Hermine's life until it became impossible to ask questions about her life. I wondered then: Who is hiding what, and why? The Vital Statistics Office in Nova Scotia allowed me to purchase the short version of her marriage certificate for C$26.50 in 2004. Although it looks like a benign piece of paper, it is an informative auto/biographical fragment, a trace that put me on the right track with Braunsteiner, her various names, and her great fortune (in the short term) to have gained safe haven in North America. The important markers are these:

1) Bride's Name: Hermine Braunstein
2) Groom's Name: Russell Ryan
3) Date of Marriage: 29 October 1958, six days after landing (23 October).
4) Place of Marriage: Halifax

I surmised that Ryan and his fiancée had arranged to meet in Halifax and marry there, it being easier at that time for Russell Ryan, an American citizen, to cross the border into Canada than for Braunsteiner, a newly landed Austrian "fugitive from justice," to cross the border into the United States. Hermine Braunsteiner had been living with Ryan in Queens since arriving in New York City on the *Stavangerfjord* on 21 April 1959 as a privileged "non-quota immigrant." The address is printed clearly on her visa application: 54–44, 82nd St., Elmhurst 73, Queens, NY.

We can assume that Ryan returned to Elmhurst to prepare the bridal home for his wife and settle down to a "normal" life. Mrs. Hermine Ryan must have thought that Miss Hermine Braunsteiner was now a mirage, a forgotten trace of a former life and not life itself. How wrong she was. US bureaucratic practices ensured that Immigration and Naturalization Service (INS) case files related to Braunsteiner's extradition hearing and eventual deportation to Germany to stand trial (from 26 November 1975 to 30 June 1981) were held in storage in Kansas. I saw the files in New York City's National Archives and Records Administration (NARA) office in 2005. Copies of identity papers that had been filed in Halifax upon her arrival in 1958 were in the file box—so, in the end, this life story remains, as do the two identities.

For me, Hermine Braunsteiner Ryan's life has significant autobiographical and historical value for a number of reasons:

1) The anti-heroic nature of her life helps us fill in some important blanks as to the full scope of the tragedy that was the Holocaust unleashed by Hitler's Nazi regime.

2) The relative ease with which a low-level camp guard such as Hermine Braunsteiner was able to disguise the facts of her involvement in the Nazi genocide, even in the aftermath of its defeat, helps fill in some additional blanks with respect to the indifference that Canada and the United States showed to the migration patterns of such persons. Their "unauthorized entry" into Canada in this crucial period (1946–59) has been documented by Howard Margolian, Alti Rodal, Reg Whitaker, and others.[14]

3) The creative and intellectual power of even the smallest trace of knowledge cannot be overlooked. Sometimes, however, that knowledge is only available through tedious archival research, supported by a research plan that is able to establish the story while always remaining open to its shifting shape, its ambiguities, and both productive and unproductive discoveries as time passes (Kadar 2005).

4) Because one thing really does lead to another, the value of time passing must be highly respected, and conclusions must be provisional for much longer than a scholar-biographer might prefer or easily tolerate. It is better never to assume that a trace is too faint to be plumbed.

5) Earlier radical-feminist claims about the ethical and moral superiority of women remain questionable in this context. At one time, theorists such as Andrea Dworkin and Catharine MacKinnon claimed a special place for women as nurturers, as better than men when it comes to treating our brothers and sisters well. I still meet

students and colleagues who find it hard to believe that women were employed as guards in Hitler's camps, or that they could be "just as brutal as" or "worse than" their male counterparts. Yet they were, according to survivors Hanna Narkiewicz-Joklo and Helen Farkas. *New York Times* writer and memoirist Joseph Lelyveld (2005) captured Russell Ryan's sentiments: "My wife, sir, wouldn't hurt a fly. There is no more decent person on this earth."

Gender, brutality, archival confusion, sobriquets, multiple languages and halting translations, errors of transcription, intentional misinformation, the passing of time, the frailty of human memory—all of these lead to a life-writing subject, but a provisional one that not everyone will want to read.

INTRODUCTION: RESISTING REMEMBERING

When Hermine Braunstein/er ordered a Ravensbrück guard to push away the stool from under a nameless fourteen-year-old girl, that girl was heard to say in Polish to the assembled inmate witnesses, "Remember me."[15] After that, so it was reported, there was a "great silence."[16] That great silence has continued off and on until today, yet it was at that moment that Hermine sealed the girl's fate. As Jill Scott writes in *A Poetics of Forgiveness*, the deafening silence is "symptomatic of the monumental interruption of the Holocaust itself, symbolizing the end of civilization and history as it had been conceived prior to 1933" (2010, 99). The woman who was ordered to translate instructions to the girl as she approached the gallows lived to tell the tale in testimony against the woman she now called "Mrs. Ryan." Mrs. Ryan, writes journalist Howard Blum, "wanted the girl to step up into the noose" (1977, 16–17). The nameless girl's invocation to remember her can also mean, "Remember this event, who was here, who did what."[17] Seventy years later, we can also say that there has been resistance to remembering the horror on a number of levels—we resist weighing the circumstances, assessing the desires at play, imagining the scene—yet several versions of this particular story about Braunsteiner and the girl do circulate in protocols and testimonies. Becoming Mrs. Ryan did not erase Hermine Braunsteiner; it just covered her up, veiling her identity for a time (with Canada's help).

This chapter is a response to the nameless girl's request, but here, she and her fellow prisoners of Ravensbrück are not my focus—an approach that has taken some working through on my part. At the girl's request, I have tried to remember her in the name of other girls and women who, named and nameless, suffered at the hands of an army of *Aufseherinnen*/overseers/guards/matrons who managed/controlled the only large concentration (extermination) camp devoted primarily to women and youth in Hitler's prison system. I followed the trail of Hermine

Braunstein/er that led from that spot on the *Appell* (roll call) grounds in 1943[18] to a farm road in Middle Musquodoboit, Nova Scotia, in 1956, and then on to Maspeth, Queens, New York, from 1958 to 1963, where the trail went cold for a time. Following Hermine has been an international, cross-border project filled with detours that I could not have anticipated ten years ago—identity switches, inauthentic auto/biographical identity markers, Nazi misinformation, and the politics of immigration and data collection, and of remembering guilt and death.

Following Hermine gave me the opportunity to face personal resistance and fear, but also institutional and state-protected resistance, both accidental and intentional. The ironies of place and time haunt us: it is a belaboured but still fraught story of the wretched contradiction we witness between youngish women like "Kobyla" knowingly killing other young girls and women in Germany, Austria, and Poland, and women in Canada enjoying freedoms resulting from the employment "opportunities" of the war effort. Women like Kobyla appear to be protected by their employer, the *Politische Abteilung* (Political Department or, casually, "Camp Gestapo") of the Third Reich/SS[19]—the same contingent that oversaw men commandants in Ravensbrück and other nearby camps, such as Sachsenhausen, a few kilometres to the south at Oranienburg. Scholars often refer to *Aufseherinnen* as members of the SS, but this is an error. Women guards could belong to SS women's auxiliary units, but the SS itself was comprised exclusively of men. We encounter a number of contradictions as soon as we speak these words: women were women and men were men, unless of course women had to stand in for men in the system. As we know from Sybil Milton, Claudia Koonz, and others,[20] the anti-feminist principle of "the 3 Ks"—*Kinder, Küche,* and *Kirche* (children, kitchen, church)—applied to Aryan women unless, of course, a woman worked the *Lager* beat.[21] Although nobody would say that Rosie the Riveter found gender/racial equality in a Canadian munitions factory, let us not forget that Hermine was also never the equal of her male counterparts in the camp hierarchy, and what the impact of that difference might signal.

Apart from my own impatience with this work of remembering, I bristle with confusion when I remember the resistance of national institutions that may find the facts too bold, too incriminating, or simply too painful to pull into a current memory. Here I speak of two major controversies relating to Hermine's story, one having to do with access to immigration screening documents in Canada, the other having to do with security in the US Immigration Service:

1) As I mentioned earlier, none of Hermine's Canadian immigration documents exist (in Canada) because none from the period of German and Austrian immigration most pertinent to our work (1945 to 1960s) have been saved in the national archives. Alti Rodal has

written about the tragedy of the 1982–83 destruction of records in Annex 4 of the government-commissioned *Nazi War Criminals in Canada: The Historical and Policy Settings from the 1940s to the Present* (1986). This loss became public when the Royal Canadian Mounted Police (RCMP) could not locate identity documents in the extradition case of Helmut Rauca (1982–83). The RCMP wrote, "The loss of these records, whose destruction should not have taken place, has seriously impaired the ability of Canadian authorities, notably the RCMP, to investigate and take effective action against war criminals in Canada" (Rodal 1986, 4).[22] We learn through the commission that "Application for Admission to Canada" forms (IMM. O.S. 8) were routinely destroyed, but that original case files were not destroyed until the 1980s.

2) When it became clear to Vincent Schiano (a trial attorney) and Anthony DeVito (an INS investigator) that someone was betraying their cause—stealing DeVito's summaries of interviews with survivor witnesses of Majdanek (incriminating Hermine)—the prosecuting attorneys in the United States decided they had to carry all their files on their person. Seven of the twelve summaries had been removed from "the bottom drawer of one of the chief trial attorney's filing cabinet" the next morning (Blum 1977, 15).

The Austrian amnesty of 1957 resulted in the quashing of a large number of proceedings, and, as a consequence, in the downplaying of Nazi crimes—a tendency that had been clear already for five to six years.[23] The same amnesty marked a turning point in Hermine's life. "Reborn" by her release from Austrian prison and her national pardon, Hermine planned her exodus from Europe quietly and cleanly, leaving no certain historical evidence about how that exodus transpired, or where or when. We might argue, as Paul Ricoeur does, that both forgiveness and justice are, as a result, foreclosed upon, prevented—that amnesty, in other words, *does* mean amnesia or, as Ricoeur says, "commanded forgetting" (2004, 452–56). The idea here is that amnesty creates a new kind of double-bind memory—that is, Hermine could make assumptions about her past, and the mourning public could then either accept her amnesty or disregard it, since there was no person to touch or address, no body to hold accountable. Hermine could easily evade the security radar, perhaps having been advised that Canada's was a porous border. Irving Abella (2000) has suggested that Canada was "a Nazi Haven." We also know that in the 1950s, 25,300 Austrian immigrants were allowed entry (Szabo 1996, 110–11), and that their numbers increased after 1955, after the Allies left Austria and the country was declared neutral. Among the newcomers were around four thousand men—war criminals (Abella 2000).

Was Canada a haven, as Irving Abella asks in his review of Howard Margolian's *Unauthorized Entry*? I cannot attest, but we do know that war criminals entered, that at least one of them was a woman, and that it was not difficult for her to cross the ocean on a signatory shipping line, disembark in Halifax, be married by Canadian authorities, change her name, and get farm work on the east coast (as did Helmut Rauca).

As Ricoeur declares, "certain crimes should not be subject to statutes of limitation because they belong to the domain of justice … these crimes themselves have long-lasting effects," and as a result, we remain "in a domain of complete confusion between the private world of forgiveness and the public world of justice" (Ricoeur and Anhohi 2005, 10). In other words, Hermine has put me in a difficult situation, in the middle of Deborah Britzman's "difficult knowledge" (1998, 119), which can no longer end. The social ego wants to console itself by "freezing" the events of history as if they did not have any present. We see this defence at its worst in Holocaust denial, and at its best in the separation of the present from the anguish about war criminals who entered Canada illegally (Ricoeur 2004, 473). The long reach of the Holocaust is current and deep, and mixed in with other issues—such as immigration, border security, refugee status, gender, Canada–US relations, anti-Semitism (both overt and subtle forms), and, much more recently, anti-Gypsyism (again raising the matter of a good refugee)—that complicate the key questions.

Standing in for auto/biography by or about Hermine is the idea of a life-writing "limit-case"—to use Leigh Gilmore's juridical term—a limit-case "from the other side" of the courtroom but where representations of honourable actions and difficult forgiveness still operate (Ricoeur 2004, 457–58) even though no other just recourse is possible. A limit-case represents the victim's testimony when no court of law can "hear" a case because it is too old, or too frightening to repeat, or is in a form that does not comply with the rules of autobiographical writing. "In their exposure of the link between illegitimacy and fiction in self-representational projects, limit-cases expose the conditions in which alternative forms of knowledge about justice are compelled to appear, and how subjects who produce this knowledge are marked" (Gilmore 2001, 135). As all great life-writing theorists have declared, "great auto/biographers have generally been heroes, personalities whose memoirs are justified by exemplary lives," even if the subjects' stories are "not without taint" (Rosen 2001, 553), but Hermine does not fit the mould, and this may be an incidence of a limit-case subject, although I am certain that Gilmore did not intend unsavoury characters to perform this role. If I am writing the limit-case about Hermine, we can hope that an alternative form of justice is the end result—a form in which Hermine's absent victims are acknowledged and questions of citizenship and belonging are hailed as complex representations that lend "substance to the national fantasy of belonging" (Gilmore 2001, 135) and its potential for forcing its cruel opposite—not belonging. In any case, Gilmore's theory allows the possibility that an auto/biographical subject leaks through "against-the-grain engagements" at the limit of autobiography—and limit is as pressing as a visa or a marriage certificate, generic types that reveal "what more conventional autobiographies [necessarily] obscure" (137). Hermine's story is "characterized by a profound indecency" (Rosen 2001, 553) about a woman subject who is guilty of crimes against women, children, babies, and others. Why would Hermine write anything about herself, apart from filling in the applications for the visas and marriage certificates that became my limit-cases, the punch cards and shift forms that became evidence of work details, and the addresses in Nova Scotia farm country and in the working-class districts of Queens that became my settings? The confessing murderer/war criminal must confront "greater resistance than any other category of writers" in order for "his assertions [to be] taken seriously" (Carl Lovitt, quoted in Rosen 2001, 553–54).[24] At the negative limit of biographical writing, following Hermine cancels out this resistance and replaces it with another: the resistance of the incredulous researcher who longs to know how it could happen. As Deborah Britzman gently suggests, the learning about and learning from that Freud distinguishes are all the more fragile in difficult knowledge because the learner resists insight, since what "tends to be projected is the learner's undisturbed present and not the way the learner's life has become her present" (1998, 118).[25]

Following Hermine is about following someone who tried very hard to prevent us from following. When prisoners blessed her with nicknames, they did so as a way of communicating with a future jurisdictional environment. Nicknames allowed prisoners to deliver warnings about their captors—that she was on the beat, or in a mood, or spying on the political prisoners, such as Gemma La Guardia Gluck, Geneviève de Gaulle, Nanda Herbermann, or Johanna Krause—without being "caught." They function as an epistle to us to remember. Sobriquets betray Kobyla; her trials really began when she ordered that stool to be pulled out from under the nameless fourteen-year-old girl who either stole food or denied she was Jewish.

Twenty years after the liberation of Ravensbrück camp, three Jewish survivors, upon recognizing Simon Wiesenthal in a Tel Aviv café, asked him, *What ever happened to Kobyla?* At this moment, remembered sobriquets—*Kobyla*, or *Die Stutte von Ravensbrück*—ensured Hermine's place in our collective memory. Hermine kicked her victims to death, and used her whip and boots to harm other women. As Sara Horowitz tells us, this is not the way it is supposed to happen. Men abuse women, men are naturally violent, and men—not women—are Nazis. In a 2005 essay, Horowitz tells us that women are still excluded from the realm of evildoing. She writes, "there is a particular anger reserved for the female collaborator, a special horror at something seen as particularly monstrous, above and beyond the act of collaboration itself" (172).

Feminist scholars in Holocaust studies have made a huge contribution to helping us understand how gender constructs our subject when it is not always easy for history to assess the genocide in this way.[26] At the same time, we acknowledge that Hermine is subject to SS misogyny and postwar sexist practices. Can we talk about how she was a victim of the Third Reich's employment practices?

Liz Stanley writes that "if feminist auto/biography departs from [the conventional, coherent norm of a celebrated hero] … then it is no longer 'auto/biography' but something different in kind: an entirely different genre" (1992, 253). Most biographies mirror the "spotlight approach" (216), but Stanley says that feminists have taken risks with the form and tried to do something else (162–65). Jana Evans Braziel suggests an "alter-biographical" form (2009)[27] that resists "the fixed relations of self, life, and writing in traditional conceptions of autobiography as a literary genre" (2001). I want to resist the biographical approach to Hermine's life, even as I follow her, because it is her context that interests us—the shadows and what "memory" or "secret"[28] they contain. However, Freud advised tact, and even a resisting construction of Hermine must be tactful because it is more importantly a response to the Holocaust, and thus a matter of ethics. Jennifer Geddes (2009) explains that there are two temptations that face ethical responses to the Holocaust:

1) The temptation to mythologize banal evil, à la Arendt, because it is relational and does not exist merely in the mind of an individual evildoer (120). (We must remember that Hermine was a cog in the wheel, so it is not helpful to demonize her.)
2) The temptation to domesticate suffering, to find good in it, or, as Charlotte Delbo says, to make good of the "useless knowledge" it provides. (We must remember not to draw too much on sympathy for the suffering, as it is too close to pity—and more about the pitier—and makes us talk about useless knowledge.)

Following Hermine has made it possible for me to see these temptations more clearly. In addition, while pursuing the traces of history in this woman's life, I have tried to unlearn inherited "outsider" knowledge I may have harboured to protect myself from knowing what Giorgio Agamben has called "the bare life" of *l'univers concentrationnaire*,[29] the other-world of the camps that Hermine maintained and repaired, training others to do the same. As Britzman writes, the "interminable work of social justice and ethical understanding," whether in literature studies or feminist activism, is only accomplished when the learner "comes to identify and disidentify with difficult knowledge" (1998, 119) by activating conundrums and contradictions, and not always/only/just feeling the pressure to resolve them, especially when they cannot, in truth, be resolved. We want to avoid any focus on hope or courage as the "adequate lesson to be made from difficult knowledge," both of which are too often "seen as a bridge to continuity and expectation" (119) (my deepest wishes). Expectation would have us demonize Hermine, and hope would have us punish her interminably, or delete her. Neither leads us back into the work of social justice, ethical understanding, or learning to look carefully at a dark side that is not just "over there"—as many before me have demonstrated, including the late Sharon Rosenberg and Gina Feldberg, Yvonne Singer, Belarie Zatzman, and Brian Osborne[30]—but is also "over here."

NOTES

I want to thank the Centre for Jewish Studies, especially Sara Horowitz and Marty Lockshin, and the Social Sciences and Humanities Research Council (SSHRC) for their kind support of this project. I also want to thank my dear colleagues in Miners Sabbatical Research Group, Humanities and Women's Studies, for listening and responding to my queries and concerns about Hermine over the years. Thanks also goes to my life-writing colleagues in the MCRI Autobiography project and to wise readings by Jeanne Perreault, Susan Ehrlich, Gary Penner, Linda Warley, and Belarie Zatzman. Finally, I am grateful to Eleanor Ty and Russell Kilbourn for inviting me to be a featured speaker at "Memory, Mediation, Remediation: An International Conference on Memory in Literature and Film" on 29 April 2011 at Wilfrid Laurier University in Waterloo.

1   The complete quotation is, "Both thinkers struggle with the uncomfortable but necessary distinction between forgetting without amnesia, and forgiving without erasing memory." By "both thinkers," Whitehead means Jacques Derrida and Paul Ricoeur. See Derrida, "On Forgiveness."
2   About Hermine's first trial, Allan A. Ryan Jr. writes, "[Simon] Wiesenthal found that Hermine Braunsteiner had been convicted in 1949 by a low-level court in Austria for her role, not at Maidanek [Majdanek], but as an overseer at Ravensbrück.... She had been sentenced to three years' imprisonment. Because she had been in confinement awaiting trial, she was released shortly before her conviction" (1984, 46–47). More reliable are the Headnotes of Case No. 68-C-848, "United States of America, Plaintiff, v. Hermine RYAN, a/k/a Hermine Braunsteiner, a/k/a Mrs. Russell Ryan, Defendant, 360 F. Supp. 265; 1973 U.S. Dis. LEXIS 13916, 24 April 1973.
3   See Lebert and Lebert, 2001.
4   The address is Hattingerstrasse 44879. I thank my assistant, Violetta Damm, for this information.
5   Boxes 8–14, Case Files Released under the Nazi War Crimes and Japanese Imperial Government Disclosure Acts, 1947–1994, RG 85, MLR Entry P-3, ARC 1766791.
6   Though unlikely, it is possible that another guard with the name "Braunstein" worked at the camps and was prosecuted. There is mention of a "Braunstein" in the Trial of the Major War Criminals before the Military Tribunal (1947), downloadable at HeinOnline: http://heinonline.org. The reference to Braunstein and other supervisors is on page 452.
7   *Dokument 22.966 des Dokumentationsarchiv des österreichisches Widerstandes*, Vienna, Austria.

8   Under cross-examination, it was not uncommon for an indicted woman guard to make this claim. The Blue Sisters Institute was devoted to the care of children and to a life of obedience to God and Christian values. More about the Religious Family of the Incarnate Word can be found at http://www.iveamerica.org.

9   Wages for women guards trumped average wages for women working in factories, such as at Henkel, where Hermine was working when she was "recruited" for duty at the "new camp for women," Ravensbrück. This camp was in Furstenberg, a quaint village about eighty-seven kilometres north of Berlin, half an hour farther than the Sachsenhausen camp at Oranienburg.

10 It is striking that on her US visa application, under "occupation," Braunsteiner wrote "hotel manager."

11 My appreciation goes to Dorota Nycz, of Toronto, for conversations about the translations.

12 Canada has not had much success prosecuting war criminals. After its failure to obtain a conviction in the Imre Finta case, the federal government gave up on prosecuting World War II criminals on the grounds that it was impossible to prove crimes to the criminal standard of "beyond reasonable doubt" fifty years after the fact.

13 See a cogent explanation of the "monumental blunder" in Cook (2002).

14 Although Canadian historians did not seem to know about Hermine Braunsteiner Ryan's escape into Canada, they had analyzed the period and documented other war criminals' escapes. See Margolian (2000); Rodal (1986); and Whitaker (1987).

15 This story, and the quoted lines, are taken from Blum's text in which he is telling the story of the prosecuting attorney, Anthony DeVito, and what he heard in the Brooklyn courtroom that day in "Mrs. Ryan's" trial. Ryan had apparently "ordered an SS man, named Ender" to bring the stool (1977, 16–17).

16 Stories like this one are also to be found in a more recently published memoir by Lanck-orońska (2005).

17 Mark Twain's oft-quoted quip points to the frailty of human memory: "When I was younger I could remember anything, whether it happened or not; but my faculties are decaying, now, & soon I shall be so I cannot remember any but the latter. It is sad to go to pieces like this, but we all have to do it" (Twain, edited by Neider, 1959, 210).

18 Quoted in protocol taken in 1964 in Warsaw by Hanna Mierzejewska (Majdanek Archives APMM, VII 135/173.)

19 Commandant, Adjutant (the commandant was also the supervisor of the guards). *Schutzhaftlagerfuhrer* ("head of protective detention camp"; in many camps, also the adjutant); *Verwaltungsfuhrer* ("head of administration").

20 See Milton (1984, 297–307); Ringelheim (1991, 243–64); Heinemann (1986); and Koonz (1981).

21 See Hutton (2005).

22 There is more about this on pp. 230–41, missing from my manuscript copy.

23 See also Garscha and Kuretsidis-Haider (1997).

24 See also Abella (2000).

25 See also Simon, Rosenberg, and Eppert (2000).

26 A few important references: Schaffer and Smith (2004); Stanley (1990); Reid (2008).

27 Braziel (2009, 13) defines the term "alter-biography" within a genre discussion by remark-ing that alter-biography is a "deconstructive or degenerative force within life-writing—one that erodes and contests the boundaries of genre as they are predicated on notions of genealogy, genius and race."

28 These are two variations of translations of titles of Philippe Grimbert's 2004 novel based on the French title, *Un Secret*.

29 According to Norris (2005),

> The *Lager* is a threshold in which human beings are reduced to bare life; and the torture this life suffers is nothing else but its exclusion from the *polis* as a

distinctively human life. The bare life that is produced by this abandonment by the state is not biological life; "not simple natural life, but life exposed to death (bare life or sacred life) is the originary political element." This is the *Muselmann* as described by Primo Levi in *If This Is a Man*. One speaks of the Shoah as industrialized mass death, and of the camps as "factories of death." But the product of these factories is not death but, as Arendt puts it, a mode of life "outside of life and death." If for Arendt, however, the production of *Muselmänner* is anti-political, in that the camps are spaces in which plurality is foreclosed, for Agamben it is the emergence of the essence of the political.

See also Agamben (translated by Rocke, 1995).
30 Osborne (2002), with thanks to my late colleague, Barbara Godard.

WORKS CITED

Abella, Irving. 20 May 2000. "Was Canada a Nazi Haven?" *Globe and Mail*. D15.

Agamben, Giorgio. 1995. "We Refugees." Translated by Michael Rocke. *Symposium* 49 (2). European Graduate School.

Bartov, Omer. 2000. *Mirrors of Destruction: War, Genocide and Modern Identity*. New York: Oxford University Press.

Blum, Howard. 1977. *Wanted! The Search for Nazis in America*. New York: Quadrangle/New York Times Book Co.

Britzman, Deborah. 1998. *Lost Subjects, Contested Objects: Toward a Psychoanalytic Inquiry of Learning*. Albany: SUNY Press.

Brown, Daniel Patrick. 2002. *The Camp Women: The Female Auxiliaries Who Assisted the SS in Running the Nazi Concentration Camp System* (Schiffer Military History). Michigan: University of Michigan Press.

Cook, Terry. 2002. "A Monumental Blunder: The Destruction of Records on Nazi War Criminals in Canada." In *Archives and the Public Good: Accountability and Records in Modern Society*, edited by Richard J. Cox and David A. Wallace, 37–65. Westport: Quorum.

Derrida, Jacques. 2001. "On Forgiveness." *Cosmopolitanism and Forgiveness*. Translated by Mark Dooley and Michael Hughes. London and New York: Routledge.

Freud, Sigmund. 1952. *An Autobiographical Study*. Translated by James Strachey. New York and London: Norton.

Garscha, Winfried, and Claudia Kuretsidis-Haider. 1997. "War Crime Trials in Austria." *Dokumentationsarchiv des Österreichischen Widerstandes*. Presented at the 21st Annual Conference of the German Studies Association (GSA) in Washington, 25–28 September 1997.

Geddes, Jennifer. 2009. "Banal Evil and Useless Knowledge: Hannah Arendt and Charlotte Delbo on Evil after the Holocaust." In *The Double Binds of Ethics after the Holocaust: Salvaging the Fragments*, edited by Jennifer L. Geddes, John K. Roth, and Jules Simon, 119–32. New York: Palgrave Macmillan.

Gilmore, Leigh. 2001. "Limit-Cases: Trauma, Self-Representation, and the Jurisdiction of Identity." *Biography* 24 (1): 128–39.

Heinemann, Marlene. 1986. *Gender and Destiny: Women Writers and the Holocaust*. Westport: Greenwood.

Horowitz, Sara. 2005. "The Gender of Good and Evil: Women and Holocaust Memory." In *Gray Zones: Ambiguity and Compromise in the Holocaust and Its Aftermath*, edited by Jonathan Petropoulos and John K. Roth, 165–78. New York: Berghahn.

Hutton, Margaret Anne. 2005. *Testimony from the Nazi Camps: French Women's Voices*. London: Routledge.

Kadar, Marlene. 2005. "The Devouring: Traces of Roma in the Holocaust: No Tattoo, Sterilized Body, Gypsy Girl." In *Tracing the Autobiographical*, edited by Marlene Kadar, Linda Warley, Jeanne Perreault, and Susanna Egan, 223–46. Waterloo: Wilfrid Laurier University Press.

Lanckoronska, Karolina. 2005. *Michelangelo in Ravensbrück: One's Woman War Against the Nazis*. Translated by Noel Clark. Cambridge: Da Capo.

Lebert, Stephan, and Norbert Lebert. 2001. *My Father's Keeper: Children of Nazi Leaders—An Intimate History of Damage and Denial*. Translated by Julian Evans. London: Little, Brown.

Lyotard, Jean-François. 1984. *The Postmodern Condition: A Report on Knowledge*. Translated by Geoff Bennington and Brian Massumi. Minneapolis: University of Minnesota Press.

Majdanek Archives. 1964. APMM, VII 135/173.

Margolian, Howard. 2000. *Unauthorized Entry: The Truth about Nazi War Criminals in Canada, 1946–1956*. Toronto: University of Toronto Press.

Meek, Allen. 2010. *Trauma and Media: Theories, Histories, and Images*. New York: Routledge.

Milton, Sybil. 1984. "Women and the Holocaust: The Case of German and German-Jewish Women." In *When Biology Became Destiny: Women in Weimar and Nazi Germany*, edited by Renate Bridenthal, Atina Grossman, and Marion Kaplan, 297–307. New York: Monthly Review.

Morrison, Jack. 2000. *Ravensbrück: Everyday Life in a Women's Concentration Camp 1939–45*. Princeton: Markus Wiener.

Norris, Andrew, ed. 2005. *The Exemplary Exception: Philosophical and Political Decisions in Giorgio Agamben's Homo Sacer*. Durham: Duke University Press.

Osborne, Brian S. 2002. "The Place of Memory and Identity." *Diversities* 1 (1): 9–13.

Rabinowitz, Dorothy. 1976. "Portrait of a Survivor." *Commentary Magazine*.

Reid, Donald. 2008. "America so Far from Ravensbruck." *Histoire-Politique*.

Ricoeur, Paul. 2004. *Memory, History, Forgetting*. Translated by Kathleen Blamey and David Pellauer. Chicago: University of Chicago Press.

Ricoeur, Paul, and Sorin Anhohi. 2005. "Memory, History, Forgiveness: A Dialogue Between Paul Ricoeur and Sorin Anhohi." *Janus Head* 8 (1): 14–25.

Ringelheim, Joan. 1991. "Women and the Holocaust: A Reconsideration of the Matriarch." In *Jewish Women in Historical Perspective*, edited by Judith R. Baskin, 243–64. Detroit: Wayne State University Press.

Rodal, Alti. 1986. *Nazi War Criminals in Canada: The Historical and Policy Setting from the 1940s to the Present*. Prepared for the Commission of Inquiry on War Criminals. Canada: Commission of Inquiry on War Criminals.

Rosen, Alan. 2001. "Autobiography from the Other Side: The Reading of Nazi Memoirs and Confessional Ambiguity." *Biography* 24 (3): 553–69.

Ross, Nancy L. 6 August 1972. "From a Dark Past, a Ghost the U.S. Won't Allow to Rest." *Washington Post*.

Ryan, Allan A., Jr. 1984. *Quiet Neighbors: Prosecuting Nazi War Criminals in America*. London: Harcourt Brace Jovanovich.

Sayner, Joanne. 2007. "Memories of Victimhood: Nazism and the Challenge of the Autobiographical." *Forum for Modern Language Studies* 43 (3): 301–15.

Schaffer, Kay, and Sidonie Smith. 2004. *Human Rights and Narrated Lives: The Ethics of Recognition*. New York: Palgrave Macmillan.

Schwarz, Gudrun. 1994. "SS-Aufseherinnen in nationalsozialistischen Konzentrationslagern 1933–1945." *Dachauer Hefte* 10: 32–49.

Scott, Jill. 2010. *A Poetics of Forgiveness: Cultural Responses to Loss and Wrongdoing*. New York: Palgrave Macmillan.

Simon, Roger, Sharon Rosenberg, and Claudia Eppert. 2000. *Between Hope and Despair: Pedagogy and the Remembrance of Historical Trauma*. Lanham: Rowan and Littlefield.

Stanley, Liz. 1992. *The Auto/Biographical I: The Theory and Practice of Feminist Auto/Biography*. Manchester: Manchester University Press.

Stanley, Liz. 1990. "Moments of Writing: Is There a Feminist Auto/biography?" *Gender and History* 2 (1): 58–67.

Szabo, Franz, ed. 1996. *Austrian Immigration to Canada: Selected Essays*. Ottawa: Carleton University Press.

Twain, Mark. 1959. *The Autobiography of Mark Twain*. Part 1. Edited by Charles Neider. New York: Harper Collins.

Whitaker, Reginald. 1987. *Double Standard: The Secret History of Canadian Immigration*. Toronto: Lester and Orpen Dennys.

Whitehead, Anne. 2009. *Memory*. New York: Routledge.

Wiesenthal, Simon. n.d. "Some Significant Cases: Hermine Braunsteiner." Simon Wiesenthal Archive.

"SNOW WHITE IN AUSCHWITZ"
The Tale of Dina Gottliebova-Babbitt

Natalie Robinson

They belong to me, my soul is in them, and without these paintings I wouldn't be alive, my children and grandchildren wouldn't be alive.
—Dina Gottliebova-Babbitt

When we come to the other world and meet the millions of Jews who died in the camps and they ask us, "What have you done?" I will say, "I did not forget you."
—Simon Wiesenthal

The story of Dina Gottliebova-Babbitt's life is a survivor's tale. Her story begins in 1923, when she is born into a Jewish family in Brno, Czechoslovakia. The young girl displays an early artistic talent nurtured by her family and community. As Dina grows, so does the power of Hitler's Third Reich. In 1942, Dina is studying at the Academy of Fine Arts in Prague when she and her mother are arrested and imprisoned in Theresienstadt, a Nazi transit camp in the Czech city of Terezín. A year later, they are sent to Auschwitz, a Nazi concentration camp complex near the Polish town of Oświęcim.[1] The young woman's gift for painting comes to the attention of her captors when she paints a mural of the characters from the 1937 Disney animated film *Snow White and the Seven Dwarfs* on the wall of a children's prison barrack in the camp. Her talent is useful to the chief doctor of the camp, Dr. Josef Mengele, the infamous "Angel of Death." Dina's ability to paint saves her life and that of her mother.

Among her paintings of prisoners and the pseudo-medical experiments performed by the Nazi doctors are several portraits of Roma prisoners, the subjects all soon exterminated by the Nazi regime. These paintings become documents of lives lived and lost, entwined with the story of the artist who created them. Evacuated from Auschwitz in January 1945, Dina and her mother survive the "death march" to Ravensbrück camp, and they live to see the defeat of the Nazis and the end of World War II in April of that year.[2] The young survivor then meets a dashing American animator, whom she marries. They settle in Hollywood, California with their two daughters, and Dina works as an artist and animator, drawing iconic images for cartoons and advertising. This should have been the end of Dina's tale, the peaceful ever after she so deserved. Instead, the work she produced during her imprisonment, the artifacts of her personal experience, have become contested objects entangled with the officially mandated need to control the archives of the complex history of twentieth-century Europe. This essay examines the story of one woman's work during World War II and her fight to reclaim her past.

In 1973, Dina learned from curators at the Polish, state-owned Auschwitz-Birkenau Memorial and Museum (ABMM), located on the site of the wartime concentration camp, that they had obtained six watercolour paintings for the museum's collection of archives. The paintings bore the signature "Dinah" and the date "1944" written in pencil (Milton 2003, 66).[3] Museum officials invited Dina to come to Poland to verify that the paintings were the portraits she painted during her imprisonment in the concentration camp. The ABMM had purchased the six watercolours in 1963 from a woman identified as Ewa, a Hungarian survivor of Auschwitz adopted by a local Oświęcim family after the liberation of the camp ("Museum's Position"). Another survivor of the camp had reportedly given the paintings to the teenage son of the family in appreciation for their generosity and care for Ewa (Szymanska 2003, 139). The Museum Artifacts Purchase Committee's official record from December 1963 states, "The Committee members bought on purpose all paintings for the Museum collections as the portraits of the Gypsies are closely connected with the camp history (Gypsy camp).… It has been determined that the portraits of Gypsies were probably painted in the concentration camp at the time of its existence, in all likelihood by a prisoner" ("Museum's Position"). At that time, museum officials, working under the Communist government of the Polish People's Republic, did not know the identity of the artist "Dinah," nor were they aware of the circumstances surrounding the creation of the portraits.

In 1969, the head of the museum's Collections Department recognized the signature on a painting in a published book of artwork. The signature was the same as the one on the watercolours in the museum, and the book listed the name of the artist as Dinah Gottliebova. The museum now had the name of the artist and began a search to locate her ("Museum's Position").[4] Travelling to Poland in January 1973, Dina verified the paintings as the products of her forced labour under extreme duress: the threat of death for her and her loved ones at the whim of Mengele. The museum officials acknowledged the paintings as her work, but they refused to relinquish possession of them and offered to produce facsimiles for Dina to take home with her. As the acknowledged artist of the works, and as a survivor of the systematic brutalization of the Nazi regime, Dina believed the paintings to be her property, an idea that goes beyond any notion of sentimental value or international copyright. The paintings are her only extant objects from the nightmare of the camps that claimed the lives of her father, her grandmother, and her two half-siblings.

I first came to know Dina's story while I was researching contemporary revisions of the *Snow White* fairy tale. A graphic novel/comic strip biography of Dina had the intriguing subheading "Snow White in Auschwitz." The comic strip, entitled *The Last Outrage*, was created as a joint project between Rafael Medoff, director of the David S. Wyman Institute for Holocaust Studies, and comic-book artists and creators Neal Adams, Joe Kubert, and Stan Lee (Gustines 2008).[5] Medoff and the institute have long supported Dina Gottliebova-Babbitt's efforts to reclaim her work. The mandate of the David S. Wyman Institute for Holocaust Studies is to teach "the history and lessons of America's response to the Holocaust, through scholarly research, public events, publications, and educational programs" (David S. Wyman Institute). Medoff and J. David Spurlock of Vanguard Productions were the organizers behind a series of petitions sent to the ABMM's director, Piotr M.A. Cywiński, on behalf of Dina, garnering support from hundreds of comic-book artists, animators, attorneys, museum officials, curators, and painters ("Dina Babbitt," 2009).

The six-page comic strip (Figures 6.1–6.6) tells Dina's story, beginning with her childhood in Brno and her art studies in Prague. The story follows her deportations and her arrival in Auschwitz, where, at the request of fellow prisoner Freddy Hirsch, a youth leader Dina knew from her time in Theresienstadt, she painted a mural on the wall inside the Block 31 barracks at the camp (Koren and Negev 2004, 104). She began the mural by painting a meadow, flowers, and animals. Dina then asked the children what they wanted her to paint next. She recalls, "One morning, I started painting the view of a Swiss alpine meadow. Then I noticed I was surrounded. There were kids all over behind me. And I asked them what would you like me to paint for you now? Several of them said, 'We want Snow White and the Seven Dwarfs.'... I saw that movie seven times. And I was enthralled. So I was doing the stuff on the wall, and the kids loved it" (quoted in Haase 2000, 372). She remembers Freddy Hirsch bringing her the materials and starting the mural with the idea to paint the view as if the observers were on the deck of a Swiss chalet looking out upon the meadow (Helstein 2008).[6] The mural inspired the child prisoners to stage their own version of the fairy tale, and they named the play *Snow White in Auschwitz* (Koren and Negev 2004, 104).

The quality of Dina's artwork on the mural caught the attention of Dr. Franz Lucas, the SS physician assigned to the Theresienstadt Family Camp and Gypsy Camp in Auschwitz-Birkenau (Milton 2003, 66). Lucas recommended her skills to Mengele, who was seeking a way to replicate the skin tones of his Roma prisoners to document his racist theories—theories of ethnic inferiority based on physical characteristics. Dina states that the Nazi doctor was unsatisfied with the results of colour photography of the time and sought to have a more realistic representation of the prisoners' bodies to document his experiments (Helstein 2008). Mengele asked Dina if she could paint the colours more realistically than the garish results achieved with photographs. He told her that if she could, she would work there under his orders, and her prisoner number, the number tattooed on her left forearm, would be placed on his list of those to be spared death. She stated that she could do the work, but, fearing that her mother would soon be sent to the gas chamber, told Mengele she would commit suicide by walking into the electrified barbed wire fence surrounding the camp if her mother was not placed on the list, too (Helstein 2008).[7] Mengele sent for her mother and placed both prisoner numbers on the list. Dina began her work painting portraits in February or March of 1944. She and her mother were among only twenty-seven Czechoslovakian Jews to survive from the group of approximately five thousand people who arrived in their transport from Theresienstadt on 8 September 1943 (Friess 2006; Helstein 2008).

The young artist would go each day under guard to Mengele's office and work in a "small office adjacent to Mengele, where she received cardboard, brushes, watercolours, and two chairs to paint portraits of Roma subjects used in Mengele's notorious genetic and medical experiments. She later recalled that she had painted between ten and twelve portraits" (Milton 2003, 66). She was permitted to sign her name "Dinah" and the date "1944" in pencil on the paintings.[8] Dina remembers, "I painted slowly, conserving the work that was light, giving me a better opportunity of living through the camp. One portrait took about two weeks. Dr. Mengele examined each portrait very carefully; on some, he asked me to make minor changes or additions" (quoted in Milton 2003, 66). Her first portrait was of a young Roma woman named Céline who had recently lost her newborn baby to starvation (Friess 2006). One of Mengele's interests was the shape of the ears of the Roma people—he believed he could prove his racist theories through physiognomy. He posed Céline with a blue scarf covering her shaved head with one ear protruding and ordered Dina to paint her this way (Figure 6.4). The portrait of Céline survived the war, and the painting is among the works in the possession of the ABMM. In later years, Dina recreated some of these paintings, and, in a haunting remembrance of the Roma woman, painted Céline as she felt the young woman would rather have appeared, with the scarf covering her ears and softly draped around her head. This act is both a tribute to Céline and a repudiation of Mengele's ideas.

The documentary film *As Seen Through These Eyes*, directed by Hilary Helstein, examines the role of art and artists in the documentation of the Holocaust and highlights the importance of visual representation of the genocide and the experience of the camps. Dina features in the film, and she speaks about the people in her portraits, how she learned their stories, bringing the surreal conditions under which she painted the portraits into context. Dina remembers, "Céline, she was French, she was so beautiful … like a porcelain doll, you know … and she looked very sick so I asked her if I could do anything to help her … we became friends.… I wanted to keep Céline with me there for as long as I could" (Helstein 2008). The two women were both twenty years old in 1944. Céline's two-month-old daughter died of starvation in Auschwitz, as the young mother was unable to supply enough milk to the baby on her prisoner food rations (Koren and Negev 2004, 104). Dina recalls that Céline was very ill from malnutrition, so Dina would secretly share with her the larger rations of bread that she received as a prisoner working on Mengele's projects. Over the course of the time it took to complete the portrait, the two women became friends despite the language barrier, and Céline taught Dina a French song (Koren and Negev 2004, 105). The act of giving Céline her food and delaying the completion of the portrait was an expression of Dina's rebellion within the confines of her forced labour. In the film, Dina speaks of the executions of all the people she painted that happened soon after she completed the portraits. The trauma of the memory is still evident in the expressions of despair on the artist's face. Her work assignment in the Roma camp (commonly referred to as the "Gypsy Family Camp") "continued until August 2, 1944, the day thousands of Roma prisoners were murdered in the Birkenau gas chamber" (Milton 2003, 66).[9]

Dina continued to paint under extreme duress. Her work included painting pictures to replicate the pseudo-scientific procedures performed on children and adults, often without anaesthesia. She worked tracing the x-rays of many of the doctor's subjects, including the Ovitz family, seven members of which were dwarves.[10] Dina recalls how, in the midst of her work, one day she saw

> a column of dwarfs trotting toward me, like a film scene. There were seven; I could not believe my eyes. It was as if all my animated dwarfs—Dopey, Grumpy, Sneezy and all the rest—had descended from the mural in the children's barrack and come to life. But I was no Snow White, and they were real. I could not help smiling in response to the dwarfs, and to the magic number of seven—there was something optimistic and encouraging about such fragile beings managing to survive here. (quoted in Koren and Negev 2004, 106)

At the end of August 1944, Mengele gave Dina a large roll of paper and ordered her to map out the complex family tree of the Ovitz family and note the members who were dwarves and those who were of average size (131). Mengele even ordered Dina to paint his own portrait.

Prisoners produced many forms of artwork while in concentration camps during World War II (Milton 2003, 62). They created artwork for propaganda, drafting diagrams of camps and buildings, visually documenting events, and painting portraits of Nazi officers, among other tasks (62). Dina's work on the Roma portraits differed from the mass-produced art of the camps in that the artist was face to face with her subjects immediately before their murders. The time it took to produce the work allowed Dina to speak with her subjects of their mutual hopes and dreams for freedom and survival in secret while Mengele was away from the room. Dina survived the camps and the war, but the subjects of the paintings and their families did not.

RECLAIMING DINA GOTTLIEBOVA-BABBITT'S WORK

After learning that the paintings were in the possession of the ABMM, Dina believed she had a legal case to reclaim them, but the officials at the museum repeatedly refused her requests. Dina's work, which she wished to claim as personal objects from her lived experience, was taken from her in the context of her forced labour and is still held at the site of her imprisonment. She states, "My paintings saved my life and thanks to them I lived to raise a family.... They are part of my soul, and I won't be complete without them. As long as they are there, I'll still be a prisoner in Auschwitz" (quoted in Koren and Negev 2004, 217).

The ABMM states that under Polish law, the museum is the rightful owner of the portraits and Dina Gottliebova-Babbitt holds what are termed "the author property rights" ("Museum's Position"). Therefore, the ABMM "is allowed to use them within the limits of permissible public use of protected artifacts determined in regulation regarding author rights and relation rights" ("Museum's Position"). Examining both sides of the legal argument in the case, law scholar Kristen Messer states that the ABMM's position "focuses on the premise that the paintings fall under the principle of work for hire, or commissioned artwork. Under this principle, it is the patron, not the artist who holds the property rights in the work. Thus, the museum purports that Dr. Mengele, the commissioner of the portraits, would be the only individual who would legally have a claim" (2008, 22). While Messer's statement is provocative, the ABMM does not claim Mengele would be the owner, but that the portraits are part of the Nazi doctor's archives held by the museum. In its official position on Dina's case, the ABMM states that after the initial visit in 1973, the museum sent Dina a recorded copy of her testimony about the portraits and two sets of photographs of the paintings, after which it received no further contact from the artist. The museum officials concluded, incorrectly, that "Mrs. Gottliebova, in regard to tragic memories connected with the camp, did not want to stay in touch with the institution and recall the tragic past" ("Museum's Position"). Dina felt "betrayed and used by the museum to authenticate the works" (Passamano 2011, 10) after receiving the photographs and letters. She could not bear to respond during the 1970s and '80s, but she decided to resume correspondence with the museum in the 1990s (10).

The ABMM has a complex history. Jonathan Huener, in his book *Auschwitz, Poland, and the Politics of Commemoration, 1945–1979*, explores the challenges of establishing and maintaining the historical site within the context of Poland's postwar reconstruction and the commemoration of the country's enormous wartime losses. Huener chronicles how the memorial at Auschwitz "was constructed, maintained, and modified within a political and cultural framework" (2003, xiv) that has changed in step with the political and cultural shifts in Poland through the past decades. The site's symbols, exhibitions, and public demonstrations both explain the history of the events that occurred at the site and misinterpret that history (23). As Huener explains, the ABMM "has honoured the dead and, at times, been selective about those whom it chooses to honour; it has shown reverent silence and has also engaged in noisy demonstrations; it has been an indicator of liberalizing transformation in the cultural policy of the Polish People's Republic and has also communicated the ideological rigidity of that state" (23). From its beginnings as a site of evidence collection for war crimes tribunals to its present status as a UNESCO World Heritage Site, the ABMM has served as a site for Polish national martyrdom, a monument to the struggle of the political prisoner (often styled as a socialist hero or resistance fighter), and a stage for political propaganda. The ABMM now exists as a commemoration of the genocide of the Jews, Sinti, and Roma, and the murder of millions by the Nazi regime.

Auschwitz is not just the site, its structures, and the memories of the individuals who documented their experiences, but also the constructed memory of the Holocaust by the ABMM over time. In the context of the ABMM, the term "memory" in relation to Auschwitz refers not to the individual memories, but to an aggregate of these memories officially sanctioned and legitimized. Huener states, "The museum has, both by accident and by design, altered and distorted the past while attempting to reconstruct it in the tangible forms of exhibitions, monuments, and demonstrations. The site has always been selective in what it has presented to the public" (2003, 25). Claims upon the site of commemoration, such as Dina's fight to reclaim her work, highlight the complexity of such collective memory building and the individual stories that exist within the framework of the officially sanctioned commemoration.

Since the mid-1990s, the ABMM has addressed Dina's claim on her paintings at several meetings of the museum's council. Rabbi Andrew Baker, the director of International Jewish Affairs for the American Jewish Committee and a member of the International Auschwitz Council, which advises the officials at the Auschwitz museum, tried to facilitate a deal between the artist and the museum. His actions brought some hope that a resolution that would satisfy both parties might occur within Dina's lifetime. Additionally, United States Representative Shelley Berkley of Nevada sponsored a congressional resolution supporting Dina's claim and requested that the US State Department take up the case with Polish government officials (Weber 2009).[11] The countless letters and petitions from those who learned of her story failed to sway the museum's official stance on Dina's request to take possession of her work.

On 15–16 June 2009, the International Auschwitz Council met to discuss issues pertinent to the museum and attention "returned once again to the issue of the seven Roma portraits painted by Dina [Gottliebova]-Babbitt. The Council emphatically reiterated its previous determination that the transfer of the originals to Mrs. [Gottliebova]-Babbitt, as she demands, is out of the question" (International Auschwitz Council 2009). The museum council further ruled that

> in this and all similar cases, the overriding consideration is the authenticity and completeness of the Memorial, with all its movable and non-moveable property. The portraits in question were painted in the camp, on orders from Dr. Joseph Mengele, as documentation for his pseudoscientific racist research. Today, they are among the very few remaining vestiges of the murdered Roma, and cannot be replaced by any copies. Respect for this principle makes it possible to avoid any sort of doubts that could be cynically exploited in the future by deniers. It must be stressed once again that the International Auschwitz Council has already expressed its position on these paintings. On a motion by Rabbi Andrew Baker, the issue was voted on once again. (International Auschwitz Council 2009)

Sadly, Dina Gottliebova-Babbitt died of cancer on 29 July 2009. Her daughters continue her claim of ownership of the paintings as a means of fulfilling their mother's last wish.[12] But Dina's case goes far beyond the desires of one woman. Her claim represents the appeal for the reclamation of rights and property of all people who have lost their possessions or the product of their work during times of state-sanctioned forced labour and confinement. Medoff states that "Dina Babbitt's passing is a double tragedy—a tragedy for Dina and her family, that she passed away without ever regaining the paintings that saved her life in Auschwitz; and a tragedy for the art world, that a museum has cruelly trampled the principle of an artist's right to her artwork. It is a tragic example of a state-sponsored institution assuming self-proclaimed and unlawful rights against the moral and lawful rights of the individual" (quoted in "Dina Babbitt," 2009). The legal designation of "forced alienation of property" applies to the conditions of forced labour and property produced within that context. The status of worker as a prisoner ordered to create a piece of work cannot be seen as relinquishing ownership rights.

Given the extraordinary circumstances of Dina's life and work, the ABMM's refusal to return the paintings to the artist (now the estate of the artist) seems contrary to any humanitarian judgment. Many recent government initiatives that reflect efforts to make reparations to groups of people systematically persecuted by former state-sanctioned policies deemed to violate human rights have restated positions and reversed previous rulings on issues involving property claims, personal artifacts, and monetary compensation.[13] Yet, in the cases of reclamation of property stolen during the Nazi regime or work created within the framework of imprisonment in Nazi concentration camps, there is a complex system of appeal even in cases where the artist/owner's name is present on the work. Of her paintings, Dina states, "They are definitely my own paintings; they belong to me, my soul is in them, and without these paintings I wouldn't be alive, my children and grandchildren wouldn't be alive…. I created them. Who else's could they be?" (Friess 2006).

The ethical implications of the ABMM's decision on Dina's claims to her work are complex and troubling. The extraordinary circumstances of forced labour within a historical system of state-sanctioned genocide cannot be evaluated within any context of worker and employer contract. Dina's position as prisoner, or slave, negates any notion of a fair exchange of labour. And what of the Roma subjects forced to sit for the portraits and the labour stolen from them? Would they not have claim on the product of their labour? The subjects were all murdered at the camp, so they cannot make a claim on the work. Officials at the ABMM sent Dina a photograph of a Roma picnic at the museum and a letter explaining the support of the Roma organization for the museum's position, suggesting that she and her family stop requesting that the works be returned to her (Passamano 2011, 10). In fact, organizations dedicated to the preservation of Roma culture and history, and to the rights of Roma people today, are divided on the issue of returning the portraits to Dina's heirs (10).[14]

The belief that the memory of the event exists primarily in the monument, both the immovable and movable objects, drives much of the ABMM's decision-making policy. Survivors' requests for property seized during times of war and within the framework of the state-sanctioned persecution during the Nazi regime prompted a summit in Prague in June 2009 to address "the problem of property plundered during the Holocaust and World War II" ("EU Summit"). The European Union summit consisted of delegations from forty-six countries, and, at its conclusion, the committee issued this declaration (the Terezín Declaration):

> As the era is approaching when eye witnesses of the Holocaust (*Shoah*) will no longer be with us and when the sites of former Nazi concentration and extermination camps, will be the most important and undeniable evidence of the tragedy of the Holocaust (*Shoah*), the significance and integrity of these sites including all of their movable and immovable remnants, will constitute a fundamental value regarding all of the actions concerning these sites, and will become especially important for our civilization including, in particular, the education of future generations. We, therefore, appeal for broad support of

all the conservation efforts in order to save those remnants as the testimony of the crimes committed there to the memory and warning for the generations to come and where appropriate to consider declaring these as national monuments under national legislation. ("EU Summit")

The protectionist action of the council reflected in the Terezín Declaration is a call for the preservation of cultural memory, overseen by a select group entrusted by state, or other governing bodies. Jan Assmann's work on cultural memory helps us to understand the ideas that inform these types of rulings. In his study of memory, Assmann differentiates between types of collective memory: communicative memory, which is shared and "based exclusively on everyday communication" (Assmann 1995, 126), and cultural memory, which begins where communicative memory ends and "is characterized by its distance from the everyday" (129). Communicative memory has "a limited temporal horizon" (eighty to one hundred years into the past) and is a private interpretation of a history, characterized by "a high degree of formlessness, willfulness, and disorganization" (127). Cultural memory "has its fixed point; its horizon does not change with the passing of time" (129). Cultural memory's fixed points are "fateful events of the past, whose memory is maintained through cultural formation (texts, rites, monuments) and institutional communication (recitation, practice, observance)" (129). Assmann asserts that in cultural formation, the collective experience "crystallizes, whose meaning, when touched upon, may suddenly become accessible again across millennia" (129). For example, the Holocaust is a fateful event of the more recent past that has become, in the twentieth century, a cultural memory. It is the work of museums, national archives, and appointed historical preservationist councils to ensure the integrity of the cultural memory of a nation and, in the case of the ABMM, the documentation of human rights violations and genocide.

Dina Gottliebova-Babbitt's personal story is entangled within the complex history that informs the cultural memory of World War II and, more specifically, the cultural memory of what happened at Auschwitz and the other death camps operated by the Nazis during this historical period. Assmann addresses the exceptional place of Auschwitz in the formation and preservation of cultural memory: the place in our world history of the name/place/concept of Auschwitz in collective memory. He states,

Auschwitz, the darkest chapter of German history, has long since assumed the dimensions of a 'normative past' that must not and cannot be allowed to fall into oblivion under any circumstances because its importance goes well beyond the memories of victims and perpetrators; it has become an instance of universalized bonding memory and the founding element of a global secular religion that is concerned with democracy and human dignity.

Its commandment is 'Never again, Auschwitz', and this means not just that there should never again be victims of a German fascism, but that we—and this 'we' includes humanity—wish never again to be perpetrators, fellow travelers, or electors of a regime that tramples on human dignity. (Assmann 2006, 24)

Perhaps more than any other historical event, and surely more than any other event in World War II, Auschwitz conveys, or, in Assmann's term, "crystallizes," the horror of the human rights violations of the totalitarian regime and genocide. But the story of Auschwitz consists of many individual, private interpretations of what happened at the camp, and these stories have many witnesses. The scope of Auschwitz's legacy spans the Jewish diaspora after World War II and falls outside of the confines of the Polish government, the ABMM, and its governing council. The demands of survivors to reclaim the objects from the past, often the only objects of family history that exist, have proven problematic for those who are the appointed keepers of cultural memory.

The ABMM's statement, via a news release, on the Terezín Declaration specifically names Dina's case as an example of the type of claims that make such a declaration necessary:

These provisions are important at a time when concrete claims are being made on the remains of the camps. An example is the desire to deprive the Auschwitz memorial of 7 watercolours that a prisoner, Dina Babbitt-Gottliebova [sic], painted on orders from Dr. Joseph Mengele. These watercolours depict the faces of Roma people who, after the portraits were completed, died within the framework of the SS doctor's pseudo-scientific experiments. The International Auschwitz Council has already denied these claims on two occasions, indicating that the paintings cannot be considered within the category of individual works of art. The basis of their worldwide significance is the fact that they are part of Dr. Joseph Mengele's pseudo-scientific archive, and represent an undeniable memento of the suffering and death of Roma victims in Auschwitz. ("EU Summit")

As the language of this statement makes clear, the organizations dedicated to preserving cultural memory must protect the state collection of objects from those with the "desire to deprive" the museum of its archives. The educational value of objects such as Dina's paintings is undeniable, and it was never her intention to deny the use of reproductions in the museum. In fact, the museum often displayed reproductions of the paintings due to the fragile nature of the materials ("Dina Babbitt," 2009). Dina wished the originals to be the property of her family upon her death and considered donating them to a museum in the United States.

Rabbi Andrew Baker states, "The people at the Polish museum are not devils.... They want to maintain Auschwitz as authentically as they can, and I appreciate the role exhibiting the paintings plays. What I've always thought is that there is no one else in the world who so values these paintings as Dina Babbitt and the directors of this museum" (quoted in Weber 2009). There are groups of people worldwide who deny that the Holocaust ever happened. Therefore, the ABMM, as a state-supported keeper of cultural memory, along with other organizations dedicated to the "Never again" commandment, must be vigilant in their documentation and educational efforts. Archives and memorials have an undeniable value for all humanity, and the lessons we learn from the tragedies of the past must pass on to future generations. But must that come at the price of one woman's right to claim her own creative work as objects of her personal history—work stolen from her under the threat of death?

TELLING DINA GOTTLIEBOVA-BABBITT'S STORY

What is the story of the Auschwitz-Birkenau Memorial and Museum without the individual stories of the people who lived through the horror of the camp during World War II? Take, for example, the story of Céline's portrait. The painting as a historical object is a document of one young woman murdered during a time of war when many perished, but combined with Dina's recollection of the creation of that portrait, the loss of the young woman seems immeasurable. Dina's recollection of the specific point in time, even mediated by the fragility of memory and passing time, makes the mistreatment and the murder of Céline personal even though we never knew her. We see Céline as a mother, a daughter, and a friend, and realize the impossibly difficult situation of the two women prisoners. The result is infinitely more powerful than just viewing a portrait on the wall, even if that wall is in the Auschwitz-Birkenau Memorial and Museum.

The problems faced by educational organizations aiming to teach the lessons of history to younger generations include the distance from the experience of those involved in the events. Dina's story has become an educational tool by which children learn about the Holocaust and the lives of survivors. The comic strip created by Medoff, Adams, Kubert, and Lee is now a motion comic as part of the series *They Spoke Out: American Voices Against the Holocaust*. The series, produced by Disney Educational Productions, consists of ten "remarkable stories of Americans of all faiths who raised their voices, marched in protest, or even helped smuggle Jewish refugees out of Hitler's Europe" (*They Spoke Out*). The classroom editions of three films that tell stories of the Holocaust, *Anne Frank*, *The Boy in the Striped Pajamas*, and *Life is Beautiful*, now include the motion comic of the printed strip as a bonus feature on the DVD. Through the wide audience of the Disney studio, Dina's story now reaches a new generation of learners.

However, scholars of Holocaust literature express caution about representations of historical events, especially in narratives designed to teach children about the lessons of the Holocaust. Efraim Sicher suggests that fictional representation of the Holocaust in "plays, novels, and movies generates cultural perceptions in ways that are particularly problematic and that stimulate further media reworking of the memory," producing "stronger images than documentary presentation of facts and testimony by witnesses, educators and historians" (2000, 56). The "fictionalization" or "Americanization" of the Holocaust has come under scrutiny since the introduction of Holocaust studies into school curricula and the subsequent demand for age-appropriate books and audiovisual materials needed to teach on the topic (Baron 2003, 394). The problems arise when, in developing the narratives for a younger audience, the texts become cultural artifacts with "tenuous relevance to the historical events" (Sicher 56–57). In her work on the Holocaust and children's literature, Adrienne Kertzer explains, "Because the child reader is presumed to be ignorant of the Holocaust and the pedagogical purpose is to produce some clear knowledge, children's books about the Holocaust have little interest in traumatized voices. By the end of the story, the child knows more, and what she knows, because it works within the representative limits of children's books, still allows her to hope" (2002, 13). The need to put a hopeful shape to the story of survival or death within the tragedy of the Holocaust, to find a lesson within the events of the story, is challenging in the context of such difficult subject matter.[15]

The connection with the *Snow White* fairy tale through Dina's drawings on the camp walls, highlighted in the narrative of the comic strip about her life, evokes a fairy tale intertext to Dina's story. Used in narrative therapy and the pedagogy of text with difficult subject matter, fairy-tale-type narratives offer a frame in which to tell both fictional and non-fictional stories to children and young adults. The familiar structure and motifs bring the incomprehensible subject matter into a safer space where readers can then interpret the difficult knowledge. In his work on the connection between the fairy tale and the trauma of children, Donald Haase stresses the importance of the fairy tale as a device used by children "to interpret their surroundings and as a psychological survival tool to transform their environment into a hopeful utopian space, a reconstituted home" (2000, 372). Haase points to the example of Dina drawing the *Snow White and the Seven Dwarfs* mural to bring comfort to the child prisoners in Auschwitz (372).

The fairy tale intertext informs readers' interpretation of the biographical comic strip and the resulting tale becomes a mode of transmission for Dina's story. The fairy tale, as a cultural institution,[16] becomes an archival source by which we may retell the story of real people. Fairy-tale-type narratives have the potential to be infinitely powerful in transmitting lessons of history, yet they are fraught with the difficulty of avoiding the trivialization of such traumatic historical events. As Holocaust survivor and author Elie Wiesel states, "If the choice is between a trivialization of the event and nothing, I prefer nothing" (quoted in Kertzer 2002, 39). Kertzer argues,

> The history that makes us wish fairy tales did happen, that life were like a children's book and we all lived happily ever after, is not an easy history to read or write. If we persist in thinking that children need hope and happy endings (and I must confess that I believe that they do), then the stories we give them about the Holocaust will be shaped by those expectations, and we will need to consider narrative strategies … that give child readers a double narrative, one that simultaneously respects our need for hope and happy endings even as it teaches us a different lesson about history. (2002, 74–75)

Dina's story fits this fairy tale narrative paradigm because she survived a perilous journey and never gave up the fight for what she believed was right. By framing her story in this type of narrative, readers can give a shape to the traumatic events of her life, and our collective memory of that particular historical period, that provides hope for a happy ending for Dina. Medoff's remarks upon the occasion of Dina's death reflect this idea:

> Dina was an inspiration to everyone who cares about justice. As a Jew who outlasted the Nazis, as a cartoonist who brought joy to an entire generation of American children, and as an artist who fought for the return of her artwork, her life embodied the principle of doing the right thing. We will do everything we can to continue Dina's fight to persuade the Auschwitz State Museum to do the right thing by returning the paintings to the Babbitt family. (quoted in "Dina Babbitt," 2009)

Dina's story continues through the efforts of those who are dedicated to reclaiming the work she created during World War II, and in the retelling of her life narrative.

Dina Gottliebova-Babbitt's story now exists within numerous archival objects that stand alongside the work she created during World War II. Documents chronicling the various rulings on her case exist in museum records—in both the United States and Poland—and there are texts such as the comic strip biography, educational materials, documentary films, and essays about her life. These archives are a testament to her extraordinary life, and they will tell her story when the limits of communicative memory expire and the tale of Dina Gottliebova-Babbitt becomes part of the cultural memory of a time the world will not, and should not, ever forget.

Figures 6.1–6.6   *The Last Outrage*, by Neal Adams, Rafael Medoff, Joe Kubert, Stan Lee, and the David S. Wyman Institute For Holocaust Studies. Marvel Comics, 2008. Courtesy of Neal Adams.

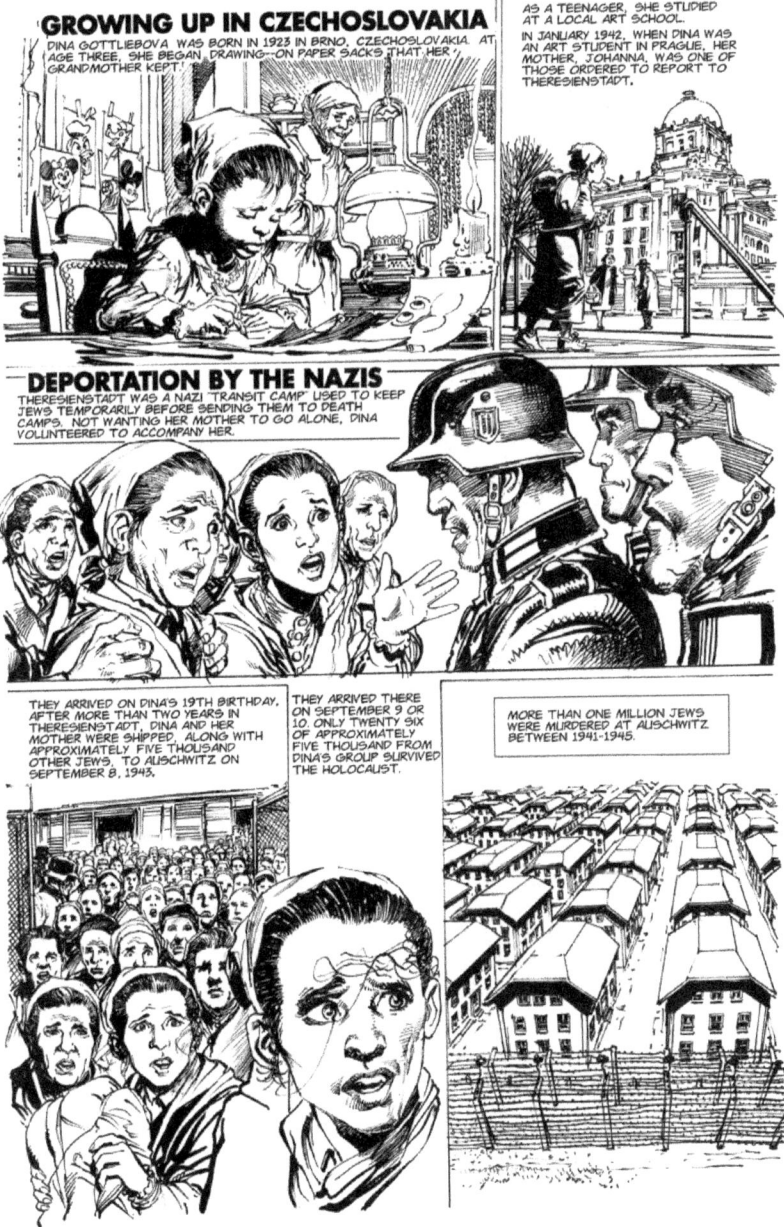

SNOW WHITE IN AUSCHWITZ

FREDDY HIRSCH WAS A ZIONIST YOUTH MOVEMENT LEADER WITH WHOM DINA HAD BEEN FRIENDLY IN CZECHOSLOVAKIA. FREDDY SPOKE TO DINA.

HE WAS THE UNOFFICIAL HEAD OF ONE OF THE CHILDREN'S BARRACKS AT AUSCHWITZ. THIS IS THE BARRACKS WHERE CHILDREN WERE HOUSED TEMPORARILY UNTIL IT WAS THEIR TIME TO BE GASSED TO DEATH.

KNOWING OF DINA'S ARTISTIC ABILITY, FREDDY ASKED HER TO PAINT A MURAL ON THE WALL OF THE BARRACKS TO CHEER UP THE CHILDREN. SHE AGREED, ALTHOUGH SHE EXPECTED SHE WOULD BE EXECUTED IF THE GERMANS CAUGHT HER. THIS WAS SOME TIME IN FEBRUARY 1944. USING PAINTS THAT WERE SMUGGLED FROM VARIOUS SOURCES, DINA SET TO WORK PAINTING A SCENE OF SNOW WHITE LOOKING OUT OVER THE SWISS COUNTRYSIDE.

DINA KNEW THAT SOME OF THE CHILDREN HAD SEEN THE MOVIE AND WOULD RECOGNIZE THE CHARACTER. SHE HAD SEEN THE MOVIE "SEVEN TIMES IN A ROW" BACK IN CZECHOSLOVAKIA.

--BECAUSE SHE SO LOVED THE ANIMATION-- THE MEMORIES OF THE CHARACTERS' FEATURES WERE STILL SHARP IN HER MIND.

WHEN THE CHILDREN SAW HER PAINTING SNOW WHITE, THEY BEGAN CLAMORING FOR HER TO ADD THE SEVEN DWARVES, AS WELL AS VARIOUS FARM ANIMALS IN THE FIELDS, WHICH SHE DID.

ENCOUNTER WITH THE "ANGEL OF DEATH"

ON FEBRUARY 22, 1944, SHORTLY AFTER THE MURAL WAS FINISHED, AN SS MAN CAME TO DINA'S BARRACKS

AND ORDERED HER TO GET INTO A JEEP. SHE BELIEVED SHE WAS ABOUT TO BE KILLED. INSTEAD, SHE WAS TAKEN TO AN AREA OF THE CAMP WHERE GYPSIES WERE HELD.

THERE SHE MET THE NOTORIOUS WAR CRIMINAL, DR. JOSEF MENGELE, WHO PERFORMED BARBARIC MEDICAL "EXPERIMENTS" ON AUSCHWITZ PRISONERS IN ORDER TO BOLSTER NAZI RACIAL THEORIES.

MENGELE HAD BEEN TAKING PHOTOGRAPHS OF SOME OF THE THOUSANDS OF GYPSY PRISONERS IN AUSCHWITZ, AS PART OF HIS EFFORT TO FIND SCIENTIFIC EVIDENCE THAT NON-ARYANS WERE GENETICALLY INFERIOR TO ARYANS. MENGELE WAS DISSATISFIED WITH THE QUALITY OF THE PHOTOGRAPHIC EQUIPMENT AVAILABLE TO HIM.

HE BELIEVED IT FAILED TO CAPTURE ASPECTS OF THE GYPSIES' SKIN TONES WHICH, HE CLAIMED, HELPED DEMONSTRATE THEIR RACIAL INFERIORITY.

HE WANTED AN ARTIST TO PAINT PORTRAITS OF SOME OF THEM, IN ORDER TO MORE ACCURATELY CAPTURE THEIR SKIN TONES.

IT WAS MENGELE'S CALM, CRUEL FACE THAT MANY OF THE JEWISH PRISONERS ENCOUNTERED WHEN THEY WERE FIRST HERDED THROUGH THE GATES OF AUSCHWITZ.

THEY CALLED HIM "THE ANGEL OF DEATH."

WITH ONE FLICK OF HIS WRIST, HE DECIDED THEIR FATE. TO THE LEFT- STRAIGHT TO THE GAS CHAMBERS. TO THE RIGHT- THE SLAVE LABOR BATTALIONS-- OR MENGELE'S LABORATORY.

HERE, MENGELE PERFORMED UNIMAGINABLE EXPERIMENTS ON PRISONERS. HOW MUCH PAIN COULD THEY ENDURE WITHOUT ANESTHESIA? HOW WOULD THEY REACT WHEN INJECTED WITH A VARIETY OF SUBSTANCES? HE SUBJECTED IDENTICAL TWINS TO VIVISECTION... (CUTTING THEM...

AS A CORONER WOULD A DEAD BODY... WHILE THEY LIVED.) TO LEARN MORE ABOUT THEIR PHYSIQUE. THE GYPSY PRISONERS WERE KEPT ALIVE... TEMPORARILY, WHILE MENGELE STUDIED THEIR SKIN COLOR.

HERE... NOW MENGELE FELT HE NEEDED PAINTINGS... TO PORTRAY GYPSY SKIN TONES. DINA WOULD BE GIVEN WATERCOLORS, TO PAINT PORTRAITS AND SPARING HER LIFE.

DINA HAD RECENTLY LEARNED THAT THE JEWS WITH WHOM SHE HAD BEEN DEPORTED FROM THERESIENSTADT WERE SCHEDULED TO DIE. AMONG THEM, HER MOTHER WAS SCHEDULED TO BE GASSED TO DEATH SOON.

SUMMONING ALL HER COURAGE, DINA TOLD THE "ANGEL OF DEATH" SHE WOULD INSTEAD COMMIT SUICIDE... UNLESS HER MOTHER WAS SPARED.

MENGELE BELIEVED HER.

MENGELE AGREED!

ON MARCH EIGHTH, THE OTHERS FROM THAT TRANSPORT TRAIN... WERE GASSED.

WHEN, WITH SOVIET TROOPS APPROACHING, THE GERMANS FLED AUSCHWITZ AND FORCED THE JEWISH PRISONERS TO UNDERTAKE A DEATH MARCH FROM THE CAMP. DINA AND HER MOTHER SURVIVED THE MARCH... AND WERE ULTIMATELY LIBERATED, FROM THE RAVENSBRÜCK CAMP, BY ALLIED TROOPS IN MAY 1945.

DINA'S POSTWAR CAREER AS AN ANIMATOR

AFTER THE WAR, DINA SETTLED IN PRAGUE, WHERE SHE MET ARTHUR BABBITT, AN AMERICAN CARTOON ANIMATOR (WHO HAD, COINCIDENTALLY, BEEN THE LEAD ANIMATOR ON THE CHARACTER OF "DOPEY" IN SNOW WHITE).

THEY MARRIED AND MOVED TO HOLLYWOOD, WHERE SHE WORKED FOR SEVENTEEN YEARS AS AN ASSISTANT ANIMATOR FOR JAY WARD PRODUCTIONS, WARNER BROTHERS, AND MGM. OVER THE YEARS, SHE ILLUSTRATED SUCH CHARACTERS AS DAFFY DUCK, WILE E. COYOTE, SPEEDY GONZALEZ, AND CAP'N CRUNCH.

DISCOVERY OF THE PAINTINGS

DINA ASSUMED THAT HER GYPSY PAINTINGS WERE GONE FOREVER. BUT IN 1963, THE AUSCHWITZ STATE MUSEUM, A POLISH GOVERNMENT-FUNDED MUSEUM ON THE SITE OF THE FORMER DEATH CAMP, WAS CONTACTED BY A LOCAL RESIDENT WHO HAD SIX OF THE PAINTINGS. THE MUSEUM PURCHASED THEM. LATER, IT BOUGHT A SEVENTH OF DINA'S PAINTINGS, FROM ANOTHER PERSON.

THE PAINTINGS WERE SIGNED "DINA 1944." EVENTUALLY, IN 1973, MUSEUM OFFICIALS IDENTIFIED THE PAINTER AS DINA BABBITT AND CONTACTED HER.

DINA FLEW TO POLAND. SHE BROUGHT A LARGE SUITCASE, EXPECTING TO TAKE HER PAINTINGS HOME. SHE WAS SHOCKED WHEN MUSEUM OFFICIALS TOLD HER THAT SHE COULD NOT HAVE THEM.

"FROM THAT MOMENT ON, I COULDN'T STOP THINKING OF THOSE PAINTINGS," SHE SAID LATER. "IT'S LIKE A PART OF MY HEART IS STILL IN AUSCHWITZ."

DINA'S SECOND AND LAST VISIT TO THE MUSEUM WAS IN 1997. SHE WAS ACCOMPANIED BY KATIE COURIC AND A CAMERA CREW FROM NBC-TV'S "TODAY SHOW." ONCE AGAIN, THE MUSEUM REFUSED TO LET DINA HAVE HER PAINTINGS.

OVER THE YEARS, THE AUSCHWITZ MUSEUM HAS OFFERED SEVERAL EXPLANATIONS FOR ITS REFUSAL TO RETURN THE PAINTINGS TO DINA.

THE MUSEUM HAS CLAIMED THAT THE EDUCATIONAL VALUE OF DISPLAYING THE PAINTINGS OUTWEIGHS DINA'S RIGHT TO THEM. DINA HAS POINTED OUT THAT THE SAME EDUCATIONAL GOAL WOULD BE ACHIEVED BY DISPLAYING HIGH-QUALITY REPRODUCTIONS. IN FACT, DURING HER VISIT IN 1997, DINA FOUND THAT SOME OF HER GYPSY PORTRAITS ON DISPLAY WERE REPRODUCTIONS, NOT ORIGINALS. THE MUSEUM ROTATES THE ORIGINALS WITH REPRODUCTIONS.

THE MUSEUM HAS ASSERTED THAT RETURNING DINA'S PAINTINGS MIGHT ENCOURAGE OTHER HOLOCAUST SURVIVORS TO SEEK THE RETURN OF THEIR PROPERTY FROM MUSEUMS, THUS DEPRIVING MUSEUMS OF SOME ARTIFACTS. BUT IT HAS NOT EXPLAINED WHY A MUSEUM'S RIGHT TO DISPLAY A PARTICULAR ITEM SHOULD NECESSARILY TRUMP AN INDIVIDUAL'S RIGHT TO HIS OR HER PROPERTY.

OFFICIALS OF THE AUSCHWITZ MUSEUM HAVE BEEN QUOTED AS CLAIMING THAT DR. MENGELE IS THE LEGAL OWNER OF THE PAINTINGS. IN RESPONSE, 50 PROMINENT ATTORNEYS SENT A LETTER TO THE MUSEUM, CALLING THAT CLAIM "PREPOSTEROUS AND OFFENSIVE." THEIR LETTER NOTED: "A WAR CRIMINAL DOES NOT DESERVE TO ENJOY THE FRUITS OF HIS CRIMES. MRS. BABBITT WAS COERCED, ON PAIN OF DEATH, TO PAINT THESE PORTRAITS. SHE DID NOT VOLUNTARILY ENTER INTO A BUSINESS RELATIONSHIP WITH MENGELE. HE CANNOT BE REGARDED AS A PATRON WHO COMMISSIONED THE ARTWORK."

IN 2001, THE U.S. HOUSE OF REPRESENTATIVES UNANIMOUSLY PASSED A RESOLUTION, SPONSORED BY REP. SHELLY BERKLEY OF NEVADA, RECOGNIZING "THE MORAL RIGHT OF DINA BABBITT TO OBTAIN THE ARTWORK SHE CREATED" AND URGING THE PRESIDENT AND THE SECRETARY OF STATE "TO MAKE ALL EFFORTS NECESSARY TO RETRIEVE" THE PAINTINGS. THE RESOLUTION ALSO INSTRUCTED THE STATE DEPARTMENT TO UNDERTAKE "IMMEDIATE DIPLOMATIC EFFORTS" TO SECURE THE RETURN OF THE ARTWORK.

BUT THE POLISH GOVERNMENT AND THE AUSCHWITZ MUSEUM HAVE IGNORED THE CONGRESSIONAL RESOLUTION. AND THE STATE DEPARTMENT HAS NOT APPLIED THE PRESSURE NECESSARY TO RESOLVE THE PROBLEM.

MEANWHILE, THE DAVID S. WYMAN INSTITUTE FOR HOLOCAUST STUDIES, A RESEARCH AND EDUCATION INSTITUTE IN WASHINGTON, D.C., MOBILIZED 450 CARTOONISTS AND COMIC BOOK CREATORS FROM AROUND THE WORLD TO SIGN A PETITION TO THE MUSEUM, URGING RETURN OF THE PAINTINGS.

AS DINA'S STRUGGLE HAS BECOME KNOWN, MANY PEOPLE HAVE WRITTEN TO THE MUSEUM (MUZEUM@AUSCHWITZ.ORG.PL) IN SUPPORT OF HER CAUSE. BUT DESPITE THE GROWING TIDE OF PUBLIC SYMPATHY FOR DINA, THE AUSCHWITZ MUSEUM HAS REFUSED TO YIELD.

AND SO DINA, NOW 84, CONTINUES TO WAIT AND HOPE THAT ONE DAY, THE MUSEUM WILL REALIZE THE WRONG IT HAS COMMITTED AND WILL FINALLY GIVE BACK HER PAINTINGS.

HOW LONG WILL THIS OUTRAGE CONTINUE? HOW LONG WILL THE INTERNATIONAL COMMUNITY ACCEPT THIS INJUSTICE? HOW MUCH MORE SUFFERING MUST DINA BABBITT ENDURE?

NOTES

The first epigraph is taken from "History Claims Her Artwork, but She Wants It Back," by Steve Friess, *The New York Times*, 30 August 2006. The second epigraph is taken from Hilary Helstein's 2008 documentary film *As Seen Through These Eyes*, which features Simon Wiesenthal, Dina Gottliebova-Babbitt, and other Holocaust survivors and artists. Simon Wiesenthal (1908–2005) was a survivor of the Nazi death camps. Wiesenthal dedicated his life to documenting the crimes of the Holocaust, and to hunting down the perpetrators still at large. "When history looks back," Wiesenthal explained, "I want people to know the Nazis weren't able to kill millions of people and get away with it." As founder and head of the Jewish Documentation Center in Vienna, the freelance Nazi hunter, usually with the cooperation of the Israeli, Austrian, former West German, and other governments, ferreted out nearly eleven hundred Nazi war criminals, including Adolf Eichmann, the administrator of the slaughter of the Jews; Franz Murer, "The Butcher of Wilno"; and Erich Rajakowitsch, who was in charge of the "death transports" in Holland. Wiesenthal was the author of *The Murderers Among Us* (1967), *Sails of Hope* (1973), *Sunflower* (1970), *Max and Helen* (1982), *Krystyna* (1987), *Every Day Remembrance Day* (1987), and *Justice Not Vengeance* (1989). In 1989, HBO produced a film based on his life entitled *Murderers Among Us: The Simon Wiesenthal Story*. See: http://www.wiesenthal.com.

1   In his essay "Auschwitz and the German Camp System," Henry Friedlander chronicles the establishment and operation of the Auschwitz concentration camp complex, which grew to encompass the camps known as Auschwitz I, Auschwitz II (Birkenau), and Auschwitz III (Monowitz). Heinrich Himmler chose the site for the camp shortly after the German invasion of Poland in September 1939. Originally used to hold Polish political prisoners and captured Soviet soldiers, "Auschwitz grew in size to become the largest of all Nazi concentration camps" (Friedlander 2003, 5). In 1941, "Himmler also selected Auschwitz as one site for the mass murder of Jews and Roma (commonly referred to as Gypsies) known as the so-called final solution" (5).

2   The concentration camp at Ravensbrück, in Fürstenberg/Havel, Germany, was evacuated by the German SS ahead of approaching Soviet troops towards the end of April 1945. Prisoners were marched or transported to Malchow or Neustadt-Glewe, satellite camps of Ravensbrück, where they were liberated by Soviet troops on 28 April 1945 (Buergenthal 2007, 154). Dina and her mother were taken to Neustadt-Glewe, where they remained until they were liberated by Allied troops (Koren and Negev 2004, 215).

3   The spelling "Dinah" represents the European/Czech spelling of her name. Dina Gottliebova-Babbitt, or Dina Babbitt, is her American name, adopted upon her marriage to American Art Babbitt, an animator who had worked for Disney Studios on, among other projects, the film *Snow White and the Seven Dwarfs*. The couple divorced in 1962 (Friess 2006).

4   The museum acquired a seventh painting in 1977 (Weber 2009).

5   The comic strip first appeared in the fifth and final issue of the Marvel Comics series *X-Men: Magneto Testament*. The five-issue miniseries focused on Holocaust-themed narratives. Joe Kubert is also the author of the graphic novel *Yossel: April 19, 1943*, which depicts the story of a young cartoonist imprisoned in the Warsaw ghetto.

6   In 1938, the Propaganda Ministry of Hitler's Nazi government allowed the purchase and import of *Snow White and the Seven Dwarfs* among a number of American movies deemed suitable for German audiences. Disney's film, based on the nineteenth-century Grimm Brothers variant, was a favourite film of Joseph Goebbels, Hitler's minister of propaganda, and Hitler himself. Esther Leslie states, "In 1938, Hitler arranged for a copy of *Snow White and the Seven Dwarfs* to be taken to his private cinema at Übersalzberg. He thought it was one of the greatest films ever" (2002, 153).

7   Suicide by walking or running into the thirteen-foot-high electrified fence that surrounded the camp was a common occurrence within the concentration camp system. Many prisoners, some driven by starvation and mental breakdown, walked to their deaths this way, and many others were forced into the fence by guards. See Huener (2003); Buergenthal (2007); Friedlander (2003).

8   See Note 5.

9   On 2 August 1944, the Nazis murdered 2,897 men, women, and children in the gas chambers at Auschwitz-Birkenau on orders from SS Officer Heinrich Himmler. The majority of victims of this massacre were Roma prisoners from the so-called "Gypsy Family Camp." Since 1997, 2 August has been observed as Roma Holocaust Remembrance Day, or *Pharrajimos* in the Romani language. See "'Voices of Memory'—'The Roma in Auschwitz.'"

10 The Jewish Romanian Ovitz family was a large extended family, many members of which were prisoners in Auschwitz during the war. The Ovitz family had seven dwarf siblings, and they, as well as their average-size family members, were subjects of interest to Dr. Mengele in his experiments at the camp. Before the war, the family travelled Europe performing as entertainers known as the Lilliput Troupe. For more about the Ovitz family, see Yehuda Koren and Eilat Negev's *In Our Hearts We Were Giants: The Remarkable Story of the Lilliput Troupe—A Dwarf Family's Survival of the Holocaust*. New York: Carroll & Graf, 2004.

11 See Bill Text, 107th Congress (2001–2002) S. CON. RES.49.IS. 14 June 2001.

12 Dina Gottliebova-Babbitt's daughters, Michele Kane and Karin Babbitt, continue to pursue their mother's claims to her artwork. In an interview, Michele states, "Her dying wish was to get her artwork back" (Weber 2009).

13 I refer here to national and international initiatives to examine and make reparations for systematic, state-sanctioned violations of human rights: the South African Truth and Reconciliation Commission, the Australian Aboriginal land rights movement, the Residential School Political Agreement/Truth and Reconciliation Commission in Canada, and the Commission on Wartime Relocation and Internment of Civilians addressing the Japanese American internment during World War II are among many committees and initiatives dedicated to the study of institutionalized human rights violations.

14 The US-based Roma organization Lolo Diklo strongly supported Dina's case and urged its supporters to write to the museum on her behalf.

15 For further critical attention to the subject of the fictionalization and Americanization of Holocaust-themed narratives, see Efraim Sicher's "The Future of the Past: Countermemory and Postmemory in Contemporary American Post-Holocaust Narratives"; Adrienne Kertzer's "'Do you know what 'Auschwitz' means?': Children's Literature and the Holocaust," "Like a Fable, Not a Pretty Picture: Holocaust Representation in Roberto Benigni and Anita Lobel," and *My Mother's Voice: Children, Literature and the Holocaust*; Lawrence Baron's "Not in Kansas Anymore: Holocaust Films for Children"; and Deborah P. Britzman's "'That Lonely Discovery': Anne Frank, Anna Freud, and the Question of Pedagogy."

16 Fairy tale scholar Jack Zipes states, "By the beginning of the twentieth century, the fairy tale had become fully institutionalized in Europe and America, and its functions had shifted and expanded. The institutionalization of a genre means that a certain process of production, distribution, and reception has become fully accepted within the public sphere of a society and plays a role in forming and maintaining the cultural heritage of that society" (1988, 21–22).

WORKS CITED

Adams, Neal, Rafael Medoff, Joe Kubert, and Stan Lee. 2008. "The Last Outrage." Marvel Comics.

Assmann, Jan. 1995. "Collective Memory and Cultural Identity." Translated by John Czaplicka. *New German Critique* 65: 125.

———. 2006. *Religion and Cultural Memory*. Translated by Rodney Livingstone. Stanford: Stanford University Press.

Baron, Lawrence. 2003. "Not in Kansas Anymore: Holocaust Films for Children." *The Lion and the Unicorn* 27(3): 394–409.

Buergenthal, Thomas. 2007. *A Lucky Child*. London: Profile Books.

"EU Summit: Better Protection for Memorials." 30 June 2009. Auschwitz-Birkenau Memorial and Museum, http://auschwitz.org/en/museum/news.

David S. Wyman Institute for Holocaust Studies, http://www.wymaninstitute.org.

"Dina Babbitt, Who Fought for Her Auschwitz Paintings, Passes Away; Museum Refused to Return Them; Family Will Continue the Struggle." 30 July 2009. David S. Wyman Institute for Holocaust Studies, http://www.wymaninstitute.org/press.

Friedlander, Henry. 2003. "Auschwitz and the German Camp System." In *The Last Expression: Art and Auschwitz*, edited by David Mickenburg, Corinne Granof, and Peter Hayes, 4–13. Evanston, IL: Northwestern University Press.

Friess, Steve. 30 August 2006. "History Claims Her Artwork, but She Wants It Back." *New York Times*, E1.

Gustines, George Gene. 9 August 2008. "Comic-Book Idols Rally to Aid a Holocaust Artist." *New York Times*, B7.

Haase, Donald. 2000. "Children, War, and the Imaginative Space of Fairy Tales." *The Lion and the Unicorn* 24 (3): 360–77.

Helstein, Hilary, dir. 2008. *As Seen Through These Eyes*. Menemsha Films. DVD.

Huener, Jonathan. 2003. *Auschwitz, Poland, and the Politics of Commemoration, 1945–1979*. Athens, OH: Ohio University Press.

International Auschwitz Council. 2009. "Meeting XVII: 15–16 June 2009." Auschwitz-Birkenau Memorial and Museum, http://auschwitz.org/en/museum/auschwitz-council/iac-meetings.

Kertzer, Adrienne. 2002. *My Mother's Voice: Children, Literature, and the Holocaust*. Peterborough: Broadview Press.

Koren, Yehuda, and Eilat Negev. 2004. *In Our Hearts We Were Giants: The Remarkable Story of the Lilliput Troupe—A Dwarf Family's Survival of the Holocaust*. New York: Carroll & Graf.

Leslie, Esther. 2002. *Hollywood Flatlands: Animation, Critical Theory and the Avant-Garde*. London: Verso.

Messer, Kristen. 2008. "Two Sides of the Same Coin: The Memory of the Holocaust at War with a Survivor." *Northern Kentucky Law Review* 35 (1): 19–35.

Milton, Sybil. 2003. "Art in the Context of Auschwitz." In *The Last Expression: Art and Auschwitz*, edited by David Mickenberg, Corinne Granof, and Peter Hayes, 60–67. Evanston, IL: Northwestern University Press.

"Museum's Position on Issue of Portraits made by Dinah Gottliebova-Babbitt." 2 October 2006. Auschwitz-Birkenau Memorial and Museum, http://auschwitz.org/en/museum/news.

Passamano, Leigh-Ayna. 2011. "Witnesses of Atrocity and the Preservation of Memory: An Analysis of and Recommendations for the Relationship Between Memorial Museums and Survivors." M.A. thesis. Rutgers, the State University of New Jersey. Rutgers Library Online.

Sicher, Efraim. 2000. "The Future of the Past: Countermemory and Postmemory in Contemporary American Post-Holocaust Narratives." In *History & Memory* 12(2): 56–91.

Szymanska, Irena. 2003. "The Collections of the Auschwitz-Birkenau State Museum." In *The Last Expression: Art and Auschwitz*, edited by David Mickenberg, Corinne Granof, and Peter Hayes, 138–43. Evanston, IL: Northwestern University Press.

They Spoke Out: American Voices Against the Holocaust, http://dep.disney.go.com/theyspokeout.

"'Voices of Memory'—'The Roma in Auschwitz.'" 3 August 2011. Auschwitz-Birkenau Memorial and Museum, http://auschwitz.org/en/museum/news.

Weber, Bruce. 2 August 2009. "Dina Babbitt, Auschwitz Artist, Dies at 86." *New York Times*, A20.

Zipes, Jack. 1988. "The Changing Function of the Fairy Tale." *The Lion and the Unicorn* 12 (2): 7–31.

PERPETUAL PIONEERS
The Library of Congress Meets Women Photojournalists of World War II

Beverly W. Brannan

World War II was so intensely and widely photographed that it became a prov-
ing ground for photojournalists, and their heroic or celebratory visual images
have shaped our national memory of this 'good war.'
—Linda Gordon, *Dorothea Lange: A Life Beyond Limits*

Perpetual pioneers. Without an official occupational history or honour roll, women photojournalists in the United States are justified in seeing themselves as pioneers in their field, despite a continuous record of gainful employment as women newspaper and magazine photographers at least since the 1890s. In the early 1900s, Jessie Tarbox Beals claimed to be the first woman newspaper staff photographer, and in the early 2000s, when *Washington Post* photographer Margaret Thomas left for graduate school at the University of Texas, she said she had felt like a pioneer in the 1960s when she was the first woman staff photographer hired for that paper. And I heard it again when I spoke about the history of women photojournalists at the women's section of the National Press Photographers Association in 2009. It is time that we remember these forerunners and take pride in their accomplishments.

In my nearly four decades of experience as curator of twentieth-century documentary photography at the Library of Congress, I have seen millions of photographs. The Prints and Photographs Division has approximately 15 million objects, and more than 9 million are photojournalistic in nature. Pictures in printed newspapers and magazines made personalities and events vivid and immediate to audiences from the late 1880s until the twenty-first century, when video began to eclipse still news photography.

The first steady flow of photographs came into the library's collections in 1870, chiefly through copyright deposit, but not until the 1940s did the library begin to acquire photo morgues as publications went out of business. Today, the library's photojournalism holdings are among the richest of any public institution in North America, and possibly the world. Though women began working in photojournalism in about 1890, each subsequent generation felt it was a pioneer. Always a minority in the field, women photojournalists lacked celebratory exhibitions and biographies. Without a written history of their work, women photojournalists lack a sense of occupational tradition. Despite the significant rise in the status of photography as a fine art, documentary photography and photojournalism have only recently shared the glory. When judged as works of art, most of these photographs miss the mark, and they are not valued as primary information for historical research. Much of photojournalism is held in the same regard as the newspaper that wrapped yesterday's fish.

Here I will focus on my work on the photographs of World War II and, in particular, on my efforts to bring attention to the significant work of the women photojournalists of that period. Although the best-known photographs from the war are heroic or celebratory or represent the military, many of those in the Library of Congress collections show a wider variety of subjects and responses. A large segment of the photographs depict the heroics of coping on the home front over extended periods of time with the absences, losses, and shortages that war brings (Figure 7.1).

In the early 1990s, I participated in two surveys of the library's photographic holdings aimed at establishing the parameters of the institution's photojournalism collection. As I assessed the nation's visual heritage as captured by news photographers, I felt like a pioneer exploring a continent of images. Searching the library's online catalogues for "photojournalism" produces few results because, until recently, the term "photojournalism" was rarely used in cataloguing either the photo morgues or the works produced by photojournalists.[1] Furthermore, histories of only a few newspapers exist, and the history of photojournalism is only beginning to be written.[2]

As the surveys proceeded, I chose to explore the work of the relatively few women photojournalists from among the thousands of photographers overall. The review of unprocessed materials revealed that women had made major contributions to World War II, but these efforts had gone unacknowledged and forgotten. Another survey of images available for immediate research use showed that newspaper morgues represented the bulk of the Prints and Photographs Division's holdings, but women photographers were rarely represented among the creators. Photo morgues consisted of work by news service staff photographers, but here women were rarely hired as staff because they were perceived as too delicate or unreliable because they might leave to marry or have children.

With these insights, I undertook to alter the under-representation and under-appreciation of news photographs by women. Though I found many

Figure 7.1 "Why greases must be saved. A soldier of the home front—and there's one in every American kitchen—saves all waste fats and greases so that they can be processed into ammunition for America's soldiers on the battlefronts." Photograph by Ann Rosener. Gelatin silver photograph, June 1942. Farm Security/ Office of War Information Collection, Library of Congress.

powerful images by women relating to World War II at the time the library was looking to mark the war's fiftieth anniversary, I had an uphill battle convincing anyone that women photojournalists had played an important role during the war. To demonstrate women's contribution to representations of the war, I had to mount a serious campaign. It took laying out the photographs, publications that used the photographs, correspondence, and journals from the period, political cartoons, motion picture films, and transcripts of radio broadcasts to assure people that women really had contributed to the war effort—that there actually was a story worth recovering. Although I eventually received authorization from the library to assemble the exhibition *Women Come to the Front*, it proved extremely difficult to secure funding for the exhibit, even in those relatively flush times.[3] Since that 1995 Library of Congress exhibition, even though a number of other studies have been published, the story of women and the war still is not widely known.

Because photographs for newspapers and magazines of World War II have been ignored until recently, they look fresh today and provide an important window into the diversity of women's experiences at the time. Some of these photographs show the camaraderie of women new to the workplace. Others explore the drudgery of sacrifice for the war and the difficulties of children forced to grow up too fast because their fathers were off to war and their mothers were off to work. Still others, such as Dorothea Lange's Japanese relocation photographs, expose prejudices that undercut the solid front that war propagandists tried to promote.

The Library of Congress Prints and Photographs Division has identified work in its collections by more than a dozen women who documented World War II, both at home, in the United States, and abroad.[4] Born between 1895 and 1921, their peak producing years were during the Great Depression and the end of World War II. Most were daughters of successful professional men, but a few struggled to escape their parents' poverty. Because there was no "old girls network," they relied on men for job connections. In the mid-1930s, photo-magazines such as *Life* (launched in 1936) and *Look* (launched in 1937) fed the public appetite for visual information and provided further opportunities for photographers.

Journalists shot mostly with black-and-white film, which they developed and printed themselves, but when Kodachrome was introduced in the late 1930s, they experimented with colour photography. Photographers had several cameras from which to choose: the Rolleiflex (5.7 cm x 5.7 cm film), the Speed Graphic (10.2 cm x 12.7 cm film) and the "miniature" (35 mm film) camera that was introduced in a standardized form in 1932. Like their men colleagues in the photojournalism world, these women were more interested in the news and informational content of their photographs than artistic considerations, but the women seem to have given more attention to the humanitarian or emotional aspects of war or the lives of those who remained at home.

WOMEN PHOTOJOURNALISTS DOCUMENTING WORLD WAR II ABROAD

Women photojournalists who went abroad, working formally or informally as photographers during the war, whose materials are archived in the Library of Congress, include Thérèse Bonney, Margaret Bourke-White, Mary Marvin Breckinridge, Toni Frissell, and Clare Boothe Luce. By outlining the activities of these women who made their way to the war zones of the European front, I hope to show that women made a significant contribution to the representation of the war. At the time, during the war years in the United States, their work was recognized and valorized. Very quickly, however, they and their contributions were (with the exception of Bourke-White) largely forgotten. What follows, then, is a reintroduction to some of the American women photojournalists of World War II.[5]

In general, these women were well educated. Most attended girls' schools. They came from wealthy families or were sufficiently upwardly mobile that they moved in elite circles as adults. They were comfortable exercising authority, physically active, and ambitious. They were not eldest children, but they were singled out for special attention in their families. They were intellectually, socially, and culturally curious, but none appeared to have shown a marked concern for social justice or ameliorating the lot of the less fortunate.

Thérèse Bonney (1894–1978) was born in New York. She obtained a B.A. at Berkeley, an M.A. at Harvard, and a Ph.D. at the Sorbonne. She settled in Paris in 1919 to pursue photography and promote cultural exchange between France and the United States, and volunteered for the Red Cross in Paris. As Parisians were forced to sell their family heirlooms to survive after World War I, Bonney and her sister published photographs of the objects in shopping guides for wealthy Americans during the 1920s.[6] The outbreak of World War II appalled her, as she feared the conflict threatened European civilization itself. Of her "truth raids" into the countryside to document the horror of war, Bonney said, "I go forth alone, try to get the truth and then bring it back and try to make others face it and do something about it" ("Thérèse Bonney").

Bonney is not known to have photographed for a specific organization (there are rumours that she was a spy for the United States), but her images did aim to bring assistance to children and adults made homeless by the war, and her exhibitions showing their plight raised funds that kept entire villages alive in France. She published picture stories in prestigious magazines for women, and she produced the photo-essay books *War Comes to the People* (1940) and *Europe's Children* (1943). She mounted one-woman shows at the Library of Congress, the Museum of Modern Art, and dozens of museums overseas. Bonney was the heroine of a wartime comic book, *Photo-Fighter* (Figure 7.2).

Bonney's concept for a film about children displaced by war became the Academy Award-winning movie *The Search* (1948), and attracted funding for the United Nations Relief and Rehabilitation Administration (UNRRA) that helped to reunite scattered family members and relocate those displaced by the war. That she is so little known today is an indication of how quickly even widely influential women photojournalists can be forgotten.

Margaret Bourke-White (1904–1971) is the best known of this group. A skilful independent photographer, she successfully commanded attention. As a child, Bourke-White accompanied her father, an engineer, photographing factories where he worked. Later, her photographs of machinery in an era enthralled

Figure 7.2   *Photo-Fighter*, July 1944. "Three-page comic strip about Thérèse Bonney as a photojournalist in Europe during the Second World War." *True Comics* 4 (37): unpaged. Chicago, IL: Parents' Institute, Library of Congress.

by industry and mass production evoked these early experiences. She studied photography at Columbia University with Clarence White, who opened the first art photography college program in the United States. Bourke-White revolutionized US magazine photography with her use of European modernist techniques of shooting up, or down, at stark angles. In 1936, Henry Luce hired her as his first woman staff photojournalist on his newly founded *Life* magazine, which she helped to make sensational with her photograph of the Fort Peck Dam on the initial cover. Bourke-White made beautiful images of equipment, machines, and engineering feats, and, like the Farm Security Administration (FSA) photographers, she put a human face on the social woes of the country.

Bourke-White was a woman of many "firsts"—she was the first photographer for *Fortune* magazine, the first Western professional photographer allowed into the Soviet Union, *Life* magazine's first woman photographer, and the first woman war correspondent permitted by the United States to work in European combat zones during World War II, among many other accomplishments. Her photographs of World War II "gave Americans an unprecedented view of the global conflict and the human suffering the war created" (Cox 2003). She was among the first photographers to enter the Nazi death camps with American soldiers, and her images of those scenes shocked the world.

Mary Marvin Breckinridge (later Patterson) (1905–2002) was the daughter of a diplomat and an heiress. In 1929, at age twenty-four, she became the first licensed woman pilot in Maine. After Vassar, she attended the Clarence H. White School of Photography and began her career with *The Forgotten Frontier*, a 1931 documentary film about the Frontier Nursing Service, which was operated in her native Kentucky by her cousin, Mary Breckinridge. In 1933, she published photographs of her trip to Africa in newspapers. She provided travel photographs to top-flight magazines until World War II broke out in 1939 while she was in London. In the basement of her hotel, Breckinridge made the first pictures of a London air-raid shelter and later photographed civil defence activities in England. Her images showing the English "stiff upper lip" helped garner support in the United States for intervention in the war. Breckinridge's friend Edward R. Murrow hired her as the first woman staff broadcaster in Europe for CBS, even though she was new to radio. One of only a handful of American women in Europe working in radio, Breckinridge was among the first correspondents to use a new shortwave transmitter to broadcast on location. She was generally assigned apolitical stories about lifestyle and culture because she was a woman, but she found clever ways and idiomatic expressions to slip in observations that censors failed to recognize.

Breckinridge established such credibility for her radio commentary that, in February 1940, she was called in as a neutral party to document a disputed incident at sea. Her photographs established German aggression against a Norwegian ship. When she married Jefferson Patterson in May 1940, Breckinridge willingly resigned from CBS radio and counted on resuming her original career in photojournalism. She accompanied her diplomat husband as he inspected prisoner-of-war camps, but the Germans soon forbade her to bring her cameras because they realized the potential effectiveness of her photographs. Claiming that her activities would compromise her husband's work in Berlin, the US Department of State barred her from publication. Frustrated in her efforts to pursue a separate career, Breckinridge gave up both photography and broadcasting to devote her energies to the role of diplomatic spouse.

Toni Frissell (1907–1988) was a New York socialite and political conservative. She graduated from Miss Porter's School for Girls. After the deaths of her two brothers and her mother, she was highly motivated to find a purpose for her life, which she did initially by pursuing fashion photography. She had

Figure 7.3 "Abandoned boy holding a stuffed toy animal amid ruins following German aerial bombing of London." Photograph by Toni Frissell, January 1945 (film negative). Toni Frissell Collection, Prints and Photographs Division, Library of Congress.

an athletic build, tomboy sensibilities, fashion sense, a flair for drama, and the social connections that enabled her to pursue fashion photography outdoors. In 1935, Frissell began making candid outdoor photographs for *Vogue* and *Town and Country* magazines showing her socialite friends wearing sports clothes. In contrast to the formal indoor photography that had previously dominated the pages of those magazines, her photographs reflected a change of lifestyle and modern sense of femininity. Her photographs helped spread the East Coast elite ideals and promote the sportswear of American designers that advanced the switch from European couture to American mass-produced clothing and desire for the accompanying lifestyle. For about five years, Frissell fought to maintain her place in the publishing hierarchy, but by 1940 she struggled to get beyond fashion photography. She crossed racial boundaries to photograph black infants being cared for by white nurses from the Red Cross. She defied gender barriers to photograph members of the Women's Army Corps in the face of smear campaigns that questioned the respectability of women who joined the military. Frissell overcame her own strong Republican preferences and parlayed her assignments into an invitation to photograph Democratic First Lady

Figure 7.4 "Black fighter pilot series: 'Escape kits' (cyanide) being distributed to fighter pilots at air base in southern Italy," 1945. Photograph by Toni Frissell (gelatin silver photographic print). Toni Frissell Collection, Prints and Photographs Division, Library of Congress.

Eleanor Roosevelt on a Red Cross goodwill tour of England. Her photographs of Londoners under bombardment helped solidify US alliances with the English (Figure 7.3).

Frissell paid personal costs for her daring. She went to England just before Christmas in November 1942. Her daughter, who was only seven years old at the time, later remembered that her father had been furious. But it was his mother who had stood up for Frissell. Frissell's mother-in-law had had a darkroom in the attic of the house she lived in as a young woman in Paris, and she supported Frissell's career.[7]

In 1945, Frissell returned to Europe, where she photographed American pilots holding a Christmas party for Jewish orphans being hidden by nuns in a convent, and exhausted soldiers sleeping in bombed-out churches in France. She was the only professional photographer to make photographs in combat situations of the racially segregated Tuskegee airmen (Figure 7.4). Although Frissell's photographs show that she wanted to be a straight photojournalist, she never violated the etiquette of her social class. On a visit to the Library of Congress to select images for her final photography book, Jacqueline Kennedy Onassis said of her, "She knew just how far to push the envelope."[8]

Clare Boothe Luce (1903–1987) was born an illegitimate child "in an impoverished household with an absentee father until her mother married comfortably when Clare was an adolescent" (Shadegg 1970, 7). She completed her education at a private girls' school and travelled abroad, where she became interested in woman's suffrage in about 1919. After a marriage to a millionaire failed, she was well off financially and began a career in magazine journalism. In 1935, she married magazine magnate Henry R. Luce of *Time, Life*, and *Fortune*. With the help of her husband and her mentor, Bernard Baruch, she travelled to Europe for four months. Based on interviews she conducted during that trip, she wrote the book *Europe in the Spring* (1940) and many on-location articles for *Life*. The best-remembered line from her book is that war will come to "a world where men have decided to die together because they are unable to find a way to live together" (Boothe 1940, 18–19).

Boothe Luce covered a variety of World War II battlefronts and endured the discomforts, frustrations, and dangers encountered by war correspondents. Besides bombing raids in Europe and the Far East, she faced house arrest in Trinidad by British Customs when a draft *Life* article about poor military preparedness in Libya proved too accurate for Allied comfort. Boothe Luce's unsettling observations led her long-time friend Winston Churchill to revamp Middle Eastern military policy. In 1941 and 1942, she reported on Asia, Africa, and Europe. In Burma, she made photographs in the China-Burma-India Theater. Her photographs, though few in number, buttress her written work about the lack of well-thought-through plans for war. Her wartime journalism and photojournalism, which circulated widely in *Life*, gave an unsanitized version of events on the ground and on the diplomatic scene.

WOMEN PHOTOJOURNALISTS DOCUMENTING WORLD WAR II ON THE HOME FRONT

Another group of women photographers of World War II whose principle production was for projects at home (mainly for the Farm Security Administration) includes Esther Bubley, Marjory Collins, Dorothea Lange, Louise Rosskam, and Marion Post Wolcott. These women photojournalists came from more modest means. Except for Esther Bubley, daughter of an immigrant family, they were born to upper-middle-class families who had lost their money. They may have enjoyed a sense of entitlement or possibility, and were certainly ambitious, but all had to struggle with economic hardships and discouragement to become photojournalists. Early in life, they were concerned with the well-being of the less fortunate.

Esther Bubley (1921–1998) was a first-generation immigrant, the daughter of a miner-turned-shopkeeper. Rejected by every photo business in St. Paul,

Minnesota, she found a job as a microfilm and darkroom technician at the National Archives in Washington, DC, and then worked as a photographer for the Farm Security Administration/Office of War Information (FSA/OWI) and Standard Oil of New Jersey (SONJ). Hoping to impress FSA project director Roy Stryker, Bubley photographed wartime subjects in the nation's capital during her off-hours between January and September 1943. Beginning with her sisters as models, she documented the lives of women who filled the many support jobs the war required. Most women lived at home until marriage, but Bubley's World War II imagery portrayed women outside the family circle. Film scholar Paula Rabinowitz credits Bubley's photographs of women away from home as an important prototype for the film noir movie genre that flourished during the 1940s and '50s.[9] Rabinowitz devotes the chapter "Already Framed: Esther Bubley Invents Noir" to analyzing Bubley's depiction of the malaise, and even rage, that women felt once war work cut them loose from traditional home-bound responsibilities without providing any socially acceptable alternative. A kosher boarding house owned and operated by Anne and Adolph Dissin in the 1940s, where Bubley photographed, supplied a place of transition for these women.[10]

Marjory Collins (1912–1985) photographed for the Office of War Information from 1941 to 1943. In her unpublished autobiography, she wrote that her family lost its money with the stock market crash of 1929. Her mother wanted to continue socializing as before, and though Collins spent the Depression trying to fulfill her upper-class-society matron role, she rebelled in order to find out what the "real" America was like. She worked for various magazines, including the left-wing publication *PM*. Collins's World War II photographs include those presented in a 1941 article in *U.S. Camera* called "Hoboken: The Photographers' Forbidden Paradise" about the government ban on picture making there that had been in place since World War I.[11]

Through the influence of Edward Stanley (then head of the Pictures and Publications Division of the Foreign Information Service), Roy Stryker soon hired Collins to produce propaganda for the Office of War Information. Her photographs of immigrant Americans in New York City were used in leaflets to be dropped behind enemy lines in Europe. Collins's *Rosie the Riveter* series included women who did not match the cultural ideal of beauty. Her sad images of children left for long days at daycare centres, at a time when most mothers stayed home with their children, evoked feelings of guilt and sacrifice. Without her photographs, we would not know nearly as much about how extensively the country supported the war effort.

Andrea Fisher and John Tagg write about a big change that took place in the country, and we see the evidence in the photographs produced by the FSA/OWI. Where early images showed a cohesive country focused on surviving the hard times, later images reveal a more contemplative, divided atmosphere.[12]

Figure 7.5 "San Francisco, Calif., April 1942—Children of the Weill public school, from the so-called international settlement, shown in a flag pledge ceremony. Some of them are evacuees of Japanese ancestry who will be housed in War relocation authority centers for the duration." Photograph by Dorothea Lange (gelatin silver photographic print). Farm Security/Office of War Information Collection, Library of Congress.

While men photographers during the OWI period rarely depicted deprivation, the women did—Dorothea Lange and Marjory Collins among them.

Dorothea Lange's (1895–1965) father was a lawyer, and initially the family lived an upper-middle-class lifestyle. From the age of seven, Lange suffered from a leg withered by polio, and after age twelve she dealt with the social disgrace of her parents' separation and divorce. She took up photography as a teenager, and later used portrait photography to support herself, her husband, and her children. The events of the Great Depression riveted her, and she spent three years employed by Stryker documenting the effects of the economic crash and the concurrent drought. She photographed the migration of dust-bowl farmers on the move to the West, where they hoped to find new homesteads but instead found themselves vying with earlier migrants and with each other for work as stoop labourers. In the course of this work, Lange produced probably the most famous documentary image the world has ever known—"Migrant Mother." In 1938, she lost her job because Stryker reportedly found her too independent.

Lange's World War II photographs for the Office of War Information documented changes on the home front. Located on the West Coast, she was especially aware of the relocation of Japanese Americans to concentration camps. In spring 1942, she photographed Japanese neighbourhoods for the War Relocation Authority. Lange showed the Japanese selling their homes and businesses at near giveaway prices as they prepared for internment. She showed their peaceable movement, and how they made the best of it in horse stables, where they were housed for the duration of the war.

Lange was unprepared for how strongly she would react to the racial and civil rights issues posed by the internment. She vigorously opposed the program and her employers, and her resulting photographs took a strong but silent stand against internment. In the eyes of historians Linda Gordon and Gary Okihiro, Lange's images "unequivocally denounce an unjustified, unnecessary, and racist policy. [Her] critique is especially impressive given the political mood of the time—early 1942, just after Japan bombed Pearl Harbor. Hysterical fears of further Japanese attacks on the West Coast of the United States combined with a century of racism against east Asians to create a situation in which [almost no "whites"] spoke publicly against sending Japanese Americans to concentration camps" (2006, 6).

Despite her anger about the incarceration of US citizens, she offered no images of Japanese-American resistance (Gordon and Okihiro 2006, 36). Nonetheless, the agency "impounded" her photographs for the duration of World War II (5). They were not seen in any number until 1972, when twenty-seven of the photographs were included in a thirtieth-anniversary exhibition at the Whitney Museum about the Japanese internment titled *Executive Order 9066*. *New York Times* critic A.D. Coleman calls Lange's photographs "documents of such a high order that they convey the feelings of the victims as well as the facts of the crime" (1972).

Another project to honour those who contributed to the war effort includes images of defence industry workers that Lange created alongside her friend Hansel Mieth, who was working for *Life* magazine. As one of the few who photographed Mexican migrant workers in California agriculture during the Depression, Lange photographed workers in California who had been rounded up and sent home. In 1943, she provided rare photographs of Mexican workers in the initial stages of the Bracero Program, during which the federal government permitted temporary migration for workers in American industry in World War II. These photographs were almost unknown when they were included in the exhibition *Women Come to the Front*.

Louise Rosskam (1910–2003) was born to an upper-middle-class family in Philadelphia that lost its immigrant savings bank and all of its money in the stock market crash of 1929. Rosskam came onto the photography scene in times everyone recognized to be eventful—FDR brought excitement to a nation burdened with financial woes, and Margaret Bourke-White was revolutionizing US photography. She married Edwin Rosskam, and together they photographed for a newspaper in Philadelphia, went to Puerto Rico to try out for *Life* magazine, and worked for the FSA. As a freelance photographer, Louise Rosskam donated to the FSA files photographs of women and children in the continental United States during the Great Depression, and of Victory Gardens early in World War II. FSA head Stryker saw Louise and Edwin as good photography partners, and hired them for his SONJ photography project telling the story of US oil production for war use. They worked on that together from 1942 through 1945. Rosskam received little acknowledgement until late in her life because of her belief that team and project affiliation were more important than receiving individual recognition, which resulted in much of her work being presented as her husband's work.

Marion Post Wolcott (1910–1990) lived in a solidly middle-class home until her parents divorced. Subsequently, she attended boarding school and, on weekends, lived in genteel poverty in bohemian Greenwich Village in New York City with her mother. When she attended college in Austria, she found the rise of Nazism terrifying, and she risked her life teaching in preschools for children of Jewish workers before terms of her father's will forced her to return to the United States. She continued learning photography with Ralph Steiner, Paul Strand, and the Photo League, and, after a stint as a newspaper photographer, gladly accepted Ed Stanley's help and art photographer Paul Strand's recommendation to become an FSA photographer. During the Depression, Post Wolcott covered thousands of kilometres in the hardest-hit areas of the American farmland. Her trailblazing mother had travelled by car throughout the United States dispensing birth control information and devices since the 1920s, so, for Post Wolcott, travel in the American south for the FSA was almost easy by comparison. She used her good looks and friendly manner to her advantage, and her social contacts gained her access to off-limits locations such as juke joints. As war talk turned from threats to action in Europe in 1939, Post Wolcott became more concerned about staying in touch with family and friends, and apprehensive about being on the road. In 1940 and 1941, she voiced disappointment with one-size-fits-all FSA projects that were implemented even though they failed to address local needs. To counter Nazi propaganda about the weakness of Depression-era America, she made photographs to show the abundance of farm produce in North Carolina and Virginia, and was happy when Stryker released her from the busy southeastern region and gave her a fresh start in Colorado, Montana, Nebraska, and Wyoming. With the demands of life brought by marriage and children, Post Wolcott left photography as a profession in 1941, and although she often considered resuming professional photography, she never did. Only near the end of her life did she begin to receive recognition for forging a new path for women photojournalists.

At present, in my capacity as curator at the Library of Congress, I am gathering materials on these women and many others. Aiming to make this rich storehouse of materials available to scholars and to the public, I am building a website that adheres to the rigorous protocols of archival development, yet brings light to the long-hidden and forgotten achievements of women. As I work on this website, I feel very much the pioneer. We are still at the discovery stage when it comes to women's photographs of World War II—still learning their names, verifying attributions, and creating contexts for them through dogged research in databases and traditional textual documents, oral histories, and films. There is no unified history of women photojournalists, and this history is difficult to reconstruct because there is no single list of practitioners or unified archive dedicated to them. The recovery of the history of women photojournalists is the recovery of the history of gender discrimination in this field. Women were not hired as staff photographers. They worked freelance, pounding the pavement for each assignment. Furthermore, relatively few collections of personal papers of women photographers have been collected or catalogued at research institutions. It is late to develop archives for women of World War II unless the photographers' families are ready to share photographs they have held on to along with contemporary publications where the pictures appeared.

Additionally, women's work has often gone uncredited, been attributed to others, or been subsumed into larger projects. In some cases, collections of the photographs and papers of the women in this exhibit have been gathered in institutions, but they have not always been studied. In the mid-1990s, when I initiated work on *Women Come to the Front*, one researcher told me that her request for grant funding had been denied because she had not examined the papers of photojournalist Thérèse Bonney, and her request for access to those papers had been denied because she did not have the endorsement of a grant review board. Feminist scholars often face this kind of Catch-22 thinking as they attempt to recover little-known women's work. Fortunately, her request and mine, and possibly others, resulted in that collection being organized for public use.

Using gender as a category to distinguish photojournalists is one way to provide finite dimensions to the study of photojournalism, which as a whole is an under-examined area of scholarship. To establish photojournalism as a field of legitimate inquiry, its dimensions must be defined. Using women as a focal point gives added clarity, use, and human boundaries to this field. Photojournalism has traditionally come into research institutions as photo morgues that cover general topics and are often overwhelming in their vast undifferentiated volume. The library's Bain News Service, 1900–1930; *New York World Telegram and Sun,* 1920–1967; and *Look* magazine, 1951–1971 collections, fall into this category. Several specialized photo news resources focus on topics. Examples of these collections are the National Child Labor Committee photos by Lewis Hine, 1908–1924, and photos from the Farm Security Administration/Office of War Information (FSA/OWI), 1935–1945. The library formerly collected entire archives of photographers, but the volume of material required making selections from modern photographers' output. Entire archives of selected leading photojournalists include Frances Benjamin Johnston, active 1890s–1940s, and Toni Frissell, active 1930s–1970. The library now collects representative prints by leading contemporary independent photojournalists such as Susan Meiselas and Brenda Ann Kenneally. Occasionally the library is able to represent international photojournalism by women such as Regina Monfort and Farzana Wahidy. The library has acquired new images by women photojournalists when it has gathered photographs for targeted areas, such as the 9/11 terrorist attacks of 2001 and Hurricane Katrina, 2005–2006.

A final source of information about images of great public concern is the Internet, which has revolutionized the study of lesser-known women photographers through Google, and through genealogy, subscription, and newspaper databases. For many years, it was nearly impossible to identify women who contributed to the photography of World War II, or to learn anything more than their names. The Internet has made it easier for archivists and scholars to track down the photographers' relatives and neighbours, and, in turn, for them to respond to inquiries about the photographers.

It is encouraging that the work of women photojournalists is now included in academic publications, and that the stories of women's experiences from all over the world during World War II are being rediscovered. As the work of women photojournalists becomes better known and their histories are documented in the written record, I hope that women entering this field will feel that their work is part of a continuum of recording news. It is my hope that the brief sketches I have made here of individual women will spark the interest of scholars and raise new questions for new generations of pioneers. Perhaps photographers, and the historians and archivists who study their work, will sense the strength of their predecessors and enthusiastically join the ranks of perpetual pioneers who create and renew women's experience.

NOTES

1   The Library of Congress definition of photojournalism, which comes from the Art & Architecture Thesaurus Online, is "The practice of using photographs as a journalistic device; especially serial photographic documentation of significant events intended for publication in magazines and newspapers."

2   In fact, the history of photojournalism is all too brief. Michael Carlebach's two volumes, *The Origins of Photojournalism in America* (1992) and *American Photojournalism Comes of Age* (Washington: Smithsonian Institution Press, 1997) are only a beginning.

3   http://www.loc.gov/exhibits/wcf/.

4   They are listed here: http://www.loc.gov/rr/print/coll/596_womphotoj.html.

5   For discussion of non-American women photojournalists, see *Photographs, Histories, and Meanings* (Kadar, Perreault, and Worley, eds., 2009).

6   See Lisa Schlansker Kolosek's *The Invention of Chic: Thérèse Bonney and Paris Moderne*, 2002.

7   Sidney Bacon Stafford in conversation with Beverly W. Brannan, St. James, New York, 16 March 2010.

8   Jacqueline Kennedy Onassis to Beverly W. Brannan, personal conversation, Prints and Photographs Division, Library of Congress, November 1992. Frissell was the photographer for the wedding of Jaqueline Bouvier and John Kennedy in 1953.

9   Paula Rabinowitz, *Black & White & Noir: America's Pulp Modernism* (New York: Columbia University Press, 2002).

10   Jean Bubley, email correspondence with the author, 4 October 2011.

11   See Marjory Collins and Wilfrid Zogbaum. "Hoboken: The Photographers' Forbidden Paradise," *U.S. Camera* 4 (2) (August 1941): 39–54.

12   See Andrea Fisher, *Let Us Now Praise Famous Women: Women Photographers for the U.S. Government, 1935–1944* (New York: Pandora, 1987); John Tagg, *The Disciplinary Frame: Photographic Truths and the Capture of Meaning* (Minneapolis: University of Minnesota Press, 2009).

WORKS CITED

Boothe, Clare. 1940. *Europe in the Spring*. New York: Knopf.

Brannan, Beverly, and Kathy Ann Brown. n.d. *Women Come to the Front*. Library of Congress Exhibition. Library of Congress, http://www.loc.gov/exhibits/wcf.

Coleman, A.D. 24 September 1972. "A Dark Day in History." *New York Times*, D19.

Cox, Patrick. 2003. "Margaret Bourke-White: History Making Photojournalist and Social Activist." *The Digital Journalist* 03 (01), http://digitaljournalist.org.

Frissell, Toni. 1945. *[Black fighter pilot series: "Escape kits" (cyanide) being distributed to fighter pilots at air base in southern Italy, 1945]*. Photograph. Toni Frissell Collection, Prints and Photographs Division, Library of Congress, Washington, DC.

———. 1945. *[Abandoned boy holding a stuffed toy animal amid ruins following German aerial bombing of London]*. Photograph. Toni Frissell Collection, Prints and Photographs Division, Library of Congress, Washington, DC.

Gordon, Linda. 2009. *Dorothea Lange: A Life Beyond Limits*. New York: W.W. Norton.

Gordon, Linda, and Gary Y. Okihiro, eds. 2006. *Impounded: Dorothea Lange and the Censored Images of Japanese American Internement*. New York: W.W. Norton.

Kadar, Marlene, Jeanne Perreault, and Linda Worley, eds. 2009. *Photographs, Histories, and Meanings*. New York: Palgrave Macmillan.

Kolosek, Lisa Schlansker. 2002. *The Invention of Chic: Thérèse Bonney and Paris Moderne*. London: Thames and Hudson.

Lange, Dorothea. April 1942. *San Francisco, Calif., April 1942—Children of the Weill public school, from the so-called international settlement, shown in a flag pledge ceremony. Some of them are evacuees of Japanese ancestry who will be housed in War relocation authority centers for the duration*. Photograph. Farm Security/Office of War Information collection, Library of Congress, Washington, DC.

Rosener, Ann. June 1942. *Why greases must be saved. A soldier of the home front—and there's one in every American kitchen—saves all waste fats and greases so that they can be processed into ammunition for America's soldiers on the battlefronts. Pan and broiler drippings, deep fats, renderings from bacon rinds, these are some of the fats which should be put through a strainer to remove meat scraps and other solids, and poured into wide-mouthed cans such as coffee or fat cans.* Photograph. Farm Security/Office of War Information collection, Library of Congress, Washington, DC.

Shadegg, Stephen. 1970. *Clare Boothe Luce: A Biography.* New York: Simon and Schuster.

"Thérèse Bonney." *Women Come to the Front.* Library of Congress Exhibition. Library of Congress, http://www.loc.gov/exhibits/wcf/wcf0007.html.

True Comics Photo-Fighter. 1944. *True Comics,* 4 (37): unpaged. Chicago, IL: Parents' Institute. Library of Congress, Washington, DC.

WORKS CONSULTED

Arnold, Rebecca. 2009. *The American Look: Fashion, Sportswear and the Image of Women in 1930s and 1940s New York.* New York: I.B. Tauris.

Bonney, Thérèse. 8 December 1940. "How Peace Came to Finland." Photogravure Section, *Washington Post.*

———. 1944a. *Europe's Children, 1939–1943.* New York: Rhode Publishing.

———. 1944b. *War Comes to the People.* London: Pendock Press.

Brannan, Beverly. 2007. "Women Photojournalists." Library of Congress, http://www.loc .gov/rr/print/coll/596_womphotoj.html.

Bromley, Dorothy Dunbar. 28 February 1943. "Thérèse Bonney Brings Back Pictoral Record of Europe's Tragic Children." *New York Herald Tribune,* V3.

Carlebach, Michael L. 1992. *The Origins of Photojournalism in America.* Washington: Smithsonian Institution Press.

———. 1997. *American Photojournalism Comes of Age.* Washington: Smithsonian Institution Press.

Collins, Marjory, and Wilfrid Zogbaum. 1941. "Hoboken: The Photographer's Forbidden Paradise." *U.S. Camera* 4 (2): 39–54.

Fisher, Andrea. 1987. *Let Us Now Praise Famous Women: Women Photographers for the U.S. Government, 1935–1944: Esther Bubley, Marjory Collins, Pauline Ehrlich, Dorothea Lange, Martha McMillan Roberts, Marion Post Wolcott, Ann Rosener, Louise Rosskam.* New York: Pandora Press.

Rabinowitz, Paula. 2002. *Black & White & Noir: America's Pulp Modernism.* New York: Columbia University Press.

Tagg, John. 2009. *The Disciplinary Frame: Photographic Truths and the Capture of Meaning.* Minneapolis: University of Minnesota Press.

"GIRL TAKES DRASTIC STEP"
Molly Lamb Bobak's *W110278—The Diary of a CWAC*

Tanya Schaap

The army from the inside as only a girl could see it.... If she had half a chance she could go places.
—A.Y. Jackson on Molly Lamb Bobak's *W110278—The Diary of a CWAC*

From first-hand authorities comes the story of this successful girl who left Hamilton Trades School as a nobody and arrived back still a nobody, but at least a nobody with a "little hour."
—Molly Lamb Bobak, *W110278—The Diary of a CWAC*

In 1942, at the age of twenty, Canadian artist Molly Lamb Bobak enlisted in the Canadian Women's Army Corps (CWAC), becoming the first government-accredited woman war artist to be sent overseas to document the Canadian war effort.[1] Born in 1922 in Vancouver, British Columbia, Bobak is considered, by many standards, a successful Canadian painter: she has received multiple awards, has enjoyed numerous national gallery showings, boasts membership with the Royal Canadian Academy of Arts, and has received funding over the years from the Canada Council for the Arts. One important aspect of her work, however, has gone largely unrecognized: her illustrated war diary. From November 1942 to June 1945, Bobak, known as Private Molly Lamb at the time, wrote and illustrated *W110278—The Diary of a CWAC*, which documents her experiences as a new recruit at various CWAC training camps across Canada. Although Bobak may call her text a diary, she creates something decidedly atypical.

W110278—The Diary of a CWAC (hereafter referred to as *W110278*, Bobak's military service number) assumes the form of a mock newspaper, comprised of 147 pages measuring 45.6 cm x 30.5 cm, incorporating a variety of media such as pencil, watercolour, charcoal, pen, and coloured ink.[2] Stylistically, *W110278* mimics a daily broadsheet, the large newspaper format used by the more respectable newspapers at the time (distinguishing it from the daily tabloids), with eye-catching headlines, handwritten accounts, letters to the editor, special features, interviews, sketches, and detailed drawings. In the persona of diarist, Bobak adopts the tone of a reporter, and even at times assumes the voice of the newspaper editor. Her principal *newsworthy* subject is the naive, often hysterical, yet unabashedly ambitious Private Lamb. Whimsical, humorous, imaginative, hyperbolic, and notably satirical, *W110278* does not attempt to reproduce conventional ideas of diary entries. Rather, it differs dramatically from traditional diaries in style, form, and content, raising questions as to the way we can and should expand our generic considerations of life writing. Configured as a mock newspaper, Bobak's war diary chronicles a distinct moment in Canadian women's history in which Canadian servicewomen assumed a significant role in the war effort. Through parody and caricature, Bobak's diary calls attention to the ways the media and the Canadian military often (mis)represented Canadian servicewomen, thus protecting the patriarchal gender ideologies of the time.

Recognizing the atypical style of *W110278*, Terresa McIntosh, art archivist for the National Archives of Canada, explains, "Unlike those kept by Bobak's fellow war artists Charles Comfort and Campbell Tinning, [Bobak's diary] does not rely merely upon the written word for the expression of thoughts.... The diary succeeds in preserving a real feeling for the daily events of the period, while at the same time tickling the reader's funny-bone with amusing personal anecdotes and visual puns" (1992, 9). While *W110278* does indeed offer a unique glimpse into the daily experiences of young women recruits in Canada during World War II—and to that some attention is due—it also functions as an outlet through which Bobak can freely (albeit discreetly) express her innate desire for a revisionary consideration of women as represented by the military and the media. Using humour, caricature, and parody as a kind of stylistic scaffolding, Bobak is able to subtly challenge dominant ideologies of the 1940s, so that her diary operates as a form of resistance, or disruption, to the public image of women in the Canadian military. While *W110278* does convey a vivid picture of daily life during training camp, this depiction is cast in a form that effectively parodies the image of women recruits as disseminated by both the military and the media. Rather than simply recording her experiences at training camp in a traditional journal, Bobak imaginatively inserts herself into the daily news. By recreating that news, Bobak validates her experience as newsworthy, authenticates her role in the war, and effectively contests the conventional notions of what a woman soldier looks like. As both a private record of personal experience and a subtle social commentary on established gender assumptions of the 1930s and 1940s, *W110278* deserves in-depth consideration since it illuminates, in satirical style, one woman's desire to find her place, and her face, in the news.

Before I examine Bobak's war diary, it is worth reflecting for a moment on her principal artistic interests, which are evident in the war art she produced in 1945 and 1946. I argue that these interests, surely present in the years leading up to her overseas appointment, inform her war diary and her choice to represent her experience in mock newspaper style. As an aspiring young artist, Bobak attended the Vancouver School of Art from 1938 to 1941, and after graduation joined the services of the CWAC in November 1942.[3] After three years of travelling back and forth to various training camps across Canada (during which time she wrote and produced her war diary), and with persistent self-determination, Bobak was finally appointed in 1945 to overseas duty as one of thirty-three government-designated war artists, the only woman to ever serve in this capacity. In a 1977 interview with curator Ian G. Lumsden in New Brunswick, Bobak recalls her ambitious wartime spirit: "At that time, I was pestering to be a war artist so often. I used to go to Ottawa and beg to be one and I'd do all kinds of things to get appointed" (quoted in Lumsden 1977, 9).[4] Artists were commissioned during World War II by the Canadian War Records Office with the understanding that "works of art would have a longer life span and would lend themselves to the visual reconstruction of important military events that had not previously been captured on film" (Foss 1993, 93). Bobak's official appointment came in June 1945, after Nazi surrender and peace in Europe was confirmed. Waiting until the war was over assured Canadian military officials that Bobak, as a woman artist, would avoid all combat situations. The delay in commissioning Bobak until the war was over reveals the Canadian military gender bias at the time. Bobak was given membership in the "boys club," but she remained, above all else, a woman. Art historian Brian Foss tells us, "In June 1943 ... Colonel A.F. Duguid, Director of Army Historical Section and the army's representative on the Committee, argued that 'from the Army's point of view [women's] appointment was not desirable as the artists were at the scene of combat'" (1993, 100). Only after peace was assured did government officials feel comfortable enough to send women like Bobak into Europe.

In her 1978 memoir, *Wild Flowers of Canada: Impressions and Sketches of a Field Artist*, Bobak considers her friend the Group of Seven artist A.Y. Jackson, whom she affectionately calls "Uncle Alex," a key supporter of her artistic aspirations: "When I had settled in the CWAC barracks at St. Clair and Avenue Road, I wrote to A.Y. Jackson and asked if I could visit him at his studio and show him my illustrated war diary.... We loved each other right from the first meeting" (44). As art historians Dean F. Oliver and Laura Brandon explain, Jackson, a painter for Canada during World War I, was influential in the push towards a government-sanctioned war art program: "Artists such as A.Y. Jackson ... were also lobbying for a war art program. Another domestic catalyst was a growing public awareness that artists had a role to play in society; if war was an important expression of society, then they should record it" (2000, 162). We know from her memoir that Bobak showed her war diary to Jackson.[5] She considers her friendship with him, his keen and favourable interest in her work, and his influence over government-commissioned art programs as important factors that effectively jump-started her official career as an artist. She also, however, acknowledges her own ambitious spirit. In her memoir, she writes, "I wanted very much to be a war artist, too, instead of going to drafting school, but there wasn't much chance then, although much later, when I did become one, I'm sure Jackson had something to do with it. I had something to do with it too, of course, I never stopped drawing. The CWACs in the bathroom, or the dining hall, or on parade, or something" (Bobak 1978, 45).

As the only woman among the thirty-three individuals that were given a posting as an official war artist, Bobak offers a unique perspective of Canada's role in the war. Rather than concentrate on postwar violence and destruction, which occupied the attention of many of her male counterparts, Bobak chose to paint Canadian servicewomen actively engaged in their jobs. For the most part, her paintings depict women in groups working in many of the military positions deemed acceptable for women soldiers: typists, drivers, seamstresses, launderers, dishwashers, and clerks. In addition, Bobak depicts groups of Canadian servicewomen conducting drills, congregating on streets, waiting at train stations, marching in parades, and lingering in local parks, stores, and canteens. Some of these women are painted faceless, some with their backs turned, others wearing gas masks. In the Lumsden interview, Bobak is questioned about the focus of her overseas war art:

> Lumsden: You have focused upon the human element in the war effort away from the battlefront as opposed to the actual machinery of war. Was this focus of your own choosing or did the government decide that perhaps it would be more appropriate for you to portray the contribution of the Women's Army Corps to the war inasmuch as you were the only female artist?

> Bobak: Well, that's true. They didn't lay down any laws but the women weren't near the battle ever. So I think that I really had, when you think of it, a terribly free hand.... The women were mostly behind the lines in Europe and the war was over anyway and so I would do things like—if I saw Amsterdam ... I would just put a few little C.W.A.C.s in the street and paint the city and that was valid. The C.W.A.C.s were there, it was part of the atmosphere.... I think the government would have liked me to have painted the activities of the women

> and I did—in laundries, as drivers and chauffeurs, and the
> pipe band, but then I also threw in a lot of my own ideas.
> (Lumsden 1977, 8)

While Bobak paints what some might describe as a fairly accurate picture of the roles and responsibilities of Canadian servicewomen during and after the war, she does take some artistic licence, such as by including women soldiers in her paintings in settings in which they would have likely congregated.

In her art, Bobak has always retained a positive spirit. Despite the desolate postwar setting, her wartime paintings have been described as celebratory, optimistic, and affirmative (Richmond 1993, 25). With a few exceptions such as her paintings *Bremen Ruins at Night* and *Ruins of Emmerich, Germany*, Bobak noticeably avoids depictions of destruction. Instead, she mostly paints Canadian servicewomen as they appear in crowds or small groups actively fulfilling their military obligations in postwar Europe. In so doing, Bobak demonstrates a kind of disengagement or detachment with the individual. She privileges public rather than private scenes, foregrounding the energy of the crowd and the camaraderie among soldiers rather than individual faces, psychological portraits, or moments of interiority. As Foss explains, Bobak's passion for painting people in groups quickly became a principal interest in her war art: "Lamb's attitude to the army was a combination of her love of the excitement, security, and camaraderie of army life.… In particular, the ubiquitous congregation of people in C.W.A.C. barracks, canteens, and parades became a focus of interest for her, and the submergence of individual identity in the amorphous life of the crowd quickly became a leitmotif of her war art" (1993, 95).

Bobak's interest in crowds and gatherings, however, does not suggest that her war art is devoid of intimacy. On the contrary, in choosing to foreground women as they appear in groups, crowds, and parades, and thereby avoiding the depiction of landscapes, wartime machinery, or physical destruction, Bobak privileges the human element of war and the comradeship among soldiers. Bobak is aware of her affinity for public gatherings. As she explains, "I simply love gatherings, minglings … and seeing crowds.… I say that it's like little ants crawling, the sort of insignificance and yet the beauty of people all getting together" (quoted in Lumsden 1977, 8). Bobak's interest in this paradox, the simultaneous insignificance and beauty of people as they appear in crowds, does not reflect a disregard for the individual. Rather, for Bobak, it speaks to a kind of shared humanity—the idea that despite our differences, we might just be "all the same." As she says in the Lumsden interview,

> When I was in the army and I was thrown in with all kinds of girls from different ethnic backgrounds … going to Alberta for basic training and meeting

all those different girls and having to live twelve to a room, I can honestly say that there wasn't a girl I didn't like. I was so relieved to know that we were all the same. We were all different but we were all the same, and its terribly simple and naïve to talk that way, but really that's what I do believe. (1977, 13)

Bobak's keen interest in crowds reflects her optimistic love of life, her interest in community, and the tremendous joy she discovered in her friendships with other servicewomen. The war gave Bobak a remarkable sense of camaraderie.

Bobak's portrait *Private Roy, Canadian Women's Army Corps* (Figure 8.1) represents one important exception to her prevailing interest in crowds, groups, and gatherings, but speaks to both her interest in disrupting male-dominated military ideologies and her enthusiasm for meeting "all those different girls." This painting, a single portrait that fills the entire canvas, depicts a black Canadian servicewoman, known only as Private Roy, at a food counter, staring straight ahead, arms crossed, sleeves rolled up. This is perhaps Bobak's most celebrated work of art since it depicts an otherwise marginalized representative of the Canadian forces during World War II—a black woman Canadian soldier. As Foss explains, this painting holds an important position in the collection of Bobak's paintings since it speaks to Bobak's unflinching realistic depiction of the military as it pertained to women: "Private Roy's status as the only person to become the subject of a wartime oil portrait by Lamb underlines how far removed the artist was from either desire or being requested to project the sort of idealized image of C.W.A.C. life that was so dear to Corps recruiters" (1993, 112–13). Bobak's painting of Private Roy succeeds in disrupting and subverting the customary, governing image of the Canadian woman soldier as a predominantly white, stylishly uniformed, appropriately groomed recruit. Private Roy is not petite, nor is she smiling. In front of her are a few coffee cups, a couple of doughnuts, some soda bottles, and fruit. Despite these ordinary canteen items, the painting appears far from typical. From the intimidating glare of Private Roy to the solid, self-assured spirit of the painting suggested by Private Roy's folded arms and the dark strokes of black, brown, and grey, one could almost imagine Private Roy asking, "Why are you looking at me? Have you never seen a black service-woman before?" The painting—unexpected, unusual, and exceptional in terms of Bobak's overall artistic style during the war years—suggests that Bobak might be the one asking the questions.

Bobak's illustrated war diary represents another atypical record of Canadian servicewomen, as Bobak playfully and satirically questions dominant military gender paradigms. Here we see the germination of Bobak's principal artistic interests at work. Similar in many ways to her work that follows, her diary fore-grounds the public over the private. Arguably, in selecting a mock newspaper format to record her experiences in the Canadian military, Bobak could not

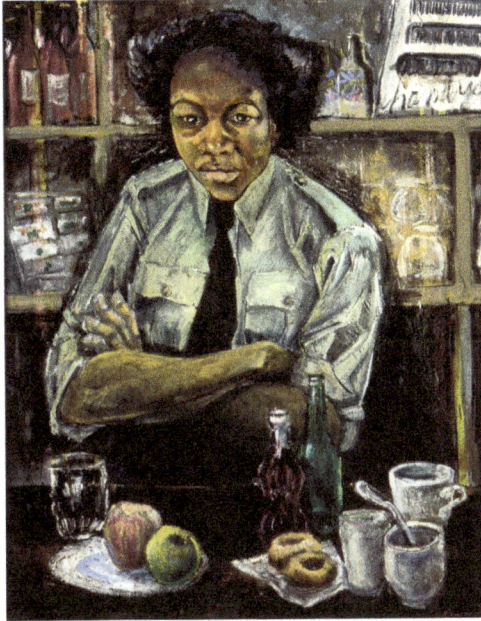

Figure 8.1 *Private Roy, Canadian Women's Army Corps,* by Molly Lamb Bobak, 1946. CWM 19710261-1626, Beaverbrook Collection of War Art, © Canadian War Museum.

have chosen a more detached, depersonalized, public genre. In their coverage of the news, newspaper reporters (whether successful or not) have claimed an allegiance to impartiality—that is, reportage that avoids, as much as possible, biased commentary. American journalist John Hersey claims, "There is one sacred rule of journalism. The writer must not invent. The legend on the license must read: *NONE* OF THIS WAS MADE UP" (2006, 153). Similarly, Stuart G. Adam and Roy Peter Clark suggest that "When journalists reflect on their role, they are likely to see themselves as standing on neutral ground—performing democratic functions.... From this imagined neutral ground, they see themselves watching the swirl of activity that marks modern government, business and commerce, science, society, culture, and civil society, and they describe themselves more as recorders and critics" (2006, xvii). Setting aside for a moment recent assertions that "neutral ground" is neither possible nor reasonable, we ought to acknowledge that for Bobak, and many like her, the newspaper in the 1940s was considered a trusted and objective authentication of lived experience. Recording her experiences in the form of a newspaper, Bobak imaginatively places herself on this neutral ground, and in so doing, grants a certain level of authenticity, impartiality, and validity to her experience. Crucial to my reading of Bobak's diary is the understanding that in the 1940s, Bobak's experience as a young CWAC private in training was not newsworthy. The experiences of these women were largely ignored by the media, deemed insignificant to the war effort, and often refuted by politicians as unnecessary. In selecting a newspaper-style format, Bobak effectively accomplishes two goals: (1) she gives her experience in the CWAC a level of legitimacy by adopting a fictitious authoritative voice; and (2) she draws attention to the often contradictory (and more often absent) news stories or advertising campaigns pertaining to women's experience in the Canadian war effort.

Bobak's diary begins with an eye-catching headline: "Girl Takes Drastic Step! 'You're in the Army Now' as Medical Test Okayed" (Figure 8.2). As Bobak places her protagonist at the centre of the news, she is quick to establish a level of emotional and psychological distance between herself, acting as "editor" and "reporter" of the newspaper, and her protagonist, Private Lamb. In this regard, Bobak's diary affirms the idea that the act of self-representation is far from straightforward, "for the teller of his or her own story becomes, in the act of narration, both the observing subject and the object of investigation, remembrance, and contemplation" (Smith and Watson 2010, 1). Thus, there exists a demarcation here between the narrating "I" and the narrated "I"—between the author of the narrative and the subject around which the narrative revolves. Bobak herself acknowledges this distinction: "My war diary which I must show you sometime, is all about this character called Lamb who goes from bad to worse in the army. Sometimes it's sentimental, sometimes it's very valid but always Lamb is the one who is laughed at as much as anybody else" (quoted in Lumsden 1977, 14). Bobak's description of herself as a "character called Lamb" might be viewed as an example of her allegiance to impartiality. She intentionally adopts a position of neutrality, which extends her role as a "reporter" documenting Private Lamb's experience. But how does this neutral ground serve to validate and authenticate her role as a woman soldier in an industry dominated by men? Sidonie Smith concludes that the woman autobiographer often "establishes the discursive authority to interpret herself publicly in a patriarchal culture" (1987, 45). As a Canadian soldier and later as an accredited war artist, Bobak is entrenched in male-dominated fields. In creating her mock newspaper diary, Bobak effectively (albeit imaginatively) adds another male-dominated industry to her resume—that of newspaper reporter and editor. In deliberately adopting a newspaper format, Bobak appropriates a respected voice of impartiality, giving her private experience in training camp a kind of public record. Bobak's diary is surely an example (although perhaps an unusual one) of what Smith means by the establishment of a "discursive authority," or a way to interpret women's experience in a patriarchal culture and/or institution, which in this case is represented by both the military and the Canadian art scene.

Figure 8.2 "Girl Takes Drastic Step! 'You're in the Army Now' as Medical Test Okayed," by Molly Lamb Bobak. Library and Archives Canada, Acc. No. 1990-255-94, Gift of Molly Lamb Bobak/C-135727.

Bobak's deliberate delineation between herself and the character Lamb represents what Mary Mason identifies as "the other voice." Mason recognizes a recurring pattern in early autobiographies by women: "The self discovery of female identity seems to acknowledge the real presence and recognition of another consciousness, and the disclosure of a female self is linked to the identification of some 'other.' This recognition of another consciousness—and I emphasize recognition rather than deference—this grounding of identity through relation to the chosen other, seems to enable women to write openly about themselves" (1980, 210). Joy Hooton suggests that Mason may be the first critic to alert us to the woman autobiographer's tendency or inclination towards defining the self in terms of alterity—that is, in terms of an "other" (1992, 27). Based on her assessment of more than six hundred published and unpublished Australian women's autobiographies, Hooton agrees with Mason's assertion: "It seemed to me, the more I read of women's life-writing, that this characteristic trait of defining the self as a self in relation, was a major historical difference between men's and women's texts" (27). While *W110278* cannot be considered an autobiography in the most complete sense of the word—that is, as a self-written account of Bobak's life over a long period of time—it does connect in some ways with the idea of an autobiographical, self-representational creation of an alter ego. On the first page of her diary, Private Lamb enlists "unwillingly and willingly, willy-nilly" to the CWAC. Rather than use first-person narration, Bobak presents herself and her experiences through fictitious reporters. She writes, "When reporters interviewed her on Wednesday night they found her in a mental state. 'I've never known so much misery,' she stated torturedly. 'Except when I didn't win the scholarship at school.'" The reporters continue to question her: "'And what was the work?' queried the press. 'If you're not bored,' continued Private Lamb, 'I'll tell you about it.'" Lamb then proceeds to inform the press about her accommodation, her uniform, and her first work detail washing dishes. The details of these first days, all rather ordinary and straightforward, give little attention to interiority. This is the "news," after all, and therefore little attention is paid to the psychological composure of the lead subject (Gossage 1992, 22).

In their early analysis of generic distinctions, Sidonie Smith and Julia Watson define the diary as a "form of periodic life writing," which records, always chronologically, the "dailiness in accounts and observations of emotional responses" (2010, 266). As the diary develops, the diarist's voice "takes on a recognizable narrative persona" (266). In contrast, they say, autobiography is more "retrospective" in its narrative and stylistic qualities (4). In other words, lacking the dailiness of a diary, autobiography is a looking back at a life lived. Bobak's text in its periodic dailiness certainly qualifies as a diary. But while the distinction and definition of the two genres is important, it is helpful to remember certain theories about women's autobiographies and self-representation in order to gain a fuller understanding of Bobak's unique diary and its effectiveness.

Smith explains that self-representation is both "discursively complex and ambiguous" due to a "radical disappropriation" of the actual life of the subject by the literary artifice of the text (1987, 47). In other words, when representing the self in a literary context, the subject (the narrated and familiar "I") is displaced by something foreign, something other (47). In trying to tell the story she wants to tell, Smith explains, the woman autobiographer "is seduced into a tantalizing and yet elusive adventure that makes of her both the creator and creation, writer and that which is written about" (46). As Bobak tells us on the first page of her diary, she wrote and illustrated the text, "In between serving soldiers in the canteen—6–10 at night," thus confirming the "dailiness" of her record-keeping (Gossage 1992, 22). However, in terms of form, *W110278* is not what one might consider a typical diary. These are not private musings quietly recorded at the end of the day in a written journal—this is extensive, detailed artwork and carefully crafted prose. Most notably, this is a work produced, it would seem, with an audience in mind. In addition to sharing her diary with Jackson, there is also evidence that Bobak shared it with fellow CWAC members. As McIntosh explains,

To others, particularly her fellow CWACs, the diary with its many insightful observations and comments about life in the CWACs represented an
invaluable record of the CWACs' role in the war effort. This idea is clearly
demonstrated in an article that was published in June 1945 in *C.W.A.C. News
Letter*: "When the war is history and army careers past, Lieut. Lamb's scrap
book should be made available to all Cwacs.... It is our story, told by one of
us as it was lived by us all." (1992, 10)

All things considered, *W110278* can be read as a public performance.
Bobak's willingness, even eagerness, to share her war diary with others in the
years following the war suggests that she wrote and illustrated it with an audience
in mind.[6] When assessed against Smith's theories of women's self-representation
and autobiography as a diary written with daily periodicity yet for public, pre-
sentational purposes, Bobak's diary becomes increasingly intriguing. *W110278*
not only demonstrates the seduction of storytelling, but also reveals the extent
to which Bobak deliberately (and perhaps strategically) stands back from the
subject of her diary, and in so doing, displaces or disappropriates the familiar "I"
with a fictitious, imagined self. As such, she becomes, through her diary art, a site
of agency—a subtle yet subversive voice challenging, through self-parody and
humour, the dominant gender ideologies in the Canadian military at the time.

While Bobak does indeed adhere in her creation of an alter ego to what
Mason identifies as a pattern of alterity, and to what Smith identifies as the
radical disappropriation of the familiar "I," she does so with specific motives. In
distancing herself from her principal character, Bobak is able freely and unabashedly to parody herself and the institution to which she now belongs. Caricature,
parody, and hyperbole (in this case, exaggerated descriptions) become the dominant devices that Bobak uses throughout the text. In the years leading up to
her more mature career as an artist, Bobak developed a passion for caricature:
"I did start out very, very much as a caricaturist," she says. "I never felt cynical
about people but I did notice their idiosyncrasies and tried to draw them in an
exaggerated way" (quoted in Lumsden 1977, 14). It is this penchant for caricature that profoundly informs her war diary. As a way of parodying what must
have seemed to Bobak an endless array of acronyms and military rankings,
she identifies her characters by a personality trait or dominant characteristic:
"Private Caneul V.N. (Very Nice)"; "Model Private O.W.K. (One Who Knows)";
"Rookie Lamb E.A.L. (Enjoys Army Life) E.F.D. (Except For Dirt)"; "Pte. M.
Gallon F.S.S. (Fat Sandwich Spreader) C.B.G.N. (Colossal But Good Natured)";
and "Corporal H. Pathetic (true name withheld) D.O.H.F. (Dead On Her Feet)".
Certainly, she would have expected this kind of mockery to garner a laugh or
two from a reader. Her readers may even have identified immediately with the
real people to whom she refers. It is these kinds of descriptions that suggest she
intended her diary as public performance.

More than anyone else in the diary, Bobak's main character, Private Lamb, is continuously lampooned, suggesting that while most of the events described in *W110278* were sure to have taken place, Bobak was able through it all to maintain a sense of humour. Some of the more comical events, or news stories, in *W110278* include "24 Hour Bedlam for Harassed Private," in which Lamb, on one of her first days at training camp, injures her thumb falling out of her bunk and is thus unable to offer an adequate fingerprint to the sergeant (Gossage 1992, 28). In "Girl Leaves Train Stockingless, Gloveless! Winter Weather of −33 Below," Lamb arrives in Alberta during winter with only her sketchpads, an "Indian sweater," and no stockings or gloves—"'But I did get a lovely ride to the Barracks and became notorious at once.' (Editor's note: It is a well known fact that Private Lamb loves notoriety)" (Gossage 1992, 31). In "Calamity on Homeward March," Lamb, in an effort to salute passing officers, drops all her Christmas parcels. "Later she told the press, 'My mind became a propeller. I felt my parcels drop and my hat get caught in some branches (see authentic flash picture). I felt my mit [*sic*] hit my cheek and I realized I had saluted. My officers smiled and said hello, but I'm afraid I couldn't manage to reply just then'" (Gossage 1992, 36). Bobak mocks her experience as a woman recruit, and thus satirizes the military institution, since she comes at it from a position of authority—she is, after all, the source of the ridicule.

In choosing to lampoon her own experience, and to never take herself too seriously, Bobak parodies and thus criticizes the institutional conventions to which she must adhere. Her experience becomes the foundational authority from which she establishes a certain freedom of expression. In keeping with Smith's theories of self-representation, Bobak's self-parody can be read as an example of how the autobiographer's narrative strategies (what Smith calls the "drift of the disappropriation") reveal the "way the autobiographer situates herself and her story in relation to cultural ideologies and figures of selfhood" (Smith 1987, 47). Smith and Watson identify these situations as "sites of agency" (2010, 57) and contend that "Situated amid multiple forms of imagined worlds, individuals as sites of agency deploy their imaginations as both a social fact and a kind of work to navigate the disjunctures of global flows" (2010, 57). In other words, Bobak's use of imagination here allows her to plot her own course in the dominantly patriarchal institutions of both the military and the art world. She becomes a site of agency and her diary becomes a form of resistance—an empowering assessment of the experience of Canadian servicewomen during World War II.

Through parody, Bobak draws attention to the differences between women's military experience in the CWAC and men's military experience on the frontlines, emphasizing the existing gender bias. One telling example, a panel entitled "Horrible Fate of Innocent Private! 'They Got Me in the Legs' Testifies Casualty as Enemy Silently Attacks," satirizes Lamb's encounter with poison ivy:

Another stinging blow was dealt to one of our troops today, when the enemy applied further atrocious tactics on our side. "It was like Pearl Harbour," admitted Pte. Lamb C. (casualty!). "The enemy dealt me a stinging blow which completely surprised me and was strictly outside the international code as set up in Geneva." … "So I went to the M.O.," went on the private, "and guess what he said?" … "Mustard gas?" queried reporters. "No," sadly smiled the private. "POISON IVY … and now, today, I look like a living ad for the BEFORE part of an eczema advertisement." Reporters confirm this and add that the private has been laid up for three days. However, morale is high and spirits are fighting mad. (Gossage 1992, 76)

As a literary device, satire employs comedy to debase, ridicule, and expose certain follies and shortcomings in society. Bobak uses satire, and its subsidiary parody, in precisely this manner. By lampooning her own calamities in the same language reserved for "newsworthy" casualties on the frontlines, Bobak draws attention to the difference between men and women's military experience in World War II. While this does not necessarily suggest that Bobak longed to join the men at the frontlines, it certainly implies that she was at least aware of the limitations imposed on women in the military, such as the inability to carry firearms and to engage in combat.

In *Greatcoats and Glamour Boots: Canadian Women at War (1939–1945)*, Carolyn Gossage tells us that more than 45,000 Canadian women volunteered for military service during World War II: close to 22,000 in the CWAC; 17,000 in the Royal Canadian Air Force (RCAF), Women's Division; and 6,781 in the Women's Royal Canadian Naval Service (the Wrens) (1991, 17). However, despite these numbers, women's presence in the Canadian military was often ignored by high-ranking officials or greeted with disapproval by politicians and outspoken military strategists. Fears over the deterioration of the family and the disruption of well-established gender roles were rampant: If women were encouraged to work outside the home, what would become of the family unit? In a parliamentary address in 1939, Member of the Legislative Assembly for Quebec René Chaloult addressed the question of women's employment in war plants (which served to accommodate for the loss of men workers travelling overseas to fight in the war): "Employing women in war plants was the 'surest way to destroy the family—Quebec's sole means of survival.' … Women, who left their villages to work in war industries, would never go back home. It is the Federal Government's duty to advise mothers of the 'dangers' awaiting their daughters in urban centres." Apparently Agricultural Minister Laurent Barré agreed, stating that a woman's place in Quebec was "on the farm, with her children and husband," while Liberal Opposition Leader Joseph-Adélard Godbout described women working in war industries as "an evil" ("Chaloult," 1945).

Others were concerned about the potential loss of a woman's "femininity"—if women were encouraged to join the "masculine" environment of the military, what would become of their inherent "feminine" qualities, and how would this affect the home to which they were intended to return? One former member of the Wrens recalls feeling out of place in her hometown wearing her uniform: "My parents lived in a small town—very much removed from the war—and I got the impression when I'd be home on leave that some people thought it was wrong for me to be in uniform. I almost felt as if they thought of me as a prostitute or something. They hardly seemed to realize there was a war on, some of them" (quoted in Gossage 1991, 190). In order to combat fears over the potential "de-feminization" of women in the military, servicewomen were often presented in a glamorous and idealistic context in both military recruitment posters and fashion advertising campaigns, with a particular emphasis on good looks, good grooming, and good lipstick.

In her extensive research of American advertising and recruitment campaigns during World War II, Linda M. Scott explains, "Highly romanticized images of women in military dress were quite common during this period" (2009). Scott reprints a number of American fashion ads containing war imagery, but one image in particular is worth contemplating for the purposes of this argument. An ad by Elizabeth Arden published in *Mademoiselle* in June 1943 portrays a servicewoman boldly and confidently staring directly at the viewer, while a man behind her gazes at her in admiration. The description reads, "Frankly, she was fascinating. She had a certain elusive charm that defied description—invariably, others appreciate the sensitive understatement of Elizabeth Arden lipstick shades which make them aware of the woman—not the make-up.… The young woman wears a burnt sugar lipstick—most effective with khaki.… Every woman should have at least four essential shades to harmonize with a wide range of costume colors and Service uniforms" (Scott 2009).

In contrast to the highly romanticized and confident servicewoman depicted by the media, Bobak portrays Private Lamb and some of the other women recruits as bewildered, often tipsy, inexperienced, and naive: "I guess we were a motley crowd—half of us in our civvies and one or two of us were a little tipsy" (Gossage 1992, 28). Other women are described in Bobak's newspaper as decidedly "unfeminine," according to 1940s standards: "I noticed one with long underwear right down her legs and grease on her face. She was huge with narrow eyes and a dominating personality" (31). Far from being the "elusively charming," "fascinating" servicewoman in the Elizabeth Arden ad, Lamb herself is depicted as confused and inexperienced. In an amusing panel in which Lamb is promoted to lance corporal, she attempts to answer her recruits' questions but fails to give them any response other than "Eh?" In a hilarious parody, she explains later to reporters that, of course, the right answers would be, "'Yes, your hair's foul.—Get a soup basin and trim it off'; 'You'll darn well go overseas when I feel like sending you…. You vile guppie!'; 'You'll get old bull for lunch and like it'; 'Stockings! What do you want them for? It's only 60 below. You fool sissy…. You—old bag!'" (40). In yet another panel, Lamb is depicted attempting to get her hair cut, military-style, at an Elizabeth Arden salon in Montreal: "Into the feminine atmosphere of Elizabeth Arden's salon of Beauty trooped the khaki-coated Lamb…. Said Lamb, 'The Army says it must be short, Monsieur.' … 'Oui,' said Marcel. But it is reported that he did not—and would not—cut it to the required length" (54). Taken together, all of these examples illustrate, quite literally, the contradiction between the media's profile of military women and the reality these women faced.

In her 1942 recruitment talk at a training facility in Kitchener, Ontario, CWAC commander Mary Dover addresses cultural fears over the potential loss of a woman's "femininity" in the military:

> I have sometimes heard it said by people who seem to think they know, that life in the Army tends to make women lose their femininity. I dispute this. If you take merely the outward and visible signs; I should like you to see the way in which the girls flutter about barracks in their pretty housecoats in their off-duty hours how welcome are all those feminine luxuries and how they enjoy the privilege of wearing civilian clothes when on their annual leave or furlough. (Thrift 2011, 48)

Rather than encouraging a new kind of thinking with regards to what the term "femininity" can and should suggest, Dover merely pacifies these fears by reaffirming the gender ideologies that were dominant before the war. However, Bobak, once again using satire and parody as her principal method, challenges these concerns in a special feature entitled "For Ladies W110278 Presents 1943 Fall Fashions" (Figure 8.3). In this supplementary coloured feature, Bobak adopts yet another alter ego: "Modom Mouton (English Pronounciation [sic] Lamb)" (Gossage 1992, 102). Perhaps Bobak's play on words here is intended to evoke the well-known idiom "mutton dressed as a lamb," a phrase intended to mock those women dressed in a style more suited to someone younger. It might also be a caustic reference to the sheep-like submissiveness of the feminized image of women soldiers. Certainly this panel parodies the magazine advertisements and supplementary fashion features that champion the 1940s woman as someone who is suitably attired, impeccably groomed, and overtly "feminine"—a woman focused primarily on modern trends and styles, despite or perhaps even because of her military career. In Bobak's version, Modom Mouton advises, "Hats will be on the face this Fall." The model posing, however, is not a high-fashion model in the latest styles, but rather a servicewoman modelling her khaki army cap. Modom Mouton's models pose in their "Battle Dress," offering both a front and rear view, and the stout rear view of the model is parodied with the caption "A Creation from the Excellent School of Cookery." In contrast, these models are then illustrated posing in their weekend wear, a new "Braemar sweater—worn after a day's work and on weekends—pearls by Birks, no less" (Gossage 1992, 102).

Bobak is clearly having some fun here with the contradictory messages sent by both the military and the media: you may be in the army, they seem to assert, but as a woman, fashion comes first. As Foss observes, "Lamb's journal poked

Figure 8.3   "For Ladies W110278 Presents 1943 Fall Fashions," by Molly Lamb Bobak. Library and Archives Canada, Acc. No. 1990-255-94, Gift of Molly Lamb Bobak/C-135764.

fun at such stereotypically feminine concerns as fashion, by pointing out the potential foolishness of attempting to combine *haute couture* with the realities of army life" (1993, 112). But while Bobak was clearly having fun, ridiculing those fears over the loss of "femininity" in the military, she was also most likely drawing on images prevalent in mainstream media. Perhaps Bobak's lampoon of military fashions is a direct mockery of images such as American war photographer Lee Miller's 1944 photo entitled "Service Women at a Fashion Salon, Paris," in which a number of uniformed servicewomen sitting in a semicircle are admiring, even fondling, the latest Parisian fashions. Or perhaps the incongruity between the lacy nightgowns and the khaki uniforms was an actual reality at the barracks. As one former member of the RCAF Women's Division recalls, "We'd go out shopping and buy sexy nightgowns trimmed with lace—and fancy bedroom slippers. After we'd reported back, we'd float around the barracks in our new outfits letting off steam before we had to get back into uniform the next morning bright and early" (quoted in Gossage 1991, 188). Regardless, Bobak exposes these incongruities by appropriating the mock-newspaper format and adopting a tone of impartiality. Without providing much in the way of editorial comments, she illuminates and illustrates the contradictions that must have been apparent to many young servicewomen.

One of Bobak's official war paintings, "Gas Drill" (Figure 8.4), also speaks to her concern about the often-contradictory gender-encoded messages for women in the Canadian military. The painting, based on a sketch that appears in *W110278* with the headline "Drill, Drill, Drill as Guppies Turn Pros Out in the Cold, Cold Snow" (Gossage 1992, 35), depicts a number of women in army coats and dark boots standing in the snow wearing gas masks. In the middle of the small crowd, one recruit in particular seems to be posing, throwing her arm back as though modelling her mask. The sketch that appears in *W110278* conveys a similar message: a recruit near the centre of the drawing models her gas mask with her chest out and her arms in full swing. Certainly, Bobak is calling attention to how strange and unfamiliar these drills must have been for many of these young women, that even when donning a gas mask, they felt the impulse to pose and poke fun at the rather serious drill at hand. It would have been a novelty for these women to wear such masks and perform such drills—surely some grandstanding would have taken place. Playfulness, laughter, and comic relief were important for these women during training camp, as Bobak's diary suggests. As one CWAC recalls, "In Basic Training, if you hadn't been able to laugh, you wouldn't have been able to retain your sanity. In fact, there were a few who didn't" (quoted in Gossage 1991, 92).

In the final pages of Bobak's diary, Private Lamb is granted the opportunity she desired: she is accredited as an official war artist for Canada and is assigned an overseas appointment. As the seriousness of her army responsibilities

Figure 8.4   *Gas Drill*, by Molly Lamb Bobak, 1944. Oil on canvas, 68.8 x 86.8 cm. CWM 19710261-1603, Beaverbrook Collection of War Art, © Canadian War Museum.

increase, so, too, does the overall tone of her diary. Elegant, descriptive phrases describe her serene early morning departure from Kitchener, Ontario: "A train shunted back and forth; a bit of dawn began to show. A crossing bell swung back and forth—dinging and donging" (Gossage 1992, 136). It is worth mentioning that Bobak does not conclude with her usual humour, parody, or caricature, but rather with solemnity and seriousness. The final sentence of her diary reads, "I walked through the carriages and saw the girls sleeping or smoking or talking sleepily to one another. They had mostly taken their tunics off and sat facing one another with their shirt sleeves rolled up" (136). Coats off, sleeves rolled up, these women are now ready and able to serve their country. This was serious business for Bobak and her language and tone suggest likewise.

Lynn Z. Bloom observes that contrary to popular perception, "not all diaries are written—ultimately or exclusively—for private consumption" (1996, 25). Most significantly, Bloom explains, "it is the audience hovering at the edge of the page that for the sophisticated diarist facilitates the work's ultimate focus, providing the impetus either for the initial writing or for transforming what might have been casual, fragmented jottings into a more carefully crafted, contextually coherent work" (25). As my argument here suggests, Bobak's *W110278* certainly constitutes a "carefully crafted, contextually coherent work." Furthermore, in its attention to detail, its use of parody and caricature, and its subtle subversive voice, *W110278* hints at public performance and speaks to an audience hovering at the edge of the page. In terms of both form and content, *W110278* must be placed in a unique category of military writings, as a sophisticated representation of army life for women holding a precarious position between private record and public document.

NOTES

All quotations from Bobak's diary are taken from Gossage, *Double Duty.*

The first epigraph is taken from a letter written by A.Y. Jackson on Bobak's behalf to H.O. "Harry" McCurry, the director of the National Gallery of Canada in 1945 (quoted in Gossage 1992, 63). The second epigraph is taken from Gossage 1992, 98.

1   Molly Lamb Bobak died on 2 March 2014 in Fredericton, New Brunswick at the age of ninety-four. For her obituary and a brief retrospective of her life and work, see Allison Lawlor's *Globe and Mail* article "Molly Lamb Bobak was First Canadian Woman Sent Overseas as War Artist."

2   In 1989, Bobak donated *W110278* to the National Archives of Canada, where it remains for public viewing today.

3   For more biographical information on Bobak, see Cindy Richmond's (curator) *Molly Lamb Bobak: A Retrospective* (Regina, SK: McKenzie Art Gallery, 1993).

4   Hereafter I will refer to this interview as the "Lumsden Interview."

5   There is also some indication that Major Charles Comfort, OC, RCA was also privy to Bobak's diary. In his foreword to the publication of Bobak's diary, *Double Duty: Sketches and Diaries of Molly Lamb Bobak Canadian War Artist,* he writes, "I first saw this unique diary in its original form and was much impressed by its unorthodox format. The essence of the diary and the events, the humour and the reality it conveys brings us Molly's zest for life and her special way of looking at things" (Gossage 1992, 7).

6   In a 1991 phone conversation with Carolyn Gossage, Bobak said that she tried to donate her diary to the war museum "ages ago, but they didn't seem to want them." The National Archives of Canada finally accepted them in 1989 (Gossage 1992, 14).

WORKS CITED

Adam, Stuart G., and Roy Peter Clark. 2006. "Introduction: Reflections on Journalism and the Architecture of Democracy." In *Journalism: The Democratic Craft*, edited by Stuart G. Adam and Roy Peter Clark, xv–xix. New York: Oxford University Press.

Bloom, Lynn Z. 1996. "'I Write for Myself and Strangers': Private Diaries as Public Documents." In *Inscribing the Daily: Critical Essays on Women's Diaries*, edited by Suzanne L. Bunkers and Cynthia A. Huff, 23–37. Amherst: University of Massachusetts Press.

Bobak, Molly Lamb. 1944. *Gas Drill.* Painting; oil on canvas. Beaverbrook Collection of War Art, Canadian War Museum, Ottawa.

———. "Girl Takes Drastic Step! 'You're in the Army Now' as Medical Test Okayed." Library and Archives Canada, Acc. No. 1990-255-94. Gift of Molly Lamb Bobak/ C-135727.

———. "For Ladies W110278 Presents 1943 Fall Fashions." Library and Archives Canada, Acc. No. 1990-255-94. Gift of Molly Lamb Bobak/C-135764.

———. 1946. *Private Roy, Canadian Women's Army Corps*. Painting (oil on canvas). Beaverbrook Collection of War Art, Canadian War Museum, Ottawa.

———. 1978. *Wild Flowers of Canada: Impressions and Sketches of a Field Artist*. Toronto: Pagurian Press.

"Chaloult Says Working Women Reduce Families." 15 March 1945. *Hamilton Spectator*, http://www.warmuseum.ca.

Foss, Brian. 1993. "Molly Lamb Bobak: Art and War." In *Molly Lamb Bobak: A Retrospective/Une rétrospective*, edited by Cindy Richmond. Regina, SK: MacKenzie Art Gallery.

Gossage, Carolyn. 1991. *Greatcoats and Glamour Boots: Canadian Women at War (1939–1945)*. Toronto: Dundurn Press.

———. 1992. *Double Duty: Sketches and Diaries of Molly Lamb Bobak Canadian War Artist*. Toronto: Dundurn Press.

Hersey, John. 2006. "The Legend on the License." In *Journalism: The Democratic Craft*, edited by Stuart G. Adam and Roy Peter Clark, 152–63. New York: Oxford University Press.

Hooton, Joy. 1992. "Autobiography and Gender." In *Writing Lives: Feminist Biography and Autobiography*, edited by Susan Magarey, 25–40. Adelaide: Australian Feminist Studies.

Lawlor, Allison. 14 March 2014. "Molly Lamb Bobak was First Canadian Woman Sent Overseas as War Artist." *Globe and Mail*.

Lumsden, Ian. 1977. *The Queen Comes to New Brunswick: Paintings and Drawings by Molly Lamb Bobak*. Exhibition catalogue. Fredericton, NB: Beaverbrook Art Gallery.

Mason, Mary G. 1980. "The Other Voice: Autobiographies of Women Writers." In *Autobiography: Essays Theoretical and Critical*, edited by James Olney, 207–35. Princeton: Princeton University Press.

McIntosh, Terresa. 1992. "Preface: A National Treasure." In *Double Duty: Sketches and Diaries of Molly Lamb Bobak Canadian War Artist*, edited by Carolyn Gossage, 9–10. Toronto: Dundurn Press.

Miller, Lee. 1944. "Service Women at a Fashion Salon, Paris," http://www.leemiller.co.uk.

Oliver, Dean F., and Laura Brandon. 2000. *Canvas of War: Painting the Canadian Experience, 1914–1945*. Vancouver: Douglas & McIntyre.

Richmond, Cindy. 1993. "Molly Lamb Bobak." In *Molly Lamb Bobak: A Retrospective/Une rétrospective*, edited by Cindy Richmond. Regina, SK: MacKenzie Art Gallery.

Scott, Linda M. 2009. "Warring Images: Fashion and the Women's Magazines, 1941–1945." *Advertising and Social Review* 10 (2): n.p.

Smith, Sidonie, and Julia Watson. 2010. *Reading Autobiography: A Guide for Interpreting Life Narratives*. Minneapolis: University of Minnesota Press.

Smith, Sidonie. 1987. *A Poetics of Women's Autobiography: Marginality and the Fictions of Self-Representation*. Bloomington: Indiana University Press.

Thrift, Gayle. 2011. "'This is our war, too': Mary Dover, Commandant of the Canadian Women's Army Corps." *Alberta History* 59 (3): 2+.

"THESE DUTCH GIRLS ARE WIZARD!"
The Dutch Resistance as Matriarchy in
One of Our Aircraft Is Missing

James D. Stone

S ilhouetted against the dawn light, a British bomber is flying over the sea. It is the wayward plane mentioned in the title of the 1942 film *One of Our Aircraft Is Missing*. Not one person is aboard. Engines hum hypnotically as we contemplate an unmanned control column, the steering device gently swaying and tilting of its own accord. A shot of an empty pilot's seat is followed by a close-up of the instrument panel, faithfully but pointlessly displaying data to the deserted cockpit. Wind howls through the cabin, bestowing upon it a desolate and apocalyptic air. It is as if the bomber's crew members have been magically snatched from their posts. As we wonder what circumstances could have led to this airborne retelling of the *Mary Celeste* legend, the plane smashes into an electricity pylon and explodes, filling the screen with an impressive fireball.

Where we expect to see airmen, there are none. The deserted aircraft is a key image in a movie filled with moments in which men are largely absent from positions of power and control. We soon discover that the crew has bailed out, parachuting into the Nazi-occupied Netherlands and leaving their stricken plane to its fate. Resourceful as they are, they must place themselves in the hands of the Dutch Resistance in order to return home. They are therefore shuttled about the countryside, from one safe house to another, with very little influence over their destiny.

The Dutch Resistance is represented mainly by women. Two women in particular, Els Meertens (Pamela Brown), a schoolteacher, and Jo de Vries (Googie Withers), an entrepreneur, are crucial to the men's survival behind enemy lines. Both are brave, strong, and intelligent leaders. Dutchmen are present in the film, but are variously portrayed as quiet, passive, quisling, or peripheral to the action. Indeed, the Netherlands under Nazi occupation seems nothing less than a matriarchal space. Surprisingly, the British airmen will embrace this world, frequently expressing admiration for women authority figures. "What a girl!" and "These Dutch girls are wizard!" are two typically appreciative exclamations.

One of Our Aircraft Is Missing is a rousing propaganda film that was designed, in the words of its co-director Michael Powell, "to show how people in the Low Countries and France were risking their necks every night to help ... [British] crews get back to their own country" (Powell 1987, 385). The movie succeeds admirably as a hymn to brave resistance members, but it is also, for several commentators, a work indelibly marked by the presence of women. In 1990, Peter Hogue noted, "The schoolmistress and the ... entrepreneur loom especially large.... The two of them are also the most memorable and genuinely heroic characters in the film" (31). Even though the six men of the aircrew claim the lion's share of screen time, a 1942 review in *The Times* made sure to reserve special praise for the actresses: "Miss Pamela Brown ... and Miss Googie Withers ... are admirable in their suggestion of the nerve and resource of Dutch women" ("One of Our Aircraft Is Missing").

In pre-production, Powell was adamant that his resistance tale would include women. In his memoirs, he states, "It was now time to think about casting, and I begged Emeric [Pressburger] to write some decent parts for women" (Powell 1987, 391). The filmmaker's emphasis on "decent parts" suggests that he sensed a dearth of substantial roles for women. As Powell undoubtedly knew, there were many British movies that focused on women's lives. However, while they might have acknowledged that the war had radically altered the landscape of gender—allowing women new opportunities in industry, agriculture, and the armed services— most of these films were quite reactionary in tone. Indeed, as feminist historian Antonia Lant argues, though British films of 1942–46 place "an emphasis on female experience" (1991, 59), they refashion "a semiotics of sexual difference in the face of wartime change" (55). Film historians Anthony Aldgate and Jeffrey Richards also suggest that, although women were a notable presence on British screens, the manner of their presentation was limited: "Only a handful of feature films were devoted exclusively to women on war service, notably *The Gentle Sex* (1943) (the ATS) and *The Lamp Still Burns* (1943) (nursing). Many more films celebrated the role of woman as housewife, maintaining the home, raising the children, acting essentially in a support role to the men at the front and stoically suffering all the stresses and anxieties that such a role entailed" (2007, 300).

To find more subversive depictions of women during the war years, we must look to the realm of the "costume drama," fantasies set safely in a mythical past. As Sue Harper argues, "Commercial films which contained more liberated images of women, such as *The Wicked Lady* (1945) [in which Margaret Lockwood plays a "highwayman"] ... avoided realistic modes of representation" (1996, 95). Lockwood's character is not only distanced from 1940s reality, but also must die for her transgressions. Pam Cook notes that even though "Audiences leaving a screening of *The Wicked Lady*" may have been thrilled to see "the stunning images of Margaret Lockwood dressed in highwayman gear astride a stallion," they were also asked to "take on board the moral implications of her punishment by death" (1996, 59).

The women of Powell and Pressburger's film stand in stark contrast to such portrayals. Els and Jo are not homemakers, but tough leaders who must make life-or-death decisions. They are neither doomed to die nor relegated to the realm of fantasy.[1] Indeed, the film in which they appear makes extensive use of the conventions of realism. As Scott Salwolke argues, "*One of Our Aircraft is Missing* has many of the trappings of the documentary.... The omission of any music ... adds to this quality, as does the extensive sequence that opens the film detailing the raid" (1997, 87).

It is not only the film's women who are distinctive. The aircrew, men who accept their placement under women's command with good humour and enthusiasm, are quite different from their cinematic brethren. In the war years, British cinema's men were largely defined by a physical assertiveness. According to Andrew Spicer, the dominant image of British masculinity in the early part of the conflict was provided by the "Debonair Gentleman," who, although imbued with "the delicacy and sensitivity of the cultivated Man of Feeling," also displayed "the athletic, vigorous manliness of 'muscular Christianity' and the Protestant success drive" (2003, 8). Spicer also describes the qualities of the wartime British "Action Hero" embodied by Lawrence Olivier's Henry V, whose "athletic manliness and ardent love-making contrast with the decadent, febrile effeteness of the French aristocracy" (12). Moreover, men characters forced to confront the social changes wrought by war frequently react to women's authority with distaste. Lant notes that in *Great Day* (1945), the male protagonist "constantly makes disparaging remarks of the type, 'No wonder the country's going to the dogs, with a pack of women running it'" (1991, 60). In the comedy *Bees in Paradise* (1944), comedic leading man Arthur Askey scolds the queen of a matriarchal island for "presiding over a distaff tyranny in which males cannot win no matter how they behave" (Spicer 2003, 21–22). *One of Our Aircraft Is Missing* presents men who are defined neither as muscular men of action nor as anxious misogynists. Instead, they display great respect for authoritative women and are notably passive, frequently finding themselves in situations where action is impossible.

Powell and Pressburger's film responds to wartime change by offering new, thought-provoking portrayals of femininity and masculinity rather than attempting to reinscribe dominant definitions of "woman" and "man." The movie refuses an approach to gender in which men are regarded as embodiments of activity and women as passive entities—a construction that philosopher Hélène Cixous refers to as "patriarchal binary thought." As Cixous points out, in patriarchal culture, the opposition "Man/Woman" corresponds to the binary opposites "Activity/Passivity," "Culture/Nature," and "Head/Emotions." As Cixous's interlocutor, Toril Moi, sagely concludes, "The 'feminine' side is always the negative, powerless instance" (Moi 1993, 104). *One of Our Aircraft Is Missing* mocks the patriarchal binary by flipping it entirely. By offering us a world in which women are active and men are relatively passive, the film is not arguing for a new essentialist paradigm. Instead, its radical reversal of the norm exposes a structuring element of culture that, because it perpetuates inequality, is ripe for interrogation.

The patriarchal binary, as its nomenclature would suggest, exists to maintain men's power over women. Gender theorist Riki Wilchins makes the valuable point, "In the end, binaries are not just a curious way of understanding the world. They are political. They are about power. They create hierarchies—male/female, white/black, colonial/native—that produce winners and losers" (2004, 41). Nowhere in popular culture is the maintenance of men's power via the active/passive binary more noticeable than in cinema. Laura Mulvey's seminal work on mid-century Hollywood identifies "the man's role as the active one forwarding the story, making things happen," and begins a vital conversation regarding the extent to which "the man controls the film phantasy and also emerges as the representative of power" over a passive woman (2011, 720).

One of Our Aircraft Is Missing is a mid-century film that neither attempts to police the borders of gender nor sustain men's power. It takes great delight in presenting men and women characters whose actions dismantle the patriarchal binary, and, in so doing, opens up the possibility that our identities are more fluid than is commonly supposed. The movie offers a conception of gender similar to that proposed by anthropologist Matthew Guttman. Masculinity and femininity, he claims, "are not original, natural, or embalmed states of being; they are gender categories whose precise meanings constantly shift, transform into each other, and ultimately make themselves into whole new entities" (1996, 21). Underlying the propaganda elements of *One of Our Aircraft Is Missing* is an enthusiasm for such "shifts" and "transformations."

Such an enthusiasm would prove to be a recurrent element in the cinematic output of Powell and Pressburger. In a creative partnership lasting from 1942 until 1972, The Archers, as these filmmakers would become known, brought to the screen many strong-willed, free-thinking women and a series of uncommonly thoughtful, sensitive men.[2] And yet, because the very narrative of *One of Our Aircraft Is Missing* is built on the systematic transfer of power from men to women, it constitutes Powell and Pressburger's most zealous reconstruction of gendered behaviour.

The casting of Pamela Brown as Els Meertens, the schoolteacher, would suggest that Powell, in particular, wanted the film to be charged with subversive ideas regarding identity. The filmmaker wrote much about his penchant for women who, as lovers and as actors, transcended normative gender identification. Brown was one such woman. In the second volume of his memoirs, Powell opens his discussion of the actress by joyously informing us, "I have waited until now to write of Pamela Brown, and if I don't I shall bust" (Powell 1992, 96). Delighting in her ability to shift between what he calls her masculine and feminine selves, he relates an anecdote regarding the casting process for the movie *The Tales of Hoffman*. After commenting, "I was thinking of playing Pamela as the boy-girl, girl-boy Nicklaus in *Hoffman*" (96), he recalls a conversation she had with chief electrician Bill Wall:

> "Look here, Pamela," he said, "when you're acting old Nicklaus, do you feel like a boy or a girl?"
> "It depends, Bill. Sometimes one and sometimes the other."
> "Cor, having it both ways, eh!" (98)

In another discussion of Brown, Powell suggests that she was not alone in her ability to accommodate a masculine and feminine self: "All actors are continually experimenting and inventing with their hormones, their male and female genes, and a few have the luck to be evenly balanced between their sexual drives. Pamela was one of these. She was a witch. Women adored her. Men feared her and for the same reason—she fascinated them" (Powell 1992, 96). The inference in Powell's analysis is that all of us, not just actors, are vessels for "male and female genes."

THE NETHERLANDS: QUEEN WILHELMINA AND THE EMASCULATED MALE

It is extremely fitting that a British movie so intent upon toying with ideas about masculine and feminine behaviour should take place in the Netherlands. For several years before 1942, the British had repeatedly associated their European neighbour with feminine strength. In British newspapers, books, and radio programs, Holland was embodied by the figure of its queen, Wilhelmina. *The Times* reported in August 1940 that "Holland lives in her Queen" (Abrahamson 1940, 5). Wilhelmina's gender was central to her myth. Her actions and decisions were often discussed, not only as those of a national icon, but also as those of a woman. May 1940 found *The Times* opining, "The Queen's proclamation made a great impression and was described as a 'true woman's utterance'" ("Holland Meets the War"). Wilhelmina's advanced age at the time of her country's occupation meant that she would naturally assume the role of matriarch. In a 1941 essay published in Britain, Dutch writer Louis de Jong describes Wilhelmina's escape to England:

"On the day of the capitulation it was the heart alone which spoke; and that heart could not coolly accept the fact that the country's Mother had left her children" (1943, 21). Wilhelmina's frequent radio addresses in which she referred to the Netherlands as a "Motherland" would reinforce the notion that the queen was indeed the mother of her nation ("The Unconquerable Netherlands").

The rhetoric employed by this emphatically feminine monarch was tough-minded and dramatic. A typical utterance railed against the German invasion of her country: "I here launch a flaming protest against this unprecedented violation of good faith and all that is decent between cultured States" ("Queen Wilhelmina's 'Flaming Protest'"). Her tough talk was regularly quoted in the British press and rendered her a personification of strength and defiance. She would become the voice of Holland's underground. And it wasn't just her words that were impressive. She could be regarded as a de facto resistance member. As Louis de Jong argues, she "completely identified herself with the men and women of the Dutch underground" (1990, 49).

Wilhelmina appeared even stronger in comparison to the Dutch people. In Britain, Wilhelmina's subjects did not enjoy the same reputation as their queen. In the late 1930s, many in British government and diplomatic circles regarded the Dutch as weak, dithering, and scared. A British Foreign Office staffer wrote disparagingly, "A people who select as leaders in an emergency M. de Geer and M. van Kleffens deserve to be overrun and enslaved" (Moore 1992, 472). Even more disappointing to British civil servants was the fact that this pair had assumed power after, as historian Bob Moore puts it, "the downfall of Dutch strongman Colijn" (470). Lord Halifax noted in 1939, "the smaller states, such as the Scandinavians, Holland, Belgium ... are very frightened and might be expected to go for peace at any price" (471).

The Times echoed such opinions during this period. A 1937 article on Holland's colonial possessions claimed, "Not for 100 years have the Dutch in the Netherlands Indies been so worried as in the last five years" ("Holland in the East"). Two years later, the newspaper implied that Dutch citizens were fantasists, ill-suited to *realpolitik*: "Many of them ... appear to be looking forward to the day when the world returns to 'normal' and seem to base their political and economic theories on the economic freedom of the pre-War days. This appears to be their chief weakness." Unsurprisingly, the article concludes with an admiring portrait of a queen attempting to bring much-needed strength to her society: "Queen Wilhelmina, in her appeals for national unity and the ending of party strife and religious quarrels ... is doing her best to rouse the people to the reality of the world around them" ("The Spirit of Holland"). The queen, it was frequently argued, distinguished herself from her fellow citizens by displaying fortitude and pragmatism.

If Holland was defined by feminine strength, it was equally associated with emasculated men. *The Rape of the Netherlands*, a book by Dutch Foreign Minister Eelco van Kleffens, presents the nation's defeat as a specifically male humiliation: "One of the oldest self-governing countries in the world suddenly found itself treated as if it were the home of eight million minors, incapable of looking after themselves. Humiliation and disgust haunt the soul of every Dutchman" (1941, 174). It is notable that, instead of casting his nation as feminine—the "motherland" Wilhelmina frequently refers to—van Kleffens repeatedly portrays Holland as masculine. Employing language commonly used to describe fist fights between men, he tells us that the Netherlands has been "beaten to the ground." His country is embodied by images of the male body laid low. He describes a corpse he saw during the invasion: "A little further on lay the uniformed body of a young Dutchman, his pale face turned towards the sky, a large pool of blood around him—a symbol of his country, attacked by ruthless superior force" (122). Van Kleffens discusses the decimation of the Dutch army not with neutral words such as "soldiers" or "troops." Rather, he is very specific in claiming that the Nazis destroyed "young men" and "manpower." He tells us, "The Dutch army lost thousands of its young men. The toll taken on some regiments attained a very high figure: let us remember here with deep respect our gallant Grenadiers who, after storming two airdromes in one day, had lost eighty percent of their manpower" (144). After reading this catalogue of assaults on men and masculinity, it is reasonable to wonder whether the sexual assault mentioned in the book's title may have been perpetrated, at least in van Kleffens's imagination, against a man.

The Rape of the Netherlands was a well-known book in Britain,[3] but it was hardly an isolated meditation on Dutch emasculation. *The Times*, echoing the opinion of those aforementioned civil servants who ridiculed dithery Dutch politicos, painted a picture of Dutch manhood as a precarious entity. A 1940 story casting the Dutch as a "subjugated people" focused on "attempts by the German Occupiers to toughen-up Dutch boys" ("Holland Under the Yoke"). When the newspaper informed its readership of the German wish to deport Dutchmen to work in foreign factories, it presented the policy as an attack on manhood. The Nazis were trying to "transplant 3,000,000 Dutchmen in the flower of manhood from 'overcrowded' Holland to that wilderness which the Germans have made of a large part of Eastern Europe" ("Nazi Plans for Holland"). Dutch masculinity, already compromised by invasion, was apparently under constant threat.

By late 1941, when Powell and Pressburger began planning their film, it appears that they had thoroughly absorbed the prevailing notion of the Netherlands as a land headed by a strong woman and peopled by emasculated men. Their portrayal of the Dutch Resistance as a matriarchy in which men play a relatively minor role seems highly influenced by this reductive characterization. Of course, in reality, the Dutch underground was made up of both sexes. Historian Pierre Janssen informs us, "There were men of the resistance; men who talked with England in secret by radio, men who fought the Germans with arms, men who printed newspapers in which Dutch people could read the truth" (1970, 29). And yet, *One of Our Aircraft Is Missing* keeps men who were engaged in these activities entirely off the screen.

While the movie downplays the role of men, it simultaneously implies that women constituted the leadership of the Dutch underground. Women certainly played a very significant role in the Resistance. A common task for women was to chaperone downed Allied airmen. Historian Herman Bodson contends, "Women played a part in the World War II lines.... Young girls were predominantly the ones to carry messages along the chains of command as well as to guide airmen from one location to another.... In the safe houses women had the basic responsibilities of cooking, caring, providing for, and sometimes even nursing the wounded or burned" (2005, 155). Walter Maass notes that "the resistance had to rely on courier services, most of them composed of young women. One group which called itself with irony 'Rolls Royce,' established a real itinerary between Amsterdam and The Hague. All the work was done by girls on bicycles. They were in less danger of being controlled by German guards, and ladies' bicycles were rarely confiscated" (1970, 218). *One of Our Aircraft Is Missing* does a good job of highlighting the importance of women in the Dutch Resistance. However, the film's women are not message bearers, cooks, or nurses. We do witness the women guiding the British airmen from place to place, but Powell and Pressburger present them as far more than brave guides. In this movie, women are the face of the underground, its leaders, and its most active members.

Inspired, it seems, by a zeitgeist that hummed with ideas about the men and women of the Netherlands, rather than the realities of a Nazi-occupied nation, Powell and Pressburger constructed their own version of Holland. Theirs is a nation in which a formidable breed of women takes the helm.

ONE OF OUR AIRCRAFT IS MISSING: MASCULINE ABSENCE, FEMININE PRESENCE

After an early scene in which the loss of the plane and its occupants is established in highly atmospheric fashion, *One of Our Aircraft Is Missing* takes us back in time to the day preceding the mission. We meet the six crewmen whose story we will follow as they eat in the mess, ready themselves for the journey, climb aboard their plane, and carry out the bombing run. This first section of the movie is defined by events and conversations that revolve around masculine absence and feminine presence. Powell and Pressburger waste no time in suggesting that manhood is under threat of disappearance, while womanhood will stamp its presence on the proceedings.

The motif of the absent man is woven through the film's early scenes. The startling image of a plane devoid of crewmen draws us into the narrative. At the aerodrome where the crew awaits its mission, a Canadian flyer, Sergeant Hopkins (Robert Beatty), is ordered to stand down. A close-up of his name being wiped from a chalkboard stresses his excision. In another vignette, men listening to a radio broadcast of a soccer game are surprised to find that the player they expect to take a penalty kick has been replaced at the last second. Men seem unable to hold on to their customary positions. Where we expect to find them, they are missing.

Perhaps the most prominent "man" to disappear in the film's early scenes is the bomber flown by the crew. Great stress is placed on the plane's gender. Its code name is "B for Bertie." Bertie is presented as "one of the boys"—a key member of the all-male group. The plane's mechanic enthuses, "New Coat. Full Stomach. Bertie's a gent." Bertie has impeccable masculine forebears. He is a Wellington bomber and therefore related to an iconic British military leader, Arthur Wellesley, 1st Duke of Wellington. The loss of Bertie—an event significant enough to be enshrined in the title of the movie—can be construed as a loss for masculine, not just national, pride.[4]

While men have a precarious hold on the movie, women will not be so easily dismissed. Just after Bertie goes missing, we are informed that another, emphatically feminine plane, code-named "M for Mother," has landed safely. Michael Powell himself, playing the role of the dispatching officer, tells us, "M for Mother landed 0426. No sign of any other aircraft about. Still no sign of B for Bertie." The masculine plane is defined by its absence, the feminine by its presence.

Even in the homosocial space that is the Royal Air Force (RAF) mess hall, women are very present. The assembled crewmen discuss girlfriends, fiancées, and wives, thereby allowing femininity a foothold in this most masculine of realms. The women discussed are notably forthright. Co-pilot Tom Earnshaw (Eric Portman) receives mail from his fiancée. The package contains no love letter, but two photographs, one of a sheep, the other of a ram. Tom and his fiancée, both children of the wool business, intend to interbreed their stock. A woman actively involved in the family business is displaying a proactive nature by suggesting they move ahead with the breeding program. It seems that she is taking a dominant role, not only on the farm, but also in the bedroom. Surely she is casting herself as the sheep and Tom as the ram, a cheeky and sexually assertive gesture that marks her as somewhat out of step with prevailing sexual etiquette. Her suggestiveness is not lost on Navigator Frank Shelley (Hugh Willams), who, looking at the two pictures, quips "I'm dying to see those two noble animals in the same meadow."

Frank then discusses his wife's impending radio broadcast, in which she will sing on the BBC's *Home and Forces Program*. She has sent Frank a letter reminding him and his compatriots to listen. "Hazel says, 'don't forget tomorrow night,'" Frank announces. Hazel, a woman of some celebrity, has a prominent voice, not just in the world of song, but also in the lives of the crew members. In the face of her performance, all other activities must be cancelled. Rear Gunner George Corbett (Godfrey Tearle), who had intended to pack his kit on the night of the broadcast, is informed by Frank, "No, no, no, you're listening to my wife."

The Canadian airman, Sergeant Hopkins, once again highlights the indelible stamp of femininity upon these men's lives. He reveals that he wears his girl-friend's silk stockings under his flying suit. "They keep you warm as toast," he claims, but worries what will happen if his "girl ever finds out." Hopkins is not the only man to covet feminine hosiery. The garments are apparently a prized possession among a great many of the flyers. An airman asks the grounded Hopkins, "If you're not going, can I have your silk stockings?" Even though a portrait of King George VI, a symbol of masculine power, presides over the mess, it would seem that all things feminine—women's words, voices, and even clothes—hold the greatest sway.

During the mission to bomb Germany, other formidable women are discussed. The pilot, John Glyn Haggard (Hugh Burden), and the front gunner, Geoff Hickman (Bernard Miles), begin to wax nostalgic about women they've known who possessed decidedly maternal qualities. Amazingly, both men have enjoyed relationships with nurses from Stuttgart. Nurses, of course, are traditionally associated with the nurturing and authoritative qualities of mothers. This pair is no exception. Geoff describes his ex-girlfriend as "a big blonde job." "Couldn't half cook too," he adds enthusiastically. The ample figure and the culinary skill endow her with a motherly air. He continues, "She used to sing that song, 'I Kiss Your Little Hand, Madame.'" The fact that she sang the song to Geoff constitutes an amusing gender reversal in which she, like a chivalrous man, kisses his hand and refers to him as "Madame." John reveals that his blonde nurse, who would read him the newspaper "out loud," was actually his nursemaid when he was a toddler. "I was only two you see," he tells us, stressing once again a submissive role to a powerful woman. These anecdotes are fittingly followed by another nod to women's dominance. As the men fly over their target, they see a huge fire below. "Bet that's Queenie on the job," says Geoff, admiring the destructive capabilities of a bomber code-named "Q for Queenie."

Figure 9.1 *One of Our Aircraft Is Missing.* © 1942 Melange Pictures LLC. Used with permission.

IN HOLLAND: STRIPPING AWAY MASCULINE POWER

While the men certainly seem to have a penchant for authoritative women, they are—until the moment that their plane is hit by anti-aircraft fire—very much in charge of their mission. They perform their duties with great care and skill, waging war—firing guns and dropping bombs—in the efficient manner we would expect from a film's male heroes. In the confines of the plane, they are at their most powerful. Indeed, the men's power, and their ability to share their strength with the beleaguered Netherlands, is suggested by a moment in which they drop a bottle of Guinness, along with propaganda leaflets, over the Dutch countryside. The obvious connotation, especially for 1940s audiences, is that the bomber crew, by its very presence over Holland, brings with it the same kind of vigour that was famously obtainable from drinking Guinness, which a well-known advertising campaign claimed was "good for you."

The men's power at this point in the narrative is further underscored by several shots in which they gaze at their surroundings with laser-like concentration. The fact that the lower half of each man's face is largely obscured by an intercom, so that his eyes are greatly emphasized, means that even the most subtle ocular movement or expression takes on an enigmatic and intense quality. Whether they are reading a map or contemplating the white cliffs of Dover, their gaze is freighted with great significance. We might say that the flying sequence reduces the male body to nothing more than a pair of eyes. And the efficiency of those eyes is an integral part of the men's aura of power. The whole sequence is built around shots of the watchful men, checking the skies for enemy aircraft, surveying the ground below, and carefully charting their course. Their eyesight proves admirably sharp since they are able to hit their target and complete the mission. However, just as the pilot announces, "Mission completed," there is an enormous explosion, wrenching the men from a space they were able to control.

After they abandon their plane and parachute to earth in Holland, the edifice of masculine power starts to crumble. The dawn chorus alerts us to the fact that the predictable and ordered world of the plane has given way to the more chaotic space of nature. Most of the crew is in a rural field, lost. The whereabouts of Radio Operator Bob Ashley (Emrys Jones) are unknown, a situation that threatens the efficiency of the team. John, the pilot, climbs a tree to survey the countryside. It is an image that renders him boyish. As the other men call up to him, the scene begins to resemble a children's adventure story more than a war film. John climbs down and begins to suck thoughtfully on a piece of grass. The talk turns to Bob, the missing crew member, and specifically his vulnerability. In civilian life, he was a soccer player travelling from place to place with his team and, therefore, it is claimed, possesses no sense of direction. "Bob will get lost on his own," laments Geoff. Pinpoint accuracy and skilled navigation have given way to uncertainty. As the men squat in the grass and exchange rather ludicrous ideas about how to avoid detection (George suggests that he strip off his clothes to pose as a "swimming Dutchman"), they appear increasingly helpless.

The first Dutch citizens onscreen are four children chasing a runaway pig. The airmen are forced to scramble for cover, all choosing to hide in the nearby tree. Their attempt at evasion is quickly foiled and the crew strikes up a conversation with the youthful band. There is a rapid affinity between the two groups. On discovering that the men are members of the Royal Air Force, a Dutch boy asks if they have come to invade Holland. "What with?" comes Frank's sardonic reply, emphasizing their somewhat impotent position, bereft of their plane and its weaponry. The children are surreptitiously wearing safety pins, a symbol of the Dutch underground that means, they reveal, "keep together, keep your mouth shut." The mention of the safety pin, an object associated with infants and motherhood, is pertinent as the men are about to encounter the Dutch matriarchy. The children decide to take the crew to see Els Meertens, the local schoolmistress and resistance leader. A scene in which the men appear notably childlike climaxes with them being taken to see a teacher like naughty schoolboys.

The following scene reinforces the suggestion that the airmen are about to be disciplined. They have been taken to a large farmhouse that functions as a base for the Resistance. Standing in an imposing antechamber, before an antique door, they look remarkably like a group of wayward boys nervously awaiting their fate outside a head teacher's study. Beyond the door is a large room full of highly animated Dutch citizens all chattering at once. Most of the room's approximately twenty occupants are women. A particularly vociferous woman pounds a table with her fist and shouts. Only three men are present, two of who remain seated. All three men choose to be silent amid the clamour.

Els Meertens appears in the doorway, beautiful and unsmiling. She certainly possesses the bearing and tone of a strict schoolmistress, and the men are suddenly children again in the face of her questioning. She wants to be sure of their identities, and, taking hold of Tom's hand, she tells Geoff, "I'm sure you can tell me your friend's name." Geoff is suddenly a tongue-tied youngster. "Well, can you or can't you?" she adds testily. The situation has apparently reached an impasse when the men are saved, in a sense, by a woman. Frank's wife, the singer Hazel Mason, is known to each of the crew members, and their shared knowledge of her upcoming broadcast on the *Home and Forces Program* proves to Els that they are indeed a downed Royal Air Force crew rather than enemies of the Resistance. The men's fate is now in the hands of women, even a woman who is hundreds of kilometres away in England.

The scene at the farmhouse inaugurates a series of moments that infer the deterioration of the men's eyesight. While the crew members proved to be skilled observers in the confines of their plane, they lose this capability once on the ground in Holland. Tom tells Els that he suspects her of working for the Nazis. Her riposte is a caustic, "I thought airmen had better eyesight than that." The men have completely missed the clues to her allegiance. Orange blossoms, a symbol of the underground, adorn the surrounding furniture. Els's eyesight is, by contrast, admirably sharp. "I see you wear an identity bracelet," she observes to Tom while conducting her interrogation.

We are left with no doubt that women preside over this space. The farmhouse is filled with the iconography of femininity. The men discover a portrait of Wilhelmina, which is not just a marker of Els's underground sympathies, but also a suggestion that a matriarch is in command. The portrait is an interesting contrast to the picture of King George VI that watched over the masculine space of the mess. At first, the men are unaware of the queen's portrait, since it is concealed behind that of a gentleman farmer who, ostensibly, has authority over this household. The discovery of Wilhelmina's image is highly significant, suggesting that, while the farmer may appear to be in charge, the real power in this home and, by extension, this nation, lies with women. As Els stands in front of the portrait while addressing the crew, we are asked to make a visual association between the two women. This is the first of two moments in which the movie compares a woman member of the Dutch Resistance to the admired queen.

As if to confirm the connotation that the household's patriarch is relatively powerless, the next scene presents the farmer as almost immobile and largely mute. He utters only one word—"gesundheit"—as he downs a shot of liquor, and will remain in a state of virtual inertia throughout the next scene. Two

Dutchmen give very brief welcoming speeches to the crew, but it is Els who sits at the head of the table. The focus of the scene is on women who busy themselves feeding the Britons from a table groaning with food. The composition of several shots emphasizes that a throng of women surround the crew. The safety of the environment is womb-like. Once again, our heroes have become children, embracing maternal women. Indeed, Geoff casts himself as a child with the words, "If we're going to be pushing off, I would just like another slice of that ham, Mother."

Power has been decisively handed from men to women and, after some initial suspicion from Tom, the men are happy to place themselves under women's command. Els is the subject of great admiration. "What a girl!" John will exclaim on two separate occasions. "You've got your head screwed on all right," Tom tells her. Els is even discussed in terms of the aerial dogfight, further suggesting that she has won over these RAF men and, in the process, been afforded access to a particularly male-centred realm. "She certainly shot you down in flames, Tom," notes Frank. The men's pleasurable absorption into the matriarchy continues as Frank removes his uniform and willingly disguises himself as a Dutchwoman, complete with pregnant belly. Soon afterwards, the men discover that a group of Dutch girls has transformed their parachutes into petticoats to hide them from unfriendly eyes. Having placed themselves in Els's capable hands, the crew members are taken by bicycle to a church service. Els commands a tandem bicycle and teaches John, seated in the rear position, how to handle the vehicle. "How am I doing?" he asks hopefully. "Quite well for a beginner," she judges.

Clearly, the film's men and women will not be bound by conventional gender roles. Women adopt a position of command and control that is usually the preserve of men, while men willingly take on a more passive, stereotypically feminine position. In keeping with this emphasis on gender's fluidity, the movie repeatedly points out that appearances cannot be trusted: behind the portrait of a supposedly powerful man is a portrait of an evidently powerful woman; under the RAF flying suit is a pair of women's silk stockings; under the skirt is a parachute; and the pretty schoolteacher is also a ruthless and skilled interrogator. If we look beyond the surface, we find that men and women's identities are far more complex than commonly assumed.

It is not just the notion of gender that the movie attempts to complicate. Other markers of identity—specifically uniforms and nationality—are shown to be untrustworthy. Els asks the assembled airmen, "Can any of you prove beyond a reasonable doubt that you are what you say you are?" "Well, our uniforms," Geoff replies. She discounts such simple-minded logic and suggests that the uniforms could be a disguise. With naive fervour, Geoff counters with, "But we're English, Miss. We wouldn't do a thing like that, would we, Frank?" Geoff's belief that identity is innate, easily recognizable, and understandable through the clothes we wear or the nation we call home seems a childish notion when subjected to Els's wry interrogation.

Because the film places great emphasis on the subject of role-playing, it implies that identity is a form of performance. Frank, we discover, was an actor in civilian life. As he prepares to climb aboard the bomber, a member of the ground crew asks for an autograph. "I saw you in *The School for Scandal*," claims the fan. "You played the part of Joseph Surface." The very fact that one of our main characters is a professional performer suggests that the movie is unusually concerned with artifice. Frank is not just an actor—he has appeared in the Richard Sheridan play that is famously built around the subject of deception. As the men remove their uniforms and don traditional Dutch clothing, they take a moment to discuss their acting abilities. "I never thought I'd be co-starring with the great Frank Shelley in a Dutch epic," marvels George. In Brechtian fashion, this line of dialogue reminds us that the men onscreen are engaged in layers of performance. Not only is George about to act in a "Dutch epic," but he is also acting in a movie called *One of Our Aircraft Is Missing*. Of course, George is neither a Dutchman nor an English Rear Gunner. He is Godfrey Tearle, an American-born actor appearing in the movie we are watching. This is not an isolated moment of self-reflexivity. Even the title sequence of the movie stresses that the men we are viewing are actors playing roles. As the camera tracks around the interior of the bomber, it alights on each member of the crew in turn. Each actor announces his character's name while his real name is superimposed over the image. Rather than hiding the notion of performance, the movie points out its own artificial nature from the outset.

Role-playing demands costume changes, and the movie is rife with them. The first time we meet the crew members they are weighed down with layers of clothing, almost indistinguishable from one another because of their thick, heavy flying suits and face-masking intercoms. When we next see them, the outer layers have been discarded to reveal their lighter RAF uniforms. In Holland, the uniforms will be cast aside and new costumes tried on. George almost abandons clothes entirely to complete his "swimming Dutchman" disguise. It seems that one project of the movie is to show men stripping away costumes, trying on new clothes and, with them, new identities.

DUTCHMEN: EMBRACING PASSIVITY

In the Netherlands, we encounter several Dutchmen. They are certainly not as prominent in the narrative as Dutchwomen, and, at first glance, appear to embody the much-discussed weakness and emasculation of their nation. Indeed, the first Dutchmen that the movie references are dead. The inaugural image of the film is a list of deceased men, members of the Dutch underground who have been shot dead by the Nazis. On official notepaper, headed with "The Netherland Government Information Bureau," are the words, "In the summer of 1941 five Dutchmen were executed by the Herrenvolk for assistance in the escape of a British aircrew. These are their names." There follows a list of the executed. The document concludes with the assertion, "Their names shall be remembered." However, rather than remembering their names, the film seems intent upon forgetting them. After such a compelling opening image, one might reasonably assume that *One of Our Aircraft Is Missing* will be about these men, or at least focus on the activities of men like them. Yet, this is not the case. It is as if Powell and Pressburger began their movie in such a way so that they could quickly confound our expectations. They offer the prospect of a typical male-centred war story, only to spend the rest of their film undermining the standard portrayals of men and women in wartime.

The Dutchmen we meet are proponents of "passive resistance," referring to the many low-key strategies that the Dutch used to frustrate the Germans and undermine the occupation, such as playing banned music or refusing to look at Nazi troops. When passive resistance was reported in the Allied press, it tended to be associated with Dutchmen. For instance, *Time* magazine presented a portrait of "placid Dutchmen" and characterized Holland's opposition to Reichskommissar Arthur Seyss-Inquart as a battle of wills between schoolboys and their teacher. We are asked to believe that "poor patient Dr. Seyss-Inquart was in much the same spot as a fuddy-duddy professor in a classroom full of rowdy boys" ("The Netherlands: It Beats the Dutch"). Passivity, it seems, was the result of "subjugation." The "passive resistance of the subjugated peoples" was the subject of a 1941 article in *The Times* ("Passive Resistance in Holland"). Powell and Pressburger, too, align their Dutchmen with passivity. A Nazi patrol enters a church in which a Dutch congregation, hiding the British aircrew, is singing a hymn. As a German officer menacingly surveys the faithful, the male organist protests the intrusion by playing a few notes of the Dutch national anthem.

The next scene finds the men at the house of a burgomaster who proves to be a likeable but rather silly authority figure. Played by the diminutive, hammy actor Hay Petrie, he spends his time complaining about the Germans. His shortcomings as a patriarch are stressed by an unsuccessful attempt to discipline his young son, Cornelius (Jimmy Baker), whom he chases upstairs but fails to catch. Echoing the scene at the farmhouse, this interlude with the burgomaster demonstrates how the domestic patriarch is simply a figurehead. The man's daughter, Jet van Dieren (Joyce Redman), displaying far more poise and authority than the ostensible head of the household, reveals paternal authority to be a sham. In her only scene, she speaks more lines than her father and is more insightful, telling us that her brother Cornelius is "more than meets father's eye." This further reference to the failure of a man's eyesight proves to be prophetic, since we eventually discover that the boy is passively resisting the Nazis. Cornelius has taken gramophone records to the German troops garrisoned across the street. His father is horrified at this apparent fraternization. But the boy has indulged in some rather subtle and clever anti-German activity, switching the labels on the discs and thereby tricking the soldiers into playing Dutch patriotic music. A form of aural torture ensues that apparently drives the Germans to distraction.

At a soccer game, the passive resistance strategies spearheaded by Dutchmen are presented once again. Attempting to blend into Dutch society, the British crew watches the game with the burgomaster. The Nazis are observing the crowd and judge that there are too many people. Through a loudspeaker, they order that fifty of them must leave. A conversation between Tom and the burgomaster identifies Dutchmen as particularly prone to passivity:

Tom:	"Tell 'em to go to hell."
Burgomaster:	"That would cause trouble."
Tom:	"It would that."
Burgomaster:	"Many people might be killed or injured."
Tom:	"Aye, on both sides."
Burgomaster:	"In Holland we've found a new system. If fifty are ordered to go, we all go."

And so, the crowd begins to disperse. The German overseers are confused and disoriented by this challenge to what John calls their "orderly minds." The Nazis order the crowd to reconvene and the game to continue. "Jerry seems a bit flustered," notes John with pleasure.

Even though the movie pokes fun at Dutchmen and insists that they are not taking the lead in the fight against the Nazis, the passive resistance strategies of these gentle men prove to be worthwhile. Their brand of heroism is based in psychological, rather than physical, warfare. In endorsing this subtle approach to conflict, *One of Our Aircraft Is Missing* asks us to consider a more nuanced conception of masculinity.

JO DE VRIES: EMBODYING THE FLUIDITY OF GENDER

The men conclude their sojourn in the Netherlands in the company of Jo de Vries, an aristocratic woman whose large house has been commandeered by the Nazis. A dedicated resistance member, she is tasked with hiding the crew and then spiriting them out to sea. As if to emphasize that Jo is doing a job that would traditionally belong to a man, there is some initial confusion regarding her gender. After Bob mispronounces her name as "Joe," Tom admonishes him by saying, "Yo, not Joe," and confirming, "It's a woman, not a man."

In many ways, Jo's persona is masculine. In her first scenes, she dresses in factory overalls with her long hair hidden by a scarf. Hanging from the side of a moving truck, she accepts delivery of the crew to her house. She shares the commanding tone employed by Els, and tells the men she has warmed to a life of danger just as they have. She even refers to herself as a man: "I'd rather be a Dutchman in Holland now than any German soldier." Without doubt, she is in command, asking Tom, "Are you in command of this party?" Before Tom can reply, George answers, "No, he's just a Yorkshireman." Jo persists, asking George, "Are you in command?" George graciously defers, "No, you are."

Like the other women in the film, Jo can boast effective eyesight. Tom wonders if "Mrs. de Vries has her weather eye open." Indeed she has. There are several shots of Jo looking at the men in a contemplative manner as if judging their fitness for battle. "Now, let me see you all," she says, emphasizing her tendency to cast an appraising eye across the group.

While Jo displays several qualities usually identified as masculine, she is quite able to move back and forth across the spectrum of gendered behaviour. A living example of gender's malleability, she takes off her overalls to slip into an evening dress and flamboyant diamond earrings, telling the crew, "It's nice to be a woman again, even for half an hour." Her feminine side is repeatedly highlighted when she behaves in a queenly manner. She is from patrician stock, presides over a mansion, and, when the situation dictates, launches into patriotic speeches regarding the fate of what she calls her "enslaved people." As she holds forth, eyes skyward, the camera's low angle adds to a sense of her physical and moral stature. The British crew listens to her fiery words with rapt attention and consistently treats her like royalty. Frank, the actor, adopts a courtly persona in her presence, choosing to reverently kiss her hand. "No Englishman would kiss a woman's hand, except perhaps an actor," Jo responds. But she will be kissed again, this time by George, who kisses her cheek, augmenting the farewell with a brief, stiff bow as if he were a respectful courtier. Jo's queenly qualities were not lost on the designers of the film's poster, who made sure that her disembodied face hovers next to two of the British crew members, dominating the image and seemingly presiding over the fate of the men. "Queen of the Underground," the poster proclaims, alluding to Jo and, clearly, the real-life queen of the underground, Wilhelmina.

In Jo's company, and after she has sent them on their way, the crewmen are notably passive. Their female leader outlines every stage of their escape plan, leaving virtually nothing for them to do. "Everything is prepared," she tells them. "There's nothing to do now but wait." When the time is right for escape, she leads them through the rafters above a room full of two hundred singing German soldiers. The men can do very little but follow. In a brief nod to their physical abilities, the British must overpower three German soldiers. The fight is over quickly and the focus returns to Jo, who puts the men in a rowboat and sets them adrift.

German sentries quickly spot the men and shoot at them, managing to wound the crew's leader and oldest member, George. It is perhaps fitting that before they leave matriarchal Holland, the patriarch of the group of men should take a bullet. Evading the enemy less by their own actions and more because the tide is favourable, the men drift out to sea, reaching a floating platform designed as a shelter for downed pilots. Here they bob, impotently waiting to be rescued. Their inactivity is comically underscored as one of them plays a solitary card game and another cooks soup. Eventually, a British naval vessel picks them up and tows them to shore. This ignominious and decidedly unheroic climax to their adventure is imposed upon them because George is too badly injured to be moved. Admitting that they had mistaken their saviours for Germans, the men are once again forced to confront their faulty eyesight. "Trouble with you fellas is, you can't see anything unless you're ten thousand feet up," a naval officer tells them sarcastically.

As if the filmmakers knew that leaving the men in such a powerless position would be frowned upon by Britain's Ministry of Information, the last minute of the movie sees the crew returned to a conventional world of masculine agency. Back in England, the men stride towards a new plane, bigger and better than their previous vessel. Marvelling at the bomber, George notes, "That's more my size," and in a sudden resort to triumphalism, the screen is filled with the words "The Netherlands will rise again!"

This brief coda, which rather startlingly reminds us of the film's genesis as propaganda, does little to dispel the notion that we have just witnessed a hymn to matriarchy. Powell and Pressburger used the Netherlands under the Nazis to imagine how a society run by women might look and feel. Certainly, they intended to memorialize and support the work of the Dutch Resistance, but they mainly celebrate Dutchwomen and their contribution to the war effort. It is highly probable that audiences leave the film with the impression that the Dutch underground was a feminine enterprise. And because Powell and Pressburger's films remain some of the most widely viewed and lavishly praised works of British cinema, it is likely that their conception of the German-occupied Netherlands will be one of the most indelible.

Ultimately, *One of Our Aircraft Is Missing* seems motivated less by official propaganda imperatives and more by a desire to play with the notion of gender. And yet, the film's most powerful propaganda message may lie in its realignment of men and women's roles. In suggesting that societies can function, and wars can be won, when conventional notions of gendered behaviour are jettisoned, the movie stands as a powerful anti-Nazi tract. British cinema may have taken a reactionary stance on gender, but a dichotomous approach to masculinity and femininity was never a centrepiece of official wartime policy in the United Kingdom. Indeed, the fact that women in Britain were encouraged to take the jobs left behind by the nation's fighting men suggests that there existed a certain amount of openness to social change. In contrast, Nazi Germany made sure to stress that the sexes were distinct in every way—so much so that women rarely served in industrial and military settings (Kitchen 1995, 139). German women, the National Socialist Party decreed, were defined by their duty as wives and mothers. Also as a matter of state policy, men were placed squarely in the "active" half of the gender binary. As a 1943 party pamphlet argued, "A woman who forgets her species and her position and becomes intellectual and erotic, is in a similar state of racial degeneration as a man who scorns work and action" (140). Powell and Pressburger's film stands in opposition to Hitler's Germany, not only by highlighting the ingenuity of Allied forces, but also by implicitly condemning the gender biases of Nazi ideology.

NOTES

1   *One of Our Aircraft Is Missing* might be accused of engaging in a similar strategy by relegating independent women to the safe distance of a foreign nation. However, Powell and Pressburger make clear their opinion that British and Dutch women are equally capable of proving themselves heroic, with a crewman proclaiming, "Our girls would do just the same if they had the chance."

2   *Black Narcissus* finds Sister Clodagh (Deborah Kerr) attempting to found a convent in a Himalayan palace once used as a harem; *The Red Shoes* follows dancer Vicky Page (Moira Shearer) climbing towards stardom in the physically and emotionally tumultuous world of professional ballet; and *Gone to Earth* portrays how a gypsy girl, Hazel Woodus (Jennifer Jones), tries to retain the free-spirited nature that a closed-minded society would reign in. Powell and Pressburger's men characters often display great affinity for women and femininity. During World War II, when masculine heroics would seem the obvious subject matter, the filmmakers created *An Airman's Letter to His Mother*, a quiet and moving testament to a relationship little emphasized by movies with a military theme. In *The Life and Death of Colonel Blimp*, the main character, Clive Candy, famously dons a woman's hat as he gives his blessing to a marriage that will rob him of the woman he loves.

3   *The Rape of the Netherlands* is prominently advertized in the 26 October 1940 edition of *The Times*. The advertisement includes a glowing review from *The Daily Telegraph*, calling the book "undoubtedly one of the principal documents of the war."

4   Van Kleffens notes in *The Rape of the Netherlands* that "every one of our aeroplanes was lost," thereby suggesting a link between absent planes and emasculation.

WORKS CITED

Abrahamson, H.S. 1940. "A Sovereign in Exile." Letter. *The Times*, 31 August 1940, 5.

Aldgate, Anthony, and Jeffrey Richards. 2007. *Britain Can Take It: British Cinema in the Second World War*. London: I.B. Tauris.

Bodson, Herman. 2005. *Downed Allied Airmen and Evasion of Capture: The Role of Local Resistance Networks in World War II*. Jefferson, NC: McFarland.

Cook, Pam. 1996. "Neither Here nor There: National Identity in Gainsborough Costume Drama." In *Dissolving Views: Key Writings on British Cinema*, edited by Andrew Higson, 51–65. London: Cassell.

De Jong, Louis. 1943. *The Lion Rampant: The Story of Holland's Resistance to the Nazis.* New York: Querido.

———. 1990. *The Netherlands and Nazi Germany.* Cambridge: Harvard University Press.

Guttman, Matthew. 1996. *The Meanings of Macho: Being a Man in Mexico City.* Berkeley: University of California Press.

Harper, Sue. 1996. "From *Holiday Camp* to High Camp: Women in British Feature Films, 1945–51." In *Dissolving Views: Key Writings on British Cinema*, edited by Andrew Higson, 94–116. London: Cassell.

Hogue, Peter. 1990. "One of Our Aircraft is Missing." *Film Comment* 26(3): 30–32.

"Holland in the East." *The Times*, 20 March 1937, 15.

"Holland Meets the War." *The Times*, 14 May 1940, 7.

"Holland Under the Yoke." *The Times*, 30 May 1940, 6.

Janssen, Pierre. 1970. *A Moment of Silence.* New York: Atheneum.

Kitchen, Martin. 1995. *Nazi Germany at War.* London: Longman.

Lant, Antonia. 1991. *Blackout: Reinventing Women for Wartime British Cinema.* Princeton: Princeton University Press.

Maass, Walter B. 1970. *The Netherlands at War: 1940–1945.* London: Abelard-Schuman.

Moi, Toril. 1993. *Sexual/Textual Politics: Feminist Literary Theory.* London: Routledge.

Moore, Bob. 1992. "The Posture of an Ostrich? Dutch Foreign Policy on the Eve of the Second World War." *Diplomacy and Statecraft* 3 (3): 468–93.

Mulvey, Laura. 2011. "Visual Pleasure and Narrative Cinema." In *Critical Visions in Film History: Classic and Contemporary Readings*, edited by Timothy Corrigan, Patricia White, and Meta Mazaj, 713–24. Boston: Bedford/St. Martin's.

"Nazi Plans for Holland." Editorial. *The Times*, 2 July 1942, 5.

"The Netherlands: It Beats the Dutch." *Time.com*, 6 January 1941.

"One of Our Aircraft Is Missing." Review. *The Times*, 22 April 1942, 6.

"Passive Resistance in Holland." *The Times*, 20 June 1941, 3.

Powell, Michael. 1987. *A Life in Movies: An Autobiography.* New York: Alfred A. Knopf.

———. 1992. *Million Dollar Movie.* New York: Random House.

Powell, Michael, and Emeric Pressburger, dirs. 1942. *One of Our Aircraft is Missing.* Film. British National Films.

———. 1942. *The Tales of Hoffmann.* Film. British Lion Films.

"Queen Wilhelmina's 'Flaming Protest.'" *The Times*, 11 May 1940, 5.

Salwolke, Scott. 1997. *The Films of Michael Powell and the Archers.* Lanham, MD: Scarecrow Press.

Spicer, Andrew. 2003. *Typical Men: The Representation of Masculinity in Popular British Cinema.* London: I.B. Tauris.

"The Spirit of Holland." *The Times*, 8 March 1939, 17.

"The Unconquerable Netherlands: Queen Wilhelmina's Call to Her People." *The Times*, 2 September 1941, 2.

Van Kleffens, Eelco. 1941. *The Rape of the Netherlands (Juggernaut over Holland).* New York: Columbia University Press.

Wilchins, Riki. 2004. *Queer Theory, Gender Theory.* Los Angeles: Alyson Books.

FACING DEATH
The Paintings of Australian War Artist Stella Bowen

Catherine Speck

A small number of women were appointed to the post of official war artist during World War II. Australian Stella Bowen was one of this select group. Australia appointed three women, but forty-six men, to this prestigious post. The story is similar in Britain and Canada, but Bowen was the only artist based in air stations in Britain that came under attack, and the only woman artist whose subjects were pilots engaging in daily bombing raids over Germany in 1944.

Stella Bowen was an enterprising expatriate artist who had been based in cosmopolitan London, then Paris, since 1914.[1] She mixed with leading avant-garde artists, actors, poets, writers, and left-leaning intellectuals, and was in a relationship with American writer Ford Madox Ford from 1918 to 1927. But as she noted in her autobiography, *Drawn from Life*, her painting took second place to Ford's writing, and she became "consort to another and more important artist" (1984, 92). Her small annual allowance was spent on impractical farming ventures in rural England, and, once they moved to Paris, on Ford's short-lived literary magazine, the *Transatlantic Review*.

Conversations about art with Ford, however, were particularly well informed. He grew up in artistic circles: his grandfather was British artist Ford Madox Brown, his mother was an artist, and Ford had written books on Dante Gabriel Rossetti and the Pre-Raphaelite Brotherhood, and on the portrait painter Hans Holbein. Bowen was well versed in modern British and French art. She learned from Walter Sickert at London's Westminster School, and she admired the decorative neo-impressionist art of Edouard Vuillard and Pierre Bonnard, whose work focused on interiors (Weisenfarth 2002, 32). A trip to Italy in 1923 with Dorothy and Ezra Pound, however, marked a turning point for her. She saw Giotto's frescoes and paintings by Fra Angelico that suggested a new direction for her art, and before long she was back painting in earnest and exhibiting.

Separating from Ford in 1927 due to his serial infidelities, Bowen faced life as a single mother of a seven-year-old daughter. Her art was her principal source of income. The economy in France was in decline, so she headed to America to paint portraits for the well heeled. By 1934 she was back in London, where the currency was more stable, but times were still challenging for an artist (Stephenson 1991, 35). Bowen supplemented her income by working for London's *News Chronicle* as an art critic under the pseudonym "Palette." Once World War II was declared and London experienced the Blitz, she found some work in radio journalism, talking about life in wartime England for the BBC's Pacific Service, and these tapes were played to Australian audiences. Extracts were also reproduced in the Australian edition of *Women's World* in February 1942.

This is the colourful and resourceful life framing Stella Bowen. From 1942, she was proactive in seeking out an appointment as a war artist. This was a well-paid job, but she was also keen to represent the effects of war on England, and, as she wrote home, "The damage in London affects me dreadfully, but if I can somehow come to terms with it by painting it, I shall feel better."[2] Importantly, she had support from her influential Australian friends Keith Hancock, who was working as a historian at the British Cabinet Offices on an official civil history of the war, and his wife Theaden Brocklebank, who was a producer for the BBC.

The Australian High Commission in London suggested Bowen for appointment, and her name was duly put forward to the Australian War Memorial's Art Committee in February 1943 by committee member Louis McCubbin, director of the National Art Gallery of South Australia in Bowen's hometown of Adelaide. McCubbin knew Bowen's brother, and in 1943, he arranged for the art gallery to purchase and display her eerie painting *Embankment Gardens* (Figure 10.1), showing the usually busy London landmark next to Embankment Station as forlorn and empty in the early war years.[3]

Australia's Minister for the Interior approved Bowen and another woman, Nora Heysen, for the position in February 1943 (Speck 2004, 116). This was the first time Australian women had been appointed to these posts. Australia was slower at making this move than Britain, and only ever appointed a few women as war artists.[4]

It was almost a year after the approval that Bowen started work as an official war artist. A number of issues peculiar to army culture had to be settled first. Would she need a commission in the armed forces? Should she wear a uniform? (Bowen wasn't convinced she should wear one.) These issues were even more protracted because she lived in Britain. Finally, on 24 November 1943, she was granted an honorary commission at the rank of captain in the Reserve of Officers, and her pay was two guineas per day. By February 1944, the question of a uniform was resolved: she should wear one, and it would be an Australian Women's Army Service uniform.[5]

Figure 10.1 *Embankment Gardens,* by Stella Bowen, ca. 1938. Oil on cardboard, 63.5 x 76 cm. Art Gallery of South Australia.

In the meantime, Bowen was able to give thought to her commission and how she could work on group portraits as a modern artist while drawing also on a fourteenth-century Italian style, and how the design of the portrait is central in conveying the character of the subject. In mid-1943, she wrote to Louis McCubbin about the kind of work she might do: "With regard to the human side of things, I can't do 'action' pictures with crowds of busy people. My line is portraiture. I would much welcome a chance to do group portraits treated in a formal decorative scheme with emphasis on linear design. Uniforms and symbols would lend themselves to this treatment.... It would give me particular satisfaction that the chance to do this should come through my own country."[6]

Bowen was intrigued by the idea of group portraits that morphed modern style with formal design and decorative elements. She had completed several that show these early Italian Renaissance ideas at work, including her 1927 painting of the staff at her favourite Montparnasse restaurant. *Le Restaurant Lavigne* (or *Au Nègre de Toulouse*) was painted as three panels in a narrow tonal range, and with overlapping figures stacked up the picture canvas to suggest depth. In *Drawn from Life*, Bowen said she would love to "have had a lot of nice fleshy faces to portray, surrounded by their insignia of office, symbols or what not, all woven into a formal pattern" (Bowen 1984, 231). She had in mind what she called "conversation pieces," in which the design of the composition unified the work and produced a dynamic sense of interaction: "How I longed to arrange their faces in rows or in circles and dress them up in their gowns and fal-lals and perhaps stick in a bit of gold and even scrolly tickets to say who they were" (232). These were the design ideas she brought to her commission.

Initially, her appointment was for three months. However, with several extensions, she spent twenty months as a war artist, painting and drawing aircraft crews as they were about to leave, or after they returned from bombing missions, as well as other facets of life involving Australians serving abroad. These included the eventual repatriation of Australian airmen who had become prisoners of war in German camps. Special studios were set up for her at Royal Air Force (RAF) stations where she was assigned work, although she frequently had to arrange private accommodation elsewhere, as some of the RAF stations did not have appropriate facilities for women to stay overnight. On other postings, she was able to stay with the Women's Auxiliary Air Force (WAAF), but she wrote home, "We are in Nissen huts with no central heating and a coal shortage. Pipes and boilers are bursting everywhere. No hot water.... I have never been so cold."[7] Bowen preferred to complete her paintings in her London studio, where she had a special fluorescent light fitted so that she could paint irrespective of the nightly blackout.

The work she was assigned, representing the Australian aircraft crews and their support staff, came at a time when air power finally became the decisive factor that turned the European war around in favour of the Allies, and she was on hand to witness it. She was based at RAF stations at Binbrook in Lincolnshire, Pembroke Dock in South Wales, and Driffield in Yorkshire, where Royal Australian Air Force (RAAF) members were based. The Australian airmen in these bases were in the RAF's Bomber Command, which was carrying out heavy and sustained bombing over Germany. Bomber Command lost fifty thousand airmen, of whom thirty-five hundred were Australians (Clarke 2002, 52). Not unexpectedly, Bowen's art reflects the dramatic and life-threatening nature of young pilots' missions as they flew off to drop bombs over Germany at this time. Her delicate observational studies also present an intimate glimpse into the emotions the men experienced, especially the apprehension felt by many.

Her portrayal of the "weaker" emotions, including apprehension, that might problematize warfare is at odds with the ideal—as philosophers like Immanuel Kant and G.W.F. Hegel have proclaimed—of participating in war as the highest act of citizenship (Higonnet et al. 1987, 4). Some even see taking up arms for one's country as an opportunity to leave the "feminine" behind (Lloyd 1985, 75). Kant, for example, in *Critique of Judgment*, describes the virtues of participating in war, and says there is "something sublime about it," provided that "it is conducted with order and sacred respect for the rights of citizens." He contrasts this with periods of "prolonged peace" that foster "self-interest, cowardice and effeminacy" (Kant 1952, 112–13). In *Phenomenology of Spirit*, Hegel argues along similar lines that participating in war promotes the ultimate form of ethical consciousness in civil society, but one open to men alone—he associates the female consciousness with the private realm of the family. Hegel writes that "womankind … changes by intrigue the universal end of government into a private end, transforms its universal activity into a work of some particular individual, and perverts the universal property of the state into a possession and ornament for the family" (1977, 288).

The horrors of trench warfare in World War I, and the response by British poets like Wilfred Owen to the futile loss of life, created space for questioning these long-accepted beliefs about manly citizenship and the virtues of participation in war. While there is widespread acceptance that men at the front are placed in life-threatening situations, and some historians, including Australian Charles Bean, even mythologize those soldiers, there has, until relatively recently, been little probing of the social structures that surround masculinity (Thomson 1994, 159; Connell 2005, 35). The telling daily loss of life for airmen at the Binbrook air station broke that silence—the "atmosphere [there] was a curious mixture of operational pride, psychological strain, emotional numbness and acceptance of one's own fate" (Clarke 2002, 52). While based at Binbrook, Bowen witnessed that very tension.

Bowen was in an interesting situation. As an official war artist, she was expected to bring first-hand experience to her work. Her placement in the air stations, close to the action, was deliberate, so that her paintings would be imbued with a sense of reality. She was given the freedom to interpret her subjects, who were, in essence, men under stress. She began work in February 1944, and her first placement was in March at the Binbrook Royal Air Force station with the 460 Squadron. This was the most highly decorated Australian squadron, but also the one that suffered the most casualties. As an outsider, Bowen picked up on the tension for these vulnerable airmen in Bomber Command, but she also probed the psychology of those involved.

There was some danger for Bowen working in RAF bases, which were targeted by enemy bombers. As one newspaper commented, Bowen "admitted she never did like being bombed, however safe the protection." She was also required to work "at any hour of the day or night, catching men on the hop as they were about to leave an aerodrome on a mission over enemy territory, or returning to base."[8]

The personal danger to the artist, though, was minor in comparison to that facing the aircraft crews. Bowen said she "found it unnerving and distressing to be painting fine aircrews who sat patiently, often rather amused, and then went off on a mission, never to return."[9] This occurred while she was working on a painting, which she subsequently called *Bomber Crew* (Figure 10.2), of six Australian airmen and one English airman.[10] Bowen had started the preparatory drawings when the pilots left for their nighttime bombing mission on 27 April 1944 over Friedrichshafen, an industrial centre in the south, and failed to return.[11] She had no option but to complete the painting in her London studio from the working drawings, but she found this extremely difficult. As she wrote to her brother, "It was terrible having to finish the picture after the men were lost. Like painting ghosts."[12] The only pilot subsequently found in a German prisoner-of-war camp was one of the Australians, the injured airman Thomas Lynch, who, in the painting, has a pale white face rising above the Lancaster, marking his close shave with death.[13]

Figure 10.2 *Bomber Crew*, by Stella Bowen, 1944. Oil on canvas, 86.1 x 63.3 cm. Australian War Memorial, ART26265.

This painting is rich in the application of her modernist ideas about design and composition. The overlapping figures are of men, not the angels in her Italian frescoes, but most have young and angelic faces. The limited tonal range adds to its sombre mood. The strapping of each pilot's harness is portrayed as one collective harness, as if the men are being airlifted to the heavens as a whole. Bowen's feeling that she was painting ghosts is seen in Squadron Leader Eric Jarman's hands: they already look deathly.

A decorative pink ribbon more usually associated with a memorial wreath gives the painting the quality of a monument. The ribbon winding around the base carries the names of the airmen and is punctuated by their flying wings. The memorial ribbon encircles the men at mid-torso, separating them from the earth and marking their physical change from creatures of the earth to inhabitants of the skies. Their transformation is enhanced by a cloud-like mass in the foreground that already envelops them. The name on each man's helmet, except Lynch's, has that deep, etched quality of names carved on memorial headstones. Their Lancaster bomber as the carrier of death also hovers above. This crew was one of the 763 crews shot down over Germany in bombing raids in the first three months of 1944.[14]

Another painting that Bowen completed at Binbrook is her ominous *Bombing Up a Lancaster for Wing Commander Douglas* (Figure 10.3), which points to the disparity of giant killing machines sitting in the tranquil green English countryside. The Lancaster was the main plane used in flights over Germany, and it carried a bigger bomb load than other planes. A ground crew had to service it meticulously each day, checking more than four hundred parts after each mission (Stanley 1985, 11). Bowen described this plane being loaded with its cargo of death as sinister and looking "like a terrifying insect, full of eggs" (quoted in Wilkins 1991, 495). The men loading the plane are dwarfed by its size. Wing Commander Douglas, standing to the left in the painting, checking the operations, was the youngest ever at his rank at twenty-two years of age, but died in February the following year in an attack over Germany (Clarke 2002, 53). The diminutive size of the men in the painting compared to the oversized Lancaster suggests not only a loss of human agency to the machinery of war, but also that the plane, resembling a giant insect, complete with antlers, could envelop the humans beneath it. The beguiling mauves and greens of the surrounding countryside do not obscure the fact that this is indeed a grim image.

The D-Day landing of troops at Normandy occurred while Bowen was at Binbrook. She had some warning that a significant event was about to take place. Major John Treloar, who ran the War Artists Scheme from Australia, had a cable sent to Bowen via the Australian High Commission in London, reading, "Important events will be taking place and there should be opportunities at Air

Figure 10.3 *Bombing Up a Lancaster for Wing Commander Douglas,* by Stella Bowen, 1944. Oil on hardboard, 63.4 x 76.2 cm. Australian War Memorial, ART26261.

Stations from which Australian squadrons are operating for pictures of considerable historical interest to be prepared."[15]

He was referring to D-Day, and in her painting *D-Day, 0300 Hours, Interrogation Hut, Warrant Officer George Lindenberg* (Figure 10.4), she presents this key event through women's eyes, as well as those of the men who took part. The painting is full of psychological drama between women of the WAAF, who were intelligence officers and pilots. The crew members in the rear area are attending a debriefing session with a WAAF intelligence officer. They have just returned to the Binbrook air station from their mission of silencing gun sites near Cherbourg, seven minutes prior to the first landing of troops at Normandy in France on D-Day, 6 June 1944.[16] They were part of the British bombing offensive that took place in the northwest of France at sites on the coast between Cherbourg and Le Harve, French ports under German occupation. The focus in the painting, though, is on the woman in the foreground, possibly an Australian, who is seeking information from a rather "edgy" and tentative RAAF pilot, Warrant Officer George Lindenberg, who had just come back from this key mission.[17]

Figure 10.4   *D-Day, 0300 Hours, Interrogation Hut, Warrant Officer George Lindenberg*, by Stella Bowen, 1944–45. Oil on canvas, 63.5 x 83.8 cm. Australian War Memorial, ART26266.

Their intense eye contact points to the mission's importance. The obligatory cup of tea, the plate of biscuits, and the pile of cigarettes are insignificant compared to that moment in history in the early hours of D-Day, when the offensive against Germany commenced. The space between the two figures gives the painting an electric tension, but also a warmth, which the glow of the warm orange-pink space conveys, as does the human touch of supper after a bombing raid.

Bowen was also based at Pembroke Dock in South Wales, where Sunderland seaplanes searched for enemy U-boat submarines. Her compelling 1945 painting *A Sunderland Crew Comes Ashore at Pembroke Dock* (Figure 10.5) is of an Australian crew, the ANZAC Squadron, which spent two years engaged in this gruelling work. She thought the seaplanes looked beautiful, and she gave them a portly and rather majestic presence. But they are less important to her than the men in the foreground who have just landed from a night out searching. They are coming ashore quickly, looking tense but pleased to be home.[18] As Derry Syme, the captain of that seaplane and the subject in the right foreground of Bowen's painting, recalled,

> We took off at last light and flew right through the night—we were high on tension all the time because we were flying at fifty feet above the water.

It was dangerous flying as we couldn't use the automatic pilot as it was too inaccurate. So we were hand flying on a radio altimeter to give us the fifty feet. We had to keep the needle dead on fifty. If we lost an engine we had no time to gain height. It was very, very tiring and exhausting. (quoted in Freeman 1999, 55)

Once again focusing on the psychology of the situation, Bowen explores how the men reacted to their mission. By clustering the men in the foreground, she focuses the viewer's eyes on them. In her working drawings, she was keen to capture the emotions of each Sunderland pilot. As Derry Syme recalled, "She would ask me to look out the window while she studied my expression, and described my far-away look and adventurous blue eyes like a hawk seeking prey—the prey being the submarine" (quoted in Freeman 1999, 55).

Figure 10.5   *A Sunderland Crew Comes Ashore at Pembroke Dock*, by Stella Bowen, 1945. Oil on canvas, 76.8 x 63.8 cm. Australian War Memorial, ART26275.

Bowen's final posting with Bomber Command crew members was at the Driffield air station in Yorkshire. Completed there in 1945, her painting of mostly Australian pilots in *Halifax Crew, Driffield* (Figure 10.6) is comparatively upbeat. In contrast to *Bomber Crew*, this was a crew of survivors, and this weaves itself into the painting. They had already completed thirty operations, and were midway through their second tour of twenty operations when Bowen painted them prior to their leaving on a mission (Challis 1979).[19] There was a tinge of apprehension before takeoff, but they returned from their mission.

Figure 10.6 *Halifax Crew, Driffield*, by Stella Bowen, 1945. Oil on canvas, 86.2 x 71.8 cm. Australian War Memorial, ART26268.

Bowen focuses on them as a group, with each airman's face framed by the upturned fur collar of his aviator's jacket. To enliven this composition, she gave each pilot a different point of gaze. This perspectival diffusion mirrors the differing emotions portrayed on the men's faces prior to takeoff. The artist was pleased with this painting and described its composition to her cousin: "Do you remember how in my book I longed to paint portrait groups in robes or uniforms as formal decoration and not naturalistically posed? That is precisely what I now have a chance to do. I am doing a Halifax Crew with the bunch of heads in the middle, all ensconced in the upturned fur collars of their Irving jackets, and around them is a sort of border in which you see their pairs of hands in action."[20] The seven pairs of hands in the space framing the heads carry out essential functions, including plotting the plane's course, operating the instrument panel, and navigating the bomber. A bird of prey hovering above is a reminder of the impending danger of their mission.

There was an inevitable change in Bowen's subject matter once the war in Europe was in its last stages. In May 1945, Treloar, based in Canberra, was already thinking of new subject matter for his official war artists in Britain to cover. He suggested Australian prisoners of war who were being released, and the postwar activities of servicemen.[21] Bowen's *Repatriated Prisoner of War Is Processed* (Figure 10.7) comes from this period. She was based at Gowrie House

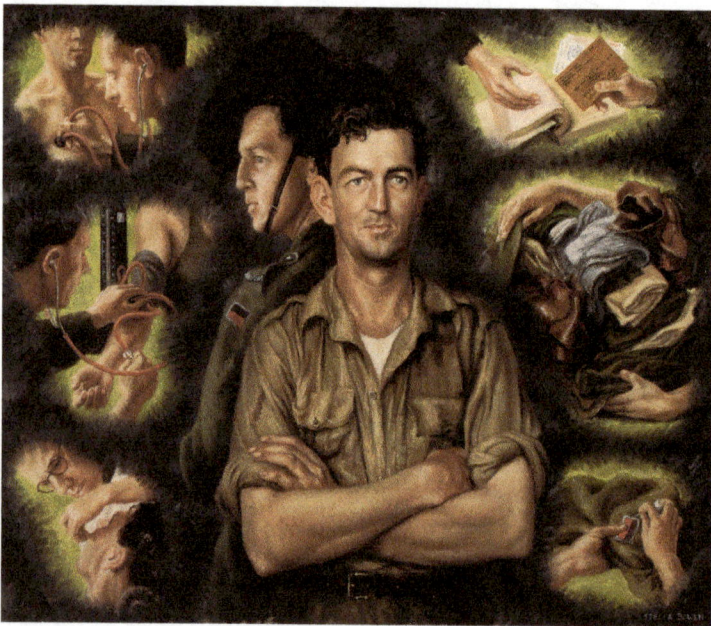

Figure 10.7 *Repatriated Prisoner of War Is Processed*, by Stella Bowen, 1945. Oil on canvas, 76.6 x 91.4 cm. Australian War Memorial, ART26272.

in Eastbourne in Sussex so she could observe how soldiers and airmen who had been prisoners of war in Germany were being debriefed. Her composition details the range of activities involved in transforming the dishevelled soldier into one immaculately dressed. The process included various health checks, having identification papers supplied, being given a uniform, and even sewing on a badge to signify rank. The dynamic design of the painting that plots this change is again inspired by the early Renaissance strategy of stacking figures up the canvas to convey spatial depth, compounded by Bowen's skill as a modern artist in employing formal decorative and design elements in her work. However, by putting her pensive soldier, who may be reflecting on his experiences as a prisoner of war, back into uniform, it is as if Bowen is closing a chapter on her probing of the many faces of masculinity. He is now defined by his uniform.

Another of her paintings from this time, *RAAF Airmen at Mongewell Park Medical Rehabilitation Unit* (Figure 10.8), focuses on the permanently injured. The mellow green and silver-grey foliage of the trees and the expansive lawns carry overtones of a cautious hope that broken bodies, even those confined to wheelchairs, can mend. The slow recuperative qualities of golf and time outdoors convey the soldiers' optimistic attempt to readjust to life after the loss of a limb.

Figure 10.8 *RAAF Airmen at Mongewell Park Medical Rehabilitation Unit*, by Stella Bowen, 1945. Oil on hardboard, 50.6 x 60.8 cm. Australian War Memorial, ART26274.

There was a surprising absence of imagery of the maimed or injured following World War I, but a differing outlook followed World War II. The latter war had permitted humans to carry out much cruelty and violence against one another, as Australian official war artist Alan Moore discovered when he accompanied the Welsh guards who liberated Belsen concentration camp in Germany in April 1945. His disturbing paintings like *Blind Man in Belsen* (1947) document the impact of Nazism on the Jewish population. Australian official war artist Murray Griffin, who was a prisoner of war and survived, similarly documented, at one camp, the Japanese treatment of Allied prisoners of war, which fell outside the rules of the Geneva Convention. His paintings of emaciated and gravely ill soldiers, such as *Roberts Hospital, Changi* (1943), are a graphic reminder of that time. When exhibited in Australian art galleries after the war, they shocked viewers.[22] In contrast, Bowen's soldiers appear to carry none of these horrific and lingering memories, but suggest a more sombre, philosophical acceptance of injury, aided by quiet healing.

Apart from portraying the men and women she encountered, Bowen had a very real interest in the ruined urban landscape. When she was appointed an official war artist, she said she would also like to pursue this in terms of its visual disparities. Writing in mid-1943, Bowen states, "I am hoping very much to be allowed to paint aspects of wartime England that appeal to me—compositions embodying the broken, makeshift appearance of what was once tidy and prosperous with strange contrasts between the still untouched, still alive elements and the dead and shattered."[23] While she was advised that her role was to focus on Australians serving in Britain, she was fascinated by the disparity between the still intact and the utterly destroyed, which sat side by side. In a letter to her cousin about life in a wartime city, she describes these incongruities:

> These sights, already commonplace to Londoners, affected me profoundly. You know that I have a rather special feeling about houses—particularly the sort that look as though they have been lived in a lot. I like to paint them ... seeing the wreck of people's homes. The rubble is all yellowish-grey. Wood and iron, plaster and bricks, armchairs, curtains and bedding, all are in the same drab monochrome. The only bits of color that remain are in the newly exposed wall-papers of the upper stories. There is something fearfully indecent about a clear bright wallpaper exposed to the wind and rain, in a room without a roof or a floor, and with perhaps a mirror still hanging over the mantle, a curtain flapping against a broken wall, an intimate garment in the branches of a tree.[24]

Prior to becoming a war artist, Bowen found herself drawn to the "psychological poignancy" of bombed buildings like these, as her 1941 painting *Flight from Reason* (Figure 10.9) shows. In essence, it is an image of these incongruities and a statement about how war itself is irrational. Much of a once-majestic church has been blown away, but some areas of the building still stand, with their interiors exposed. Surprisingly, some icons of culture endured despite the bombing. A sculpture of John Hiccocks points to how war itself is a flight from reason. The artist takes viewers, like voyeurs, over a foreground of broken masonry and the surviving sculpture, through a gap in the front wall, and into the exposed area that once provided space for contemplative inner reflection.

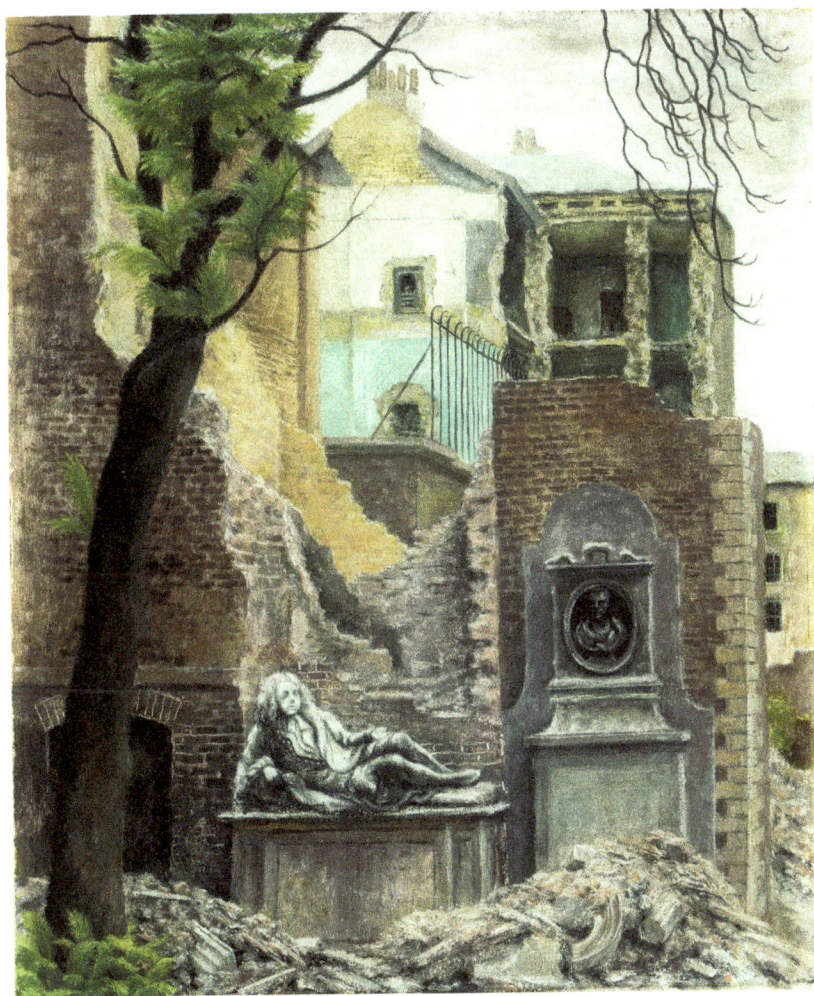

Figure 10.9 *Flight from Reason,* by Stella Bowen, 1941. Oil on cardboard, 65.4 x 54.7 cm. Australian War Memorial, ART91654.

This wartime urban landscape fascinated Bowen. As she said so piquantly, "the amazing thing is the way the horrible and the normal are jumbled together. One house is disembowelled, and next door the kettle [is] singing on gas."[25] This is the general subject she approaches in *Remains of a Flying Bomb* (Figure 10.10), in which the metal fragment of the shell of a bomb looks like a headless human figure lying amid books while a doll's head is severed from its torso. The effect is surreal and visually disturbing.

Bowen's work, and that of the other official Australian war artists—including Colin Colahan, Alan Moore, and Dennis Adams—remained in Britain until the end of the war in order to avoid loss at sea. In the meantime, the Australian High Commissioner in London sent photographs of seven of her paintings (compared to the nineteen photographs sent of Colahan's work) to Canberra's Australian War Memorial. Arthur Bazley, director of the memorial, wrote to Treloar, "I think you will agree that the work appears to be very good."[26]

By July 1946, Bowen's fifteen paintings in oil and watercolour, together with a collection of drawings, sketches, and small portraits, finally arrived in Australia. They were preceded by a Melbourne *Herald* commentary, which described them as "different from any war painting ... in Australia."[27]

Figure 10.10 *Remains of a Flying Bomb*, by Stella Bowen, 1944. Watercolour with pencil on cardboard, 51.8 x 64.7 cm. Australian War Memorial, ART26267.

Indeed, they are different. The paintings and drawings have a special quality imparted by their composition, symbolism, and an unerring sense of how a painting or drawing might function as a psychological study of the subject's character. Initially, Treloar was troubled by the relatively small number of paintings that Bowen completed compared to the output of some other war artists, but before long he was less concerned about that and more convinced of their worth as art. Even before they were unpacked, the photographs impressed him, and in January 1947 he wrote to Bowen, "I believe that they will be an important addition to our collection and will attract the attention of a number of visitors."[28] She warmed to this praise and replied that even if her paintings "do not represent an enormous output, they are, nevertheless, the result of a great deal of intensive work."[29]

Bowen's subjects are mostly Royal Air Force crew members, who were the most vulnerable to death in action in the war against Germany. The RAAF experienced the most deaths in this sphere of the conflict, and Bowen explores the psyches of those who were fully aware of the risks (Grey 1990, 188).[30] Irrespective of their age, many of her subjects look variously pensive, uncertain, worried, fearful, and relieved. This is a serious, almost personal view of war. Her work differs from the "action pictures" painted by men such as Canadian artist Miller Britain, who, in *Night Target, Germany* (1946), shows the dynamism of fighter planes carrying out attacks against the lights of night skies. Miller Britain served in the Canadian Air Force as a bomb aimer, and his first-hand experience informed his work. British official war artist Paul Nash approaches this subject in a similar vein in *Battle of Britain* (1941), in which he shows the weaving, diving action of pilots in an aerial battle over England.

Stella Bowen's paintings are complex. While the serenity of an appropriated fourteenth-century style married with her own distinctive modern practice might seem a paradoxical approach to employ for the range of emotions of her particular subjects, the thoughtful composure it conveys is an appropriate way of suggesting that these men were preoccupied with thoughts about the gravity of their mission, and their own safety. The symbolic depiction of the pilots' uniforms and insignias emphasizes the responsibility of masculine citizenship. For the women intelligence officers, the uniform displays womanly citizenship exercised by their wartime service. However, Bowen's paintings venture into human personalities and how these men and women coped in times of stress. This is a side of war many prefer not to dwell upon. She was dealing with the daily psychological reality of pilots who took to the skies to defend their country, but, in doing so, lived in some considerable fear. As Derry Syme said, "Stella seemed to get into our very souls" (quoted in Freeman 1999, 56).

It is not surprising that these paintings and drawings exist in the shadowy space occupied by a "woman war artist." *Bomber crew* has been widely exhibited, and it is an icon of youthful sacrifice, but her wartime work as a whole brings to the fore the human side of war, and the complex emotions felt by those involved.[31] Stella Bowen's uncanny method of juxtaposing seemingly contradictory features challenges viewers to read below the surface in these images.

NOTES

1   A key feature of the pre-war modern era and expatriatism was that of artists gravitating to the two cosmopolitan centres of London and Paris, and being challenged by that experience and environment. See Raymond Williams, "The metropolis and the emergence of modernism," in *Modernism/Postmodernism*, ed. Peter Brooker, 82–94 (London: Longman, 1992); and Helen Carr, "Modernism and travel (1880–1940)," in *The Cambridge Companion to Travel Writing*, ed. Peter Hulme and Tim Youngs, 70–86 (Cambridge: Cambridge University Press, 2002).

2   Stella Bowen to Kathleen Kyffin Thomas, undated, Stella Bowen Archive, private collection, Adelaide.

3   "Pictures by S.A. Artist for National Gallery," *The Advertiser*, 31 December 1943, 3; *Embankment Gardens*, ca. 1943, was the subject of an article (no author) "*Embankment Gardens* painted by Stella Bowen," *Bulletin of the National Gallery of South Australia*, 5 (3), January 1944, n.p.; Stella Bowen to Louis McCubbin, 20 July 1943: "I hear from my brother that you have been instrumental in inducing the Federal Government to consider me as a war artist, and for this I owe you my warmest thanks" (AWM File 93, 205/2/31A).

4   As the official statement said, "Due to the important part that women are playing in Australia's war effort, the War Memorial Board decided to appoint women artists from time to time to cover the activities of the women's services," "Memorandum for the Minister," 7 October 1943 (AWM File 93, 50/4/1/1/, Part 1).

5   Draft of cablegram to the High Commissioner's Office, London, 20 November 1943, AWM File 93, 205/2/5/A; cablegram from Australia House, London, cited in Bazley to Treloar, 25 January 1944, AWM File 93, 205/2/5/A; "From the High Commissioner's Office," cited in Bazley to Treloar, 19 February 1944, AWM File 93, 205/2/5/A.

6   Stella Bowen to Louis McCubbin, 20 July 1943, Art Gallery of South Australia Correspondence File A-L 1943.

7   Stella Bowen to Kathleen Kyffin Thomas, 1945, *Stella Bowen Archive*.

8   "Stella Bowen Plans Australian Visit," *Advertiser* (Adelaide), 8 May 1946, 5.

9   Ibid.

10 The six Australian pilots were E.G.D. Jarman, M.W. Carroll, R.L. Neal, T.J. Lynch, H.R. Harrison, and F.G. Jackson, and there was one English pilot, D.G. Champkin.

11 The factories in Friedrichshafen that were bombed in these attacks were staffed by Jewish prisoners from concentration camps. Stella Bowen was probably unaware of this.

12 Stella Bowen to Tom Bowen, 27 September 1944, *Stella Bowen Archive*.

13 "Death Was in a Hurry," *Australian Post*, 5 June 1958, 14.

14 Ibid.

15 Bazley to Treloar, 3 May 1944. AWM File 93, 206/2/3/A; Treloar to Bazley, 7 May 1944, AWM File 93, 205/2/3/A.

16 Cablegram from the High Commissioner's Office, London, 21 July 1944, AWM File 93, 205/2/5/A.

17 "War Exploits Recalled by Portrait," *Canberra Times*, 21 January 1979, Stella Bowen file, Australian War Memorial.

18 The crew members as they come up the steps are Derry Syme (RAAF), Ron Warfield (RAAF), Ron Tyson (RAAF), Eric Genders (RAAF), and Charlie Martin (RAAF). The

others, who are not recognizable in the painting, are Spud Murphy (RAAF), Bob Meade (RAF), Merv Pike (RAF), and John Bishop (RAF).

19 The crew members (from left to right and from top to bottom) are J. Venning (RAAF), C.J. Challis (RAAF), J. McCarthy (RAAF), J. Nicholas (RAF), G. Robinson (RAAF), J. Good (RAAF), and H.O. Stonberg (RAAF).

20 Stella Bowen to Kathleen Kyffin Thomas, 27 January 1945, Stella Bowen Archive.

21 Treloar to Bazley, 4 May 1945, AWM File 93, 205/2/5/A.

22 "Upset by Stark War Pictures," News (Adelaide), 8 January 1947; "Horrors of POW," News, 7 January 1947.

23 Stella Bowen to Louis McCubbin, 20 July 1943, Art Gallery of South Australia correspondence file A-L 1943.

24 Stella Bowen, "Letters to Kathleen," 1942, Stella Bowen Archive.

25 Ibid., ca. 1941.

26 Treloar to Bazley, 12 June 1945, AWM File 93, 205/2/5/A.

27 Elizabeth Auld, "War Artist May Visit Australia," Herald, Melbourne, 1 May 1946, Stella Bowen Archive.

28 Treloar to Stella Bowen, 19 January 1947, AWM File 93, 50/4/2/132.

29 Stella Bowen to Treloar, 28 January 1947, AWM File 93, 50/4/2/132.

30 In the war against Germany, 5,116 RAAF soldiers were killed in action or died of wounds, compared to 3,539 members of the Australian Military Forces and 876 members of the Royal Australian Navy.

31 Bomber crew was exhibited in the Shared Experiences: Art and War exhibition at the Canadian War Museum in 2005, and in the same touring exhibition at the Imperial War Museum in 2006.

WORKS CITED

"Art Gallery of South Australia Correspondence File A-L 1943." Archive. Adelaide: Art Gallery of South Australia.

"AWM File 93." Archive. Canberra: Australian War Memorial.

Bowen, Stella. 1984. Drawn from Life. London: Virago.

Clarke, Fiona. 2002. "Stella's War." In Stella Bowen: Art, Love and War, edited by Lola Wilkins. Canberra: Australian War Memorial.

Connell, R.W. 2005. Masculinities. Crow's Nest, NSW: Allen and Unwin.

Challis, C.J. RAAF News. January–February 1979, n.p.

Freeman, Gillian. 1999. "The Airman and the Artist." Wartime 6.

Grey, Jeffrey. 1990. A Military History of Australia. Cambridge: Cambridge University Press.

Hegel, G.W.F. 1977. Phenomenology of Spirit. Translated by A.V. Miller. Oxford: Clarendon Press.

Higonnet, Margaret R., Jane Jenson, Sonya Michel, and Margaret C. Weitz. 1987. "Introduction." In Behind the Lines: Gender and the Two World Wars, edited by Margaret R. Higonnet, Jane Jenson, Sonya Michel, and Margaret C. Weitz. New Haven, CT: Yale University Press.

Kant, Emanuel. 1952. Critique of Judgement. Translated by J.C. Meredith. Oxford: Oxford University Press.

Lloyd, Genevieve. 1985. "Selfhood, War and Masculinity." In Feminist Challenges: Social and Political Theory, edited by Carol Pateman and Elizabeth Gross, 63–76. Sydney: Allen and Unwin.

Speck, Catherine. 2004. *Paintings Ghosts: Australian Women Artists in Wartime*. Melbourne: Craftsman House/Thames and Hudson.

Stanley, Peter. 1985. *Australia at War: Bomber Command*. Lane Cove, Sydney: Hodder and Stoughton.

Stella Bowen Archive. TS. Private Collection. Adelaide.

"Stella Bowen Plans Australia Visit." *Advertiser* (Adelaide). 8 May 1946, 5.

Stephenson, Andrew. 1991. "Strategies of Situation: British Modernism and the Slump ca. 1929–1934." *Oxford Art Journal* 14 (2): 30–51.

Thomson, A. 1994. "Embattled Manhood: Gender, Memory and the Anzac Legend." In *Memory and History in Twentieth Century Australia*, edited by Kate Darian Smith and Paula Hamilton, 158–73. Melbourne: Oxford University Press.

Weisenfarth, Joseph. 2002. "Stella Bowen and Ford Madox Ford." In *Stella Bowen: Art, Love and War*, edited by Lola Wilkins. Canberra: Australian War Memorial.

Wilkins, Lola. 1991. "Stella Bowen: Australian War Artist." *Art and Australia* 8 (4): 493–97.

ACKNOWLEDGEMENTS

It is always a pleasure to acknowledge the rigor, enthusiasm, and patience of contributors. This group has been particularly energetic and responsive through layers of editing and revision.

The Social Sciences and Humanities Research Council of Canada's funding of this project (as part of Kadar and Perreault's ongoing work on women in the war years) has been invaluable.

We thank the Life Writing team at Wilfrid Laurier University Press and our colleagues at York University in Humanities; Gender, Sexuality and Women's Studies; and the Centre for Jewish Studies, and, at the University of Calgary, in English.

Friends and family provide supports of many kinds—intellectual, practical, emotional, and ineffable. We are grateful for all. Grateful, too, are we for the inspired diagnostic brilliance of Dr. Sandy Skotnicki.

Our greatest thanks go to Natalie Robinson, who came on as our Research Assistant in the later stages of the project. Natalie has not only written a fine essay for the collection, she has also shepherded contributions through innumerable communications regarding edits, images, and formatting. Moreover, her astute critical observations have strengthened the final draft of the volume. She accomplished all this with efficiency, tact, and grace. Natalie—thank you.

CONTRIBUTORS

Beverly W. Brannan is curator of documentary photography in the Prints and Photographs Division of the Library of Congress, Washington, DC. She is co-curator of *Women Come to the Front: Journalists, Photographers and Broadcasters During World War II* (1995) and co-author of *Re-viewing Documentary: The Photographic Life of Louise Rosskam* (2011). Brannan has in progress a website about women photojournalists in the library's collections. She has written extensively about the Farm Security Administration collection of photographs.

Charmian Brinson is a Germanist and cultural historian who has published extensively on the subject of exile from National Socialism, in particular exile in Britain, 1933–50. Her most recent book, co-authored with Professor Richard Dove, is *Politics by Other Means: The Free German League of Culture in London 1939–1946* (London: Vallentine Mitchell, 2010). She is a co-founder of the Research Centre for German and Austrian Exile Studies at the Institute of Germanic and Romance Studies, University of London, and is currently a professor of German studies at Imperial College London.

Lesley Ferris is an arts and humanities distinguished professor of theatre in the Department of Theatre at the Ohio State University. She currently serves as the director of the OSU/Royal Shakespeare Company Partnership. Her research focus is on gender and performance, Caribbean-derived carnival, and contemporary theatre practice. She has directed more than fifty productions in the United States, United Kingdom, and South Africa that include works by Catherine Filloux, Adrienne Kennedy, Caryl Churchill, and Sophie Treadwell. She is currently co-editing (with Penny Farfan, University of Calgary) a book on contemporary women playwrights.

Marlene Kadar is a professor in Humanities, and Gender and Women's Studies at York University in Toronto, Canada. She is on the advisory board of *Jeunesse: Young People, Texts, Cultures*, and she is the editor of the Life Writing series at Wilfrid Laurier University Press. She has published extensively in the field of life writing, especially in relation to traumatic historical events, archival lives, and memory studies. In the recent past, she has co-edited three collections of life-writing theory, including

Tracing the Autobiographical (2005), *ARIEL: Life Writing in International Contexts* (2008), and *Photographs, Histories, and Meanings* (2009). She is currently working with Jeanne Perreault on a study of women war photojournalists, among them Toni Frissell and Thérèse Bonney.

Eva C. Karpinski teaches feminist theory and methodology, autobiography, and translation studies in the School of Gender, Sexuality and Women's Studies at York University in Toronto. Her research interests include postmodernist and poststructuralist theories, feminist ethics and pedagogy, twentieth-century American and Canadian literature, and women's writing. She has published articles on such topics as micro-cosmopolitanism, multiculturalism, transnationalism, trauma and witnessing, fictionalysis, queer autoethnography, dystopian romance, and critical masculinities. She edited *Pens of Many Colours: A Canadian Reader*, a popular college anthology of multicultural writing. Her book *Borrowed Tongues: Life Writing, Migration, and Translation* was published in 2012 by Wilfrid Laurier University Press.

Jeanne Perreault is a professor emerita in the Department of English at the University of Calgary. She is the author of *Writing Selves: Contemporary Feminist Autography* (University of Minnesota Press), and co-editor of several volumes on life writing and on feminist theory and activism. Collections include *Tracing the Autobiographical* (Wilfrid Laurier University Press), *ARIEL: Life Writing in International Contexts*, and *Photographs, Histories, and Meanings* (Palgrave Macmillan). Her co-edited volume *Indigenous Women and Feminism: Politics, Activism, Culture* (University of British Columbia Press) won the Canadian Women's Studies Association Award for Outstanding Scholarship in 2011, and *Not Drowning but Waving: Women, Feminism and the Liberal Arts* (University of Alberta Press) was nominated for the same award in 2012. At present, Perreault is again collaborating with Marlene Kadar on a book on women photojournalists of World War II, supported by the Social Sciences and Humanities Research Council.

Natalie Robinson is a Ph.D. student in the Department of English at the University of Calgary. Her research focuses on women's writing and the fairy tale. Natalie is the author of "Exploding the Glass Bottles: Constructing the Postcolonial 'Bluebeard' Tale in Nalo Hopkinson's 'The Glass Bottle Trick'" in *Anti-Tales: The Uses of Disenchantment* (2011), and "Bella and Her Beastly Choices: Exploring the Fairy Tale in the *Twilight* Phenomenon" in *Postmodern Reinterpretations of Fairy Tales: How Applying New Methods Generates New Meanings* (2011). Recent conference presentations include "Smashing the Glass Slipper: The Fairy Tale Heroine as Action Hero in Joe Wright's *Hanna*." Natalie holds a J.A. Bombardier Canadian Graduate Scholarship from the Social Sciences and Humanities Research Council of Canada.

Tanya Schaap received a Ph.D. in English from the University of Calgary in June 2015. Her areas of research include trauma theory, women and war, and literary representations of cultural trauma. She has published on medieval marginalia in *Studies in Medieval and Renaissance History*. Tanya has presented her work at numerous conferences, including the 2011 Rocky Mountain Modern Language Association convention in Scottsdale, Arizona, and the 2012 Association for Literature, Environment and Culture in Canada conference in Kelowna, British Columbia. Tanya has won many awards, including the prestigious Izaak Walton Killam Memorial Scholarship (2011 and 2012), and she received the J.A. Bombardier Canadian Graduate Scholarship from the Social Sciences and Humanities Research Council of Canada in 2011.

Catherine Speck is the author of *Painting Ghosts: Australian Women Artists in Wartime* (Craftsman House/Thames and Hudson, 2004) and *Heysen to Heysen* (National Library of Australia, 2011), which explores the relationship between two of Australia's eminent artists, Hans Heysen and his daughter Nora. Catherine has written numerous articles and catalogue essays on expatriate artists and cosmopolitanism, the representation of war, war memorials and the memory of war, gender and war, gender and modern Australian art, and contemporary art. Current research includes the exhibitionary complex. She is an associate professor and reader in the Art History program at the University of Adelaide, and coordinates postgraduate programs in Art History and Curatorial and Museum Studies at the Art Gallery of South Australia and the University of Adelaide.

James D. Stone is an assistant professor in the Department of Cinematic Arts at the University of New Mexico, Albuquerque, United States. His writing explores British cinema (especially in relation to American culture), Hollywood's depiction of apocalyptic imagery, and the aesthetics of violence. Stone has taught courses such as the Cinema of Alfred Hitchcock, British Cinema, the History of Animation, International Horror Film, the Silent Era, and the Sound Era. His essay "Enjoying 9/11: The Pleasures of *Cloverfield*" is forthcoming in *Radical History Review* (Issue 111). Another paper, "The Meek Inherit the Earth: Celebrating the End of American Power in *Mars Attacks!*" has just been published in the Danish humanities journal *Akademic Kvarter* (Volume 2).

Mary Tarantino is resident lighting designer / professor of theatre at the Ohio State University. She also serves as the director of the Jerome Lawrence and Robert E. Lee Theatre Research Institute. Recent lighting designs include *The Secret Garden* (New Haven and Columbus), *A Midsummer Night's Dream* (Virginia Arts Festival and the Buffalo Philharmonic), and *The Camouflage Project*, which premiered at Ohio State (2011) and toured to the Clarice Smith Performing Arts Center in College Park, Maryland (2012). Recent publications include "Uncovering Gems: Theatrical Design Collections at the Wisconsin Historical Society" and an essay on lighting designer Gilbert Hemsley for *Late and Great: American Design 1960–2010*.

Patrick Taylor teaches post-colonial thought and Caribbean literature, religion, and culture in the Department of Humanities at York University. He is the past chair of Humanities and directed the Caribbean Religions Project at the Centre for Research on Latin America and the Caribbean. He is co-editor of the *Encyclopedia of Caribbean Religions* (University of Illinois Press, two volumes), editor of *Nation Dance: Religion, Identity and Cultural Difference in the Caribbean* (Indiana University Press), and author of *The Narrative of Liberation: Perspectives on Afro-Caribbean Literature, Popular Culture, and Politics* (Cornell University Press).

Julia Winckler is a visual artist whose multimedia projects have been exhibited in the United Kingdom, Canada, Italy, France, Germany, Cyprus, and Taiwan. Her interdisciplinary research focuses on archival traces, memory, and migration narratives. Together with Charmian Brinson and Anna Müller-Härlin, she has co-authored the book *His Majesty's Most Loyal Internee: Fred Uhlman in Captivity* (Vallentine Mitchell, 2009). She works as a senior lecturer in photography at the University of Brighton, Faculty of Art, School of Arts and Media.

INDEX

Books in the Life Writing Series
Published by Wilfrid Laurier University Press

Haven't Any News: Ruby's Letters from the Fifties edited by Edna Staebler with an Afterword by Marlene Kadar • 1995 / x + 165 pp. / ISBN 0-88920-248-6

"I Want to Join Your Club": Letters from Rural Children, 1900–1920 edited by Norah L. Lewis with a Preface by Neil Sutherland • 1996 / xii + 250 pp. (30 b&w photos) / ISBN 0-88920-260-5

And Peace Never Came by Elisabeth M. Raab with Historical Notes by Marlene Kadar • 1996 / x + 196 pp. (12 b&w photos, map) / ISBN 0-88920-281-8

Dear Editor and Friends: Letters from Rural Women of the North-West, 1900–1920 edited by Norah L. Lewis • 1998 / xvi + 166 pp. (20 b&w photos) / ISBN 0-88920-287-7

The Surprise of My Life: An Autobiography by Claire Drainie Taylor with a Foreword by Marlene Kadar • 1998 / xii + 268 pp. (8 colour photos and 92 b&w photos) / ISBN 0-88920-302-4

Memoirs from Away: A New Found Land Girlhood by Helen M. Buss / Margaret Clarke • 1998 / xvi + 153 pp. / ISBN 0-88920-350-4

The Life and Letters of Annie Leake Tuttle: Working for the Best by Marilyn Färdig Whiteley • 1999 / xviii + 150 pp. / ISBN 0-88920-330-x

Marian Engel's Notebooks: "Ah, mon cahier, écoute" edited by Christl Verduyn • 1999 / viii + 576 pp. / ISBN 0-88920-333-4 cloth / ISBN 0-88920-349-0 paper

Be Good Sweet Maid: The Trials of Dorothy Joudrie by Audrey Andrews • 1999 / vi + 276 pp. / ISBN 0-88920-334-2

Working in Women's Archives: Researching Women's Private Literature and Archival Documents edited by Helen M. Buss and Marlene Kadar • 2001 / vi + 120 pp. / ISBN 0-88920-341-5

Repossessing the World: Reading Memoirs by Contemporary Women by Helen M. Buss • 2002 / xxvi + 206 pp. / ISBN 0-88920-408-x cloth / ISBN 0-88920-410-1 paper

Chasing the Comet: A Scottish-Canadian Life by Patricia Koretchuk • 2002 / xx + 244 pp. / ISBN 0-88920-407-1

The Queen of Peace Room by Magie Dominic • 2002 / xii + 115 pp. / ISBN 0-88920-417-9

China Diary: The Life of Mary Austin Endicott by Shirley Jane Endicott • 2002 / xvi + 251 pp. / ISBN 0-88920-412-8

The Curtain: Witness and Memory in Wartime Holland by Henry G. Schogt • 2003 / xii + 132 pp. / ISBN 0-88920-396-2

Teaching Places by Audrey J. Whitson • 2003 / xiii + 178 pp. / ISBN 0-88920-425-x

Through the Hitler Line by Laurence F. Wilmot, M.C. • 2003 / xvi + 152 pp. / ISBN 0-88920-448-9

Where I Come From by Vijay Agnew • 2003 / xiv + 298 pp. / ISBN 0-88920-414-4

The Water Lily Pond by Han Z. Li • 2004 / x + 254 pp. / ISBN 0-88920-431-4

The Life Writings of Mary Baker McQuesten: Victorian Matriarch edited by Mary J. Anderson • 2004 / xxii + 338 pp. / ISBN 0-88920-437-3

Seven Eggs Today: The Diaries of Mary Armstrong, 1859 and 1869 edited by Jackson W. Armstrong • 2004 / xvi + 228 pp. / ISBN 0-88920-440-3

Love and War in London: A Woman's Diary 1939–1942 by Olivia Cockett; edited by Robert W. Malcolmson • 2005 / xvi + 208 pp. / ISBN 0-88920-458-6

Incorrigible by Velma Demerson • 2004 / vi + 178 pp. / ISBN 0-88920-444-6

Auto/biography in Canada: Critical Directions edited by Julie Rak • 2005 / viii + 264 pp. / ISBN 0-88920-478-0

Tracing the Autobiographical edited by Marlene Kadar, Linda Warley, Jeanne Perreault, and Susanna Egan • 2005 / viii + 280 pp. / ISBN 0-88920-476-4

Must Write: Edna Staebler's Diaries edited by Christl Verduyn • 2005 / viii + 304 pp. / ISBN 0-88920-481-0

Pursuing Giraffe: A 1950s Adventure by Anne Innis Dagg • 2006 / xvi + 284 pp. (photos, 2 maps) / 978-0-88920-463-8

Food That Really Schmecks by Edna Staebler • 2007 / xxiv + 334 pp. / ISBN 978-0-88920-521-5

163256: A Memoir of Resistance by Michael Englishman • 2007 / xvi + 112 pp. (14 b&w photos) / ISBN 978-1-55458-009-5

The Wartime Letters of Leslie and Cecil Frost, 1915–1919 edited by R.B. Fleming • 2007 / xxxvi + 384 pp. (49 b&w photos, 5 maps) / ISBN 978-1-55458-000-2

Johanna Krause Twice Persecuted: Surviving in Nazi Germany and Communist East Germany by Carolyn Gammon and Christiane Hemker • 2007 / x + 170 pp. (58 b&w photos, 2 maps) / ISBN 978-1-55458-006-4

Watermelon Syrup: A Novel by Annie Jacobsen with Jane Finlay-Young and Di Brandt • 2007 / x + 268 pp. / ISBN 978-1-55458-005-7

Broad Is the Way: Stories from Mayerthorpe by Margaret Norquay • 2008 / x + 106 pp. (6 b&w photos) / ISBN 978-1-55458-020-0

Becoming My Mother's Daughter: A Story of Survival and Renewal by Erika Gottlieb • 2008 / x + 178 pp. (36 b&w illus., 17 colour) / ISBN 978-1-55458-030-9

Leaving Fundamentalism: Personal Stories edited by G. Elijah Dann • 2008 / xii + 234 pp. / ISBN 978-1-55458-026-2

Bearing Witness: Living with Ovarian Cancer edited by Kathryn Carter and Lauri Elit • 2009 / viii + 94 pp. / ISBN 978-1-55458-055-2

Dead Woman Pickney: A Memoir of Childhood in Jamaica by Yvonne Shorter Brown • 2010 / viii + 202 pp. / ISBN 978-1-55458-189-4

I Have a Story to Tell You by Seemah C. Berson • 2010 / xx + 288 pp. (24 b&w photos) / ISBN 978-1-55458-219-8

We All Giggled: A Bourgeois Family Memoir by Thomas O. Hueglin • 2010 / xiv + 232 pp. (20 b&w photos) / ISBN 978-1-55458-262-4

Just a Larger Family: Letters of Marie Williamson from the Canadian Home Front, 1940–1944 edited by Mary F. Williamson and Tom Sharp • 2011 / xxiv + 378 pp. (16 b&w photos) / ISBN 978-1-55458-323-2

Burdens of Proof: Faith, Doubt, and Identity in Autobiography by Susanna Egan • 2011 / x + 200 pp. / ISBN 978-1-55458-333-1

Accident of Fate: A Personal Account 1938–1945 by Imre Rochlitz with Joseph Rochlitz • 2011 / xiv + 226 pp. (50 b&w photos, 5 maps) / ISBN 978-1-55458-267-9

The Green Sofa by Natascha Würzbach, translated by Raleigh Whitinger • 2012 / xiv + 240 pp. (5 b&w photos) / ISBN 978-1-55458-334-8

Unheard Of: Memoirs of a Canadian Composer by John Beckwith • 2012 / x + 393 pp. (74 illus., 8 musical examples) / ISBN 978-1-55458-358-4

Borrowed Tongues: Life Writing, Migration, and Translation by Eva C. Karpinski • 2012 / viii + 274 pp. / ISBN 978-1-55458-357-7

Basements and Attics, Closets and Cyberspace: Explorations in Canadian Women's Archives edited by Linda M. Morra and Jessica Schagerl • 2012 / x + 338 pp. / ISBN 978-1-55458-632-5

The Memory of Water by Allen Smutylo • 2013 / x + 262 pp. (65 colour illus.) / ISBN 978-1-55458-842-8

The Unwritten Diary of Israel Unger, Revised Edition by Carolyn Gammon and Israel Unger • 2013 / ix + 230 pp. (b&w illus.) / ISBN 978-1-77112-011-1

Boom! Manufacturing Memoir for the Popular Market by Julie Rak • 2013 / viii + 249 pp. (b&w illus.) / ISBN 978-1-55458-939-5

Motherlode: A Mosaic of Dutch Wartime Experience by Carolyne Van Der Meer • 2014 / xiv + 132 pp. (b&w illus.) / ISBN 978-1-77112-005-0

Not the Whole Story: Challenging the Single Mother Narrative edited by Lea Caragata and Judit Alcalde • 2014 / x + 222 pp. / ISBN 978-1-55458-624-0

Street Angel by Magie Dominc • 2014 / vii + 154 pp. / ISBN 978-1-77112-026-5

In the Unlikeliest of Places: How Nachman Libeskind Survived the Nazis, Gulags, and Soviet Communism by Annette Libeskind Berkovits • 2014 / xiv + 282 pp. (6 colour illus.) / ISBN 978-1-77112-066-1

Kinds of Winter: Four Solo Journeys by Dogteam in Canada's Northwest Territories by Dave Olesen • 2014 / xii + 256 pp. (illus.) / ISBN 978-1-77112-118-7

Working Memory: Women and Work in World War II edited by Marlene Kadar and Jeanne Perreault • 2015 / viii + 246 pp. (illus.) / ISBN 978-1-77112—035-7